Assignment Huntsville

LEE SIMMONS, General Manager, Texas Prison System, 1930–35

LEE SIMMONS

Assignment Huntsville

Memoirs of a Texas Prison Official

23919

AUSTIN

UNIVERSITY OF TEXAS PRESS

Library of Congress Catalog Card No. 57–11130

© 1957 by the University of Texas Press

Manufactured in the United States of America by the
Printing Division of the University of Texas

DEDICATED TO THE MEMORY
OF MY BELOVED WIFE

Foreword

THERE IS NO MAGIC about getting a big job done. The basis of getting it done, according to my experience, is co-operation. And the basis of co-operation is confidence—mutual confidence. Whatever success I have had in handling the lawless and violent men given into my keeping involved firmness and fairness. But I could get nowhere with being either firm or fair to five thousand convicts unless first I had obtained the loyal co-operation of the many employees of the administration of which I was the head. Beyond that, I had to get, and deserve to get, the co-operation of the prisoners as well. The astonishing thing about it all was that a great majority of the men in my keeping had a sense of fair play to which I could and did appeal in ways which worked out well for them and for me.

In the pages that follow, therefore, you will be hearing a good deal about co-operation and confidence. Confidence bestowed upon the right sort of man begets in him a worthiness of still more confidence. It was my good fortune to find and to recognize such men. As for respect, I suppose it has to come before confidence in the sense that you command respect, whereas confidence is given.

In dealing with men most of whom came to be behind walls and bars because they could not discipline themselves, I had to make it perfectly clear to everybody that I could and would discipline them, if occasion arose. Prompt and certain punishment has a justice of its own, and I believe in it.

I do not belittle the methods of correction advocated by the modern sciences, and I have made use of them, but I am a firm believer nonetheless in corporal punishment—in the home, in the schoolroom, in the reformatory, in the penitentiary. I know my notions about that are diametrically opposed to the notions of almost all present-day psychologists, psychiatrists, and penologists. I have most of the wardens and prison board members against me on that. But I came to my belief from experience, and experience is what I base my conclusions upon. Whatever else I may lack, I have had, I think, plenty of experience.

Of course, I do not claim to have all the answers to these prison mutinies and outbreaks which continue to plague our penitentiaries. But, right or wrong, in the Texas Prison System we whipped our hardened criminals, when other means of persuasion failed. And I shall be telling you, before many pages, what came of it.

I was reared in a family of children, have children and grandchildren of my own—great-grandchildren by this time. And while love and kindness, sympathy and tender care are proper requisites for developing character in the home, the rod is needed. I have no doubt about that. Discipline of like sort is needed also in the schoolroom and in the prison. It has one great advantage: It works. I know that it works.

Excessive indulgence by parents and misguided kindness go a long way, I believe, toward filling up our reformatories and penitentiaries. A little of the rod, rightly and sternly applied in childhood, I am convinced, would have saved many a grown man the pains of a prison sentence later on.

In all my early school days I never knew of a pupil's being sent home for correction. Nobody was expelled from school. The teacher handled such problems with vigor and dispatch—and discipline did the job. Parents were wise enough to leave school discipline to the teacher. And that is where it belongs.

When I entered the University of Texas, the President said to the student body: "You are supposed to be ladies and gentlemen, and we hope you are. We have no rules or regulations to give you. You are on your honor here. If we find out later that you are not conducting yourself as a lady or gentleman, you will be discharged." Few university students were sent home; discipline had been in force before their college days; character had already been formed. With many young men and women of this day and time it has not been so.

The real objective of a prison sentence is, or should be, reformation. Surely it ought not to be merely punishment. And in the prison, I freely agree, corporal punishment should be the last resort. A prison official, whether he be guard, warden, or head of the system, should have patience and use it. He should study and know the individual prisoner. You cannot use the same method of discipline with all convicts, any more than you can deal with all children or all pupils alike. There is a wide difference in temperaments. That is why a knowledge of human nature is so important in prison management.

The average conception is that the use of the "bat" in prison management is outmoded and belongs to the Dark Ages. But, to my way of thinking, the alternative of solitary confinement as practiced in nearly all present-day prisons is inhuman and should not be tolerated. Thousands of prisoners are in solitary confinement today because of supposed or real misconduct. I say that it is inhuman to place a man in solitary for thirty, sixty, or ninety days. In some cases the troublemakers are confined in isolation for years. It was never intended that man should be idle. If he is physically able, he should be at work, both for the sake of his health and for the earning of his living, whether he is in prison or out of prison.

After every warning has failed, after every attempt at guidance has been rejected, corporal punishment should be used, but used for disciplinary purposes only. I used to say to prisoners: "Outside of my mother, my father thought more of me than any other person. And yet, what would he have done to me, even when I was only a boy, if I had done such things as tear up plumbing, take out a water pipe, drive wooden pegs in it and then connect it back again—or if I had deliberately set fire to bedclothes? He would have done to me exactly what I expect to do to you boys, if you don't stop doing these things."

Did they believe me? Read the printed record. I took charge in April, 1930. For 1929: prison population, 4,868; corporal punishments, 326; escapes, 302. For 1935: prison population, 5,623; corporal punishments, 80; escapes, 71.

There were twenty bad men in solitary confinement at the Huntsville prison when I took charge. On each of the prison farms there were small strong buildings for solitary confinement. I soon did away with them all. I had other uses for such buildings. I opposed the legislators who sought to forbid the "bat," the twenty-four-inch leather strap, four inches wide, used in prison discipline. I told my friends on the legislative committee: "Gentlemen, it's just like using spurs. You get on an old cow horse without spurs—and you can't head even a milking-pen cow; but when you've got your spurs on, the old horse will do the job. And you don't have to use the spurs, because all he needs is to know that the spurs are there. It's the same with us and the 'bat.' The record shows we seldom have to use it. But the boys all know that it is there."

Committeemen smiled and failed to recommend abolition of the "bat." But, after my resignation as general manager, the next legislature forbade the use of corporal punishment—in response to the urgings of misguided and ill-informed humanitarians.

Most riots and mutinies inside prison walls are due to idleness and want of discipline. Bad food is sometimes blamed. But that is seldom the real cause. In most cases, firm discipline, fair treatment, and plenty of work to keep everybody busy will keep the riotously inclined out of mischief.

Depriving an offender of privileges, demoting him from a desired position, or cutting down his overtime credits will generally influence a wayward prisoner. But the hell-raiser fears nothing more than he fears the "bat." When I was in charge, he got it. Generally, after five lashes, the rebel raised his hand and cried, "That's enough; I'll behave." I saw only a very few take the full twenty.

Do not judge me to be a merciless brute. I believe I am as tender-hearted as the next one. My emotions often get the better of me. But in dealing with hard men you cannot go soft. For example, we had an epidemic of maiming on one of our prison farms. Men would cut the heel tendon to escape work—or even chop off a foot.

I went down to look things over. I told the men who so injured themselves that they would not be transferred to the prison hospital but that they would be treated by the prison physician right there on the farm and that, as soon as their wounds were healed, they would be put back to work, every last man of them, right there on the farm.

Foreword

Then I turned to the guards and said: "Bring them more axes, boys!"

The newspapers printed that. What they didn't print was that I got the guards off to themselves and told them privately to keep those axes out of sight for a while. We stopped the self-maiming epidemic right then and there.

Unless prison management, however, is genuinely concerned about the welfare of the prisoners, neither severe discipline nor lax discipline will be able to keep order or get a fair quota of work out of the men. A convict knows what a convict is entitled to expect as a fair, square deal. If he gets it, he can be handled—to his advantage and to the advantage of the public, whose protection is the first object of his removal from circulation.

I would not close these preliminary words without saying this: To all who have given me their co-operation I make full acknowledgment of their part in what we have done together; to all who have given me their confidence I shall ever be grateful. The full years have brought their harvest; and now the winter has come.

Lee Simmons

Sherman, Texas
   August 1, 1957

Contents

Illustrations

Assignment Huntsville

CHAPTER 1

A Youthful Tragedy

You come, I think, actually to understand the meaning of prison bars only when they stand between you and freedom. And I, who have had years of experience as the keeper of men in confinement, had my first taste of prison discipline before I was twenty-one. I had it as a prisoner, charged with murder. At times in the course of my life, this experience has been a matter of embarrassment to me, and I make mention of it, now that I am up in years, for only two reasons. In the first place, the tragedy of which I am about to tell you went a long way toward shaping my whole life. In the second place, the story which I plan to lay before you in this book will have as much to do with prisons as with Lee Simmons, and I might as well let you have it from both sides as I know it myself—from experience.

The way of it, then, was this. My brother D. E. Simmons, who later became assistant attorney general of Texas and still later United States district attorney for the Southern District of Texas, was in 1894 a member of the Texas Legislature and a practicing attorney. I myself was then on the eve of entering my fourth year at the University of Texas, having in mind my father's plan that I should join my brother in the practice of law. The thing that came upon us, however, changed all my plans.

It was in the summer of 1894 that a friend and fellow-member of the Legislature called my brother and told him of some untrue and derogatory statements being made in regard to a member of our family. The statements were coming from a prominent citizen and former public official of a west Texas county.

My brother went immediately to investigate the matter, and the guilty party not only refused to see him but kept carefully out of the way. My brother returned to make report of his findings to the entire family. This he did as we were gathered around the breakfast table. We took it pretty hard.

My brother then had to leave for south Texas on a business errand. Without his knowledge, I took it upon myself to go to west Texas to make my own investigation. I did not know a single soul in the town when I arrived, and I had considerable difficulty in finding the person I wished to see. I was cautious in my actions, as I felt that he would again leave town if he learned of my presence. There had already been a good deal of talk about my brother's having been there a few days before.

I finally found the man and came up to him to talk. He immediately went for his gun, but he lost the draw. For I was also armed.

As I have stated, I didn't know a soul in the town. So I walked up the street until I met a man with boots and a big hat. I asked him if he was an officer, and of course he was, as was easy to see. I handed him my gun and told him there had been some trouble down the street.

We started on up the street, the constable and I, when a man came running toward us and excitedly asked the officer what had happened. "I don't know," he said. "This boy here come up and give me his gun and said there was some trouble."

"Take him on to the office, and I'll be back in a minute," said our questioner, as he dashed away as fast as he could go.

"Who is that man?" I asked.

"Sheriff," said the constable.

We went on up to the courthouse and into the sheriff's office. The constable never so much as asked me a single question. Just as we reached the sheriff's office, a man ran in and said to me: "Good shot, boy; you ought to have done it!"

Then in ran the sheriff himself, through the door on the opposite

A Youthful Tragedy

side of the room, drawing his old-time .45 as he came, and crying, "Get out of the way, and I'll fix the blankety son-of-a-blank!"

The stranger who had just commended me leaped upon the sheriff, grabbed at the pistol, and deflected it just as it went off. The man who thus saved my life was County Clerk Tom Brown.

By this time, of course, excitement was running pretty high. I was a stranger, under twenty-one, and a voluntarily surrendered prisoner, whose protection was the sworn duty of the sheriff. Instead of protecting me, however, he had just attempted to assassinate me. Yes, excitement was pretty high.

The upshot of it all was that I was placed in jail, and after I was locked up, Tom Brown came in to see me. He was an old-timer in those parts and knew no fear whatever. He said things looked pretty bad on the outside. Then he told me that once when he himself was a young man in Kentucky Town, Texas, he had been in trouble and my father had befriended him.

"I've got my Winchester," he said, "and I want you to know that, if they get you, they've got Tom Brown first. I'll stay with you." And he did. I cannot hold back the tears as I recall his words. Those who know me have often remarked that I love my friends. But who would not love, almost to idolatry, a man like Tom Brown?

In a couple of days, my father arrived from Sherman, bringing with him a lawyer, C. B. Randell. By this time two factions were forming: folks were either for Lee Simmons or against him. R. E. Carswell, recognized as the ablest lawyer to be found anywhere up and down the route of the Fort Worth and Denver Railway, was hired especially to prosecute me. My family and friends retained the services of attorney Tom McMurray, and the legal battle was on.

We applied for bail, and the county attorney opposed it in the County Court. I believe the records up to that time showed that never before had an examining trial in that county been heard in the County Court. Theretofore, they had always been handled either by a justice of the peace or else by a district judge. But now, with the county judge a member of the anti-Simmons faction, the hearing on my application for bail was held in that court. Bail was refused me.

Judge J. M. Hurt, chief justice of the State Court of Criminal Appeals, was found to be at Henrietta, where he was visiting a son. He agreed to a habeas corpus hearing there, and I was transferred to the county jail at Henrietta. After an all-day session, Judge Hurt stated to the prosecution that, everything claimed by the state being admitted, the defendant was entitled to bail. Bond was set rather high, but we made it immediately, and I was released.

It was several months before the District Court convened and the grand jury was impaneled. I was indicted for murder, as was to be expected. The sheriff, however, was not indicted for assault with intent to murder. It was afterward learned that seven members of the grand jury did vote to indict him, but, as it takes the concurrence of nine grand jurors to bring in a valid indictment, the sheriff escaped. The failure to indict him neither concerned nor worried us. By this time many good citizens were openly expressing their feeling about the injustice done me. When the case was called for trial, my lawyers asked for a change of venue, as it stood to reason that I could not get a fair trial under the existing conditions.

In his argument in my behalf before the court, one of my lawyers, Mr. Randell, bitterly denounced the sheriff, the district clerk, and the county judge—the last for having denied me bail. In fact, Mr. Randell denounced just about everybody except His Honor, the district judge on the bench. The latter denied a change of venue but did grant a continuance.

It was all too clear that we could not afford to go to trial there under the circumstances prevailing at the time. For my case had become an issue in local politics, and men were elected or defeated according to which side they were on. It was not until some six months later that the court reconvened, at which time we again applied for a change of venue.

In the meantime, I had married as fine a young lady as ever went to the marriage altar. It was quite a serious step for a girl with a good home and a good name to marry a man under indictment for murder. But we had been engaged for several years before this trouble came about, and trouble or not, she stood by me.

The application for a change of venue was granted, and the case was transferred to Denton County. All we had ever sought was a fair trial, and at the first term of the District Court in Denton County we announced ready and were anxious to get on with it. The case was set, the jury venire was drawn, the jurors were selected, and the hearing of evidence began.

I was placed in jail again, as in those days no defendant was allowed to be out on bond during trial. Here, as in the course of my confincment in the other two jails where I had been held, my friends wanted to send my meals to me from the outside. But in each case I refused to let them do so. I ate corn bread, fat bacon, navy beans, and molasses. And I ate with a pewter spoon. The coffee was black and came in a tin cup. Mine was precisely the same fare that other prisoners got. And in each of the three jails where I stayed, the prisoners became my friends.

I have already said that hired counsel had been provided for the prosecution of the charges against me. Special Prosecutor Carswell pressed the case ably and severely, but honorably. We frequently met in later years, and I never had the slightest bit of ill-feeling toward him. Similarly, County Attorney Sullivan, of Denton County, bore down on the evidence against me to the best of his ability, and he was a vigorous young prosecutor. He was but doing his sworn duty, and we later became good friends. Indeed, I would have had no respect for either Carswell or Sullivan had they failed to do their best against me. Under the law, they were bound to do no less.

Associated with Carswell and Sullivan, however, was the late Clarence Wharton, of Houston, then a young lawyer of great promise and a friend of the dead man. I would have felt different, I think, about his participation had there been real need of it. But he had volunteered his services, and he made a most bitter and inflammatory speech to the jury. Then he straightway left the courtroom and the county seat before the judge had even started to read his charge to the jury. Clarence Wharton later became a prominent lawyer and one of the recognized historians of Texas. He and I met a number of times, both in Austin and in Houston, and I always spoke to him courteously. But I never shook hands with him.

Tom Brown testified on the witness stand, both in the application for change of venue and in the final trial, giving the facts as I have given them here. I hesitate to repeat his statement, but he also testified that, during the struggle to disarm the sheriff at the time of his attempt to shoot me in his office, I had said: "Give me back my gun and turn the cowardly son of a bitch loose!" I would not wish to verify the wording exactly, nor can I take any pride in it now, but it represents substantially what I had in mind at the time.

The trial judge read his charge to the jury, giving them the law applicable to the case, the evidence having already been presented under oath from the witness stand. And the twelve men retired from the jury box to consider their verdict.

My young wife and our many friends gathered about me. Perhaps it is strange, but I was neither restless nor nervous. I had not a doubt nor a fear of the result. All I ever asked—all I had a right to expect—was a fair trial by a jury of my fellow-men.

After a brief absence for deliberation the jurymen filed back into the courtroom. The verdict was: "Not guilty as charged in the indictment."

The day was September 12, 1897. It was a day of great excitement, of course, and yet far different from the tension of September 4, 1894, when the sheriff made his attempt upon my life. Later on, in a way I actually felt sorry for that sheriff. I had expected him to come to me and apologize, to say that he was sorry that he had tried to kill me and that he had lost his head at the time. But he never did, and we never spoke to each other again. From that time on his health began to fail, and in a few years he died. I believed then, and I believe now, that his death was caused by worry over his assault on an unarmed prisoner.

A few days after the trial, I received this letter, and you may be sure that it is among my most valued papers:

Pilot Point, Texas,
Mr. Simmons: Sept. 22nd., 1897.

I am so glad that you are a free man again. I am proud that I was one of the jury to turn you loose. I have received lots of praise for that good deed. I can never forget that night in the court house at Denton or that happy meeting. God bless you and your true wife, and may you live a long and peaceful life.

Yours,
[signed]   T. C. Garner

A Youthful Tragedy

In later years, as sheriff of Grayson County, as well as in all other important positions which I have held, I have always maintained that a public official charged with the enforcement of law ought, above all else, to observe that law himself. I have tried to live by that principle, and I have always instructed my employees accordingly.

CHAPTER 2

The Rod Unspared

As SLANTS THE SAPLING, they say, so is inclined the tree. But the fruitage of the oak, I have observed, is already well determined in the seed acorn. In the breeding of men, as in the breeding of cattle, bloodlines will tell. It seems proper, therefore, to go back a bit and say something of my family and of our origins.

My paternal grandfather was a Baptist preacher. My father, D. A. Simmons, was born at Townsville, Anderson County, South Carolina, on February 12, 1841. He had completed only a few months of a medical course at Atlanta, Georgia, when he quit school to join Lee's Army of Northern Virginia. He served under General Marshall and was wounded in the Battle of the Wilderness. For two years during the war he never missed a roll call. But on February 2, 1865, he took time off from military duties to marry Kate B. Swilling, a South Carolina girl not quite two years his junior.

When the fighting was over, Father returned to his young wife at Townsville, where my oldest brother, Robert, was born on January 14, 1866. Shortly thereafter, Father, Mother, and Robert, together with Jim Hollingsworth and his wife and three children, set out for Burlington, Iowa—all in one wagon. Hollingsworth and Father had been reared together, had served together in the Confederate Army, and were lifelong friends.

In Iowa, Father worked on the farm of an old Dutchman, who was as fair and square as a man could be. Father had a great liking for him and grubbed stumps for him at a dollar a stump. The work went on into the winter months, Father knocking the snow and ice away from the base of the stumps so as to get at them. Sometimes he made two or three dollars in a single day, and then he would hit a stump that would take him a day or more.

Before Father left, his employer offered to sell him a plot of land for exactly what it had cost. "You sign the note," said the Dutchman, "and you keep the land one year, and then, if you don't stay, I buy it back from you for just what you pay me for it, and I give you interest on your money."

"Thanks," replied Father, "but I am going to Texas!"

"Texas!" exclaimed the Dutchman, "If I have to go to Texas with all them cyclone and all them rattlesnake, or else I got to go to Hell, I just don't know where I better go."

But Father was determined. That Iowa land was bottom land. I well remember that Father always said to me: "Son, don't ever settle on overflow land."

By this time, my parents had a second son, David Edward, born on June 14, 1868. So, then, my family, accompanied by the Jim Hollingsworth family, came down from Iowa, traveling by wagon through the Indian Territory and crossing Red River into Texas at Colbert's Ferry, north of what is now Denison. They settled at White Mound, four miles west of Kentucky Town. Here they lived for a time in a log cabin on a rented farm, and it was here that my sister, Mollie T. Simmons, was born on April 6, 1871.

On New Year's Day, 1873, Father and Mother and their three children left White Mound for Cass County, in east Texas, where I was born on September 9, 1873, as Marshall Lee Simmons. I have not used the "Marshall" very much in my eighty-three years. In the following December the family returned to White Mound, where Father resumed farming and did right well at it in time.

Ours was a Christian home. Discipline was strict and firm. My mother was an educated and cultured woman. Father, on the other hand, despite his brief study of medicine, had little formal schooling. But he was a man of character and was widely respected for his honesty and hard work. Home life under these two demanded honesty and industry from child and grownup alike.

Man and boy, I have ridden a horse these seventy-odd years. At the age of five it was my duty to go drive up the cows from the prairie at milking time. Riding and the mastery of horses was second nature to all of us. However, we youngsters walked the mile and a half to the country school of some sixty pupils taught by Professor Dewey Langford. That was back in 1880, and I was seven years old. I learned a great deal not to be found between the blue backs of my old speller. For example, Professor Langford expected us boys to provide the firewood for the schoolhouse. His farmer patrons hauled the pole-wood for us free, but the boys were assigned the task of chopping it up into short lengths.

We also had to build the fires early on winter days, sweep the floor after school had closed at four in the afternoon, and carry drinking water two or three times a day, fetching it from a quarter of a mile away. With the exception of the fire-building before eight o'clock of a morning and the sweeping-out at four, these were welcome chores, for they gave us a desirable break from the droning duties of the school-room.

Being the youngest in our family, at home I had the job of getting in the wood and kindling. My two brothers chopped the wood, fed the livestock, and milked morning and evening, while my sister helped Mother with the housework.

For failure to get in the wood and kindling, my father would rouse me out of sound sleep and send me out to the woodpile to bring it in. I remember that one morning he whipped me for having gone to bed with my boots on. And at another time he gave me a good one for having hidden in the barn late in the evening, with the result that I fell asleep there—and all the family and hired hands were looking everywhere for me.

All this came of my conceiving that my feelings were hurt because Mother had boxed my ears. Mother was cooking supper and was very busy, while I was fooling around in the kitchen. As she passed and re-passed me, her apron strings were so inviting that I could not resist the temptation; so I caught hold of the short one and pulled it. Her apron dropped to the floor.

Without a word, Mother turned on me and gave one good slap. It was the only time, so far as I can remember, that Mother ever struck me. And that was why my feelings were hurt and why I hid in the barn.

Every Sunday morning, without fail, Mother had me take an old piepan, get some soot out of the chimney and some cream off the milk jar, mix them together, and take a rag to black my boots. Those boots had to pass Sunday morning inspection, along with my face, neck, ears, and hands. When they failed to pass inspection, it took a second going-over.

In the spring and summer it was my bare feet and not my boots that had to pass inspection. Also there was a dogwood toothbrush to be used with salt and soda for tooth powder. I give you all this detail to emphasize one thing—the value of home training. I learned the hard way to perform the duties required of me. In short, I learned responsibility.

After my punishments I never did go to bed with my boots on again. I never did hide again. In my various occupations of life, I have endeavored to keep my dress and personal appearance such as the occasion might properly demand. And I still have my teeth. These lessons cannot be taught by the preacher. They cannot be learned at school. Only the home can give this all-important training.

Of course, Mother's viewpoint occasionally differed from Father's. She used to tell how she cooked for the first year at White Mound over the open fire in the fireplace, until one day Father came home with two ten-dollar gold pieces with which to buy her a cookstove. But Mother took the money and bought two cows instead. She figured she needed milk for her little people.

Later, when I was old enough to do the milking, Father would say to me: "Son, when you're milking, leave a little more for the milk-pen calves. Those calves out on the pasture with the beef cattle are getting ahead of them."

But Mother would always say: "Son, strip those cows a little better; I'm running short of milk and butter." Father was likely to think of his livestock, but Mother looked after us children.

At the age of nine, I was teaming, hauling farm products over dirt roads, crossing fairly large creeks with no bridges, selling my load, depositing the proceeds in the bank, then buying groceries or bagging and ties for the cotton gin Father had begun operating, or bringing the money back to Father, according to his instructions. I remember that cottonseed then sold for five dollars a ton, and hulls were given away to anyone who would haul them off. Seed was stacked outside on the ground at Father's gin.

By the time I got to be ten, Father was placing all kinds of responsibility on me, as my two brothers were then attending Halsell's College at Savoy, twenty-odd miles from home. Once a month, on Friday, I rode one horse and led another to Savoy to bring the boys home. The round trip took all of Friday. After Saturday at home, the boys and I started out early Sunday morning on the journey back to college, where I left them to get back home with the horses late that evening. The round trip was well over forty miles. And I rode double, of course, when I had the boys with me.

When Father first came to Texas, he did not say anything about being a "doctor." He attended the sick only in his family. But gradually the neighbors called him in, and he sent for some doctor books and read them until at length he had a large practice taking him over the community for miles around.

It was a common thing, along about dark, for somebody to ride up and hail Father from the road: "Come quick, Doc, the wife is took bad!"

Father always said they waited until nightfall before calling him. He figured they waited until sundown to see if they could make it through the night. And then they called the doctor. Many was the night that he got on his horse to ride ten miles into the country, getting back home after midnight. But Father never refused anyone. It made no difference to him whether or not they paid; if they were sick, he was a doctor—and he answered all calls.

Father collected when, where, and if he could. He used to send me out to collect for him. I remember he sent me out one time to get a load of *bois d'arc* fence posts that old Dick Guess had cut for him. Dick was a Negro who owed Father a doctor bill. When I got to Dick's house, Dick was sick again and in bed. There was no one to help me load the posts.

I wasn't over nine or ten at the time, but I had to load up those posts. *Bois d'arc,* as you know, is a heavy, solid wood. I had to get down on the ground, drag a couple of posts up to the wagon, stand

The Rod Unspared

them on end, and lean them against the wagon bed. Then I would get up on the wagon and pull up the posts one at a time. Then down on the ground again to get two more posts, and so on. Well, I did it all by myself. I was late bringing in my load. But I brought in the posts.

One day, also when I was about ten, Father sent me on a pony to bring in a cow and a calf. He ought not to have done it, for you know how a cow and a calf will run every which way, especially when they are a little wild. It was really a two-man job. It was very late at night when I finally brought them in after we had run all over the country. Next morning, when Father went out to the barn lot, my pony was dead. But Father never criticized or rebuked me about it, either then or afterward.

On still another occasion, Father sent me out to collect from a patient who was mighty poor pay. "He owes me $40," said Father, "but take anything you can get." So off I went to see what I could do. The fellow didn't seem to have anything much except a black calf that looked as if it had been hit in the head with a churn dasher.

So I made my man a proposition. "I'll allow you $20 on your bill," I said, "if you'll give me that calf."

He hemmed and hawed, but I got out my rope, and he "reckoned it would be all right" for me to take the calf. I had started home with the animal when I met one of the traveling cattle-buyers who in those days toured the country, trading and buying as they went along. As it turned out, I sold the calf for six silver dollars.

On the way home with the six silver dollars heavy in my pocket, I got to worrying about what Father would say. After all, I had just sold a twenty-dollar calf for six dollars. When I got home, I told Father what I had done and cocked an anxious eye at him. "Well, son," he said, "six silver dollars is just six dollars more than nothing." And that is all he said.

Looking back on it now, I find it surprising what all my father put on the shoulders of a little fellow. I remember that one evening he sent me several miles into town to take seventy dollars, which was Father's part on a community carload of lumber the neighbors were ordering by freight from east Texas.

Down in my heart I was sure that everybody in the county knew

D. A. Simmons was sending that ten-year-old of his cross-country with seventy dollars cash in his pocket. Seventy dollars was seventy dollars in those days. I laid it on to my horse and made all the speed I could. I don't know what I would have done if a stray cow or something had crashed through the brush by the side of the road. I would have fainted right off the horse. But I made it into town without any trouble.

In 1885 we moved to Sherman, where I attended the public schools. When I was fifteen, Father put me in charge of a "half-circle" hay-baler and its crew of hands, and we baled hay for the farming community thereabouts during the summers.

In due time I entered Austin College at Sherman, where I completed two years, followed by three more years at the University of Texas. I have already told how I got into serious trouble, and I never returned to the university for my degree.

I had just turned twenty-two when I married as fine a country girl as ever graced a well-to-do farm home. I got a job at thirty dollars a month with R. E. Smith, then known as the "Alfalfa King of Texas," and I went to work. I have been working ever since.

At the end of a year's work as a hired hand, I bought a pair of mules and rented a little farm for two years. Next I bought ninety acres at forty dollars an acre, made a small down payment, with the remainder due in annual installments of four hundred dollars with interest at 10 per cent. I paid it out easily as it came due and then bought more land adjoining—this time at the cheap rate of 8 per cent—and soon paid that out also. Then I built the best barn in Grayson County, if I do say it myself.

Three years later I built one of the best farm homes in the county, and we moved out of our original little three-room box house. I was especially proud of our three new fireplaces, equipped, respectively, with a nice white-brick mantel, a large oak mantel, and an extra-fine one of the mission type. Our house was all paid for when it was completed.

When our crop was laid by, our custom was to hitch a pair of good mules to a covered wagon and make a trip somewhere. On this occasion we prepared for a long trip and fixed up Pullman style; bedsprings, mattress, sheet-iron cookstove, chuck box, water keg, etc.

The Rod Unspared

Mrs. Simmons was a good shot and killed many quail, one prairie chicken, and a number of small rabbits, and I had a small seine, so we had plenty of fresh meat. We carried from home ham, shoulder, bacon, potatoes and onions, meal and flour, so our entire expense on this thirty-day vacation did not exceed ten dollars and most of it was for two sacks of oats for the mules and for ferry charges. Later in life we visited a number of World Fairs, California, and Colorado, but we always agreed that this 1901 vacation trip to Indian Territory was the most interesting and finest of all.

As I figured it, we were just ready to live—really to live. We didn't owe anybody a thing except friendship and appreciation. But the lack of good roads and of school facilities caused me to sell out and move to town, where I could go into the livestock business on a larger scale. For several years I operated a mule barn in Sherman.

In 1912 lawlessness and crime conditions in general got to be so bad in Grayson County that popular demand for law enforcement became almost an uprising. In May of that year I received a long petition signed by prominent and successful citizens from all over the county. This document said I should run for sheriff. I had never had any kind of peace officer's job, nor had I held public office. But my extensive business as a trader in mules and cattle had carried me into every section of the county, and I was by that time well and widely known. A few people remembered the trouble I had been in fifteen years before. But those few were like the present mayor of Sherman, who was foreman of the Denton County jury that acquitted me. They knew the straight of that old story.

I did not decide upon my answer right away but first made a careful survey of the entire situation. Then, in the latter part of May, I made the usual formal announcement of my candidacy, subject to the action of the voters at the primary election to be held in July.

That was perhaps the hottest, and was surely the bitterest, political campaign ever waged in the county. The outcome of it was that I received the nomination by a majority of 1,208 over an old-time peace officer who was running for his second term as sheriff. The second-term tradition is strong in Texas, and this was the only time in the history of Grayson County that a sheriff failed to be re-elected for a second term.

Open violation of the law continued right on up to the general election in November. After my election I made the announcement that I intended to appoint as my deputies the best and most experienced officers I could find anywhere in the country. Evidently the criminal element saw that there would be a sweeping change when I took over my duties as sheriff in January. They decided not to wait.

One Saturday night I attended a meeting at the local YMCA, in company with my dear friend Hayden W. Head, now deceased. After the meeting, no sooner had I gone home and entered the house than I was called to the front door. As I opened it I was met by a fusillade of shots. Three of the bullets went clear through me. I finally recovered, of course—else you wouldn't be reading these lines from my hand.

The would-be assassin, I concluded at the time, was the tool of a careful plot to eliminate me so that in some manner the old regime could continue in office. Under the law, you know, an official remains in office until his successor qualifies. I came within a fraction of an inch of not being able to qualify for anything except a first-class funeral. The brains of the gang escaped prosecution, and only the triggerman went to the penitentiary.

CHAPTER 3

Bootleggers and Other Evildoers

$\mathbb{A}$ SIDE FROM the convalescent difficulties of a pretty thoroughly punctured sheriff, the shooting of which I have just told you really turned out to be a great help in my work. The natural sympathy of my friends and neighbors while I was slowly regaining my strength also won for me their support in the enforcement of the law. The records of Grayson County will show that I did enforce it.

It is not of records, however, that I now want to speak. I shall content myself with recalling that conditions in the county were so bad that a special district court had been provided to assist the two regular courts then hearing cases. Bootlegging was at that time a felony under the law. Many killings were taking place. Liquor-selling was prevalent.

One night a bootlegger stopped me and insisted upon selling me whisky. I thought at first that it was some friend jollying me. But when I saw that he actually meant it, I made the purchase. Upon learning his mistake, the fellow promptly pleaded guilty and went to the penitentiary. I am not strait-laced about liquor. I don't particularly care for it, but in my time I have taken a social drink or two. When I came to be sheriff, though, I laid off. And I never touched a drop all the time I was in office. I had promised law enforcement, and I made no exception in the case of liquor violations.

In Denison at that time there were many illegal clubs in operation.

After my election I immediately went around and told them all that they would have to close. One of the principal offenders failed to comply with my order. I made a second visit and said to him: "It is not my duty to come around here and ask you to close up. I can get a warrant and take you to jail. But I want to deal fairly with you. The next time I come, I will have a warrant and I will take you over to Sherman—you and everything you have in your joint—and I will put you in jail."

He came right back at me: "Mr. Simmons, you're not going to have to come to see me any more. I have a wife and a little girl, and I think you mean what you say. I'm closing down right now." So saying, he went out of the place with me and turned and locked the door behind us. I left him then—and, sure enough, I never had occasion to go back.

I remember another bootlegger who thought he could get rough with my deputies, and one of them worked him over a bit, knocked the fellow down, handcuffed him, and hauled him off to jail. When I got there, the jailer had the prisoner with his head under a hydrant, washing the blood out of his hair and face. Of course, I summoned the county physician, who came down and fixed up the prisoner.

Shortly thereafter, the bootlegger pleaded guilty. Still later, I recall, he made an embarrassing request of me. He said that he saw that he was going to have to change his ways or else go to the penitentiary. If he could get a steady job, he argued, he was ready to go straight. How about it? Would I help him get a job as brakeman on the railroad?

I couldn't honestly recommend him, and I told him so; but I did write a letter for him to the officials of the road. I stated to them that the man had promised to mend his ways and to do his best to render good service, if given the job. Well, he got it, and I never had any more trouble with him.

Sometimes my efforts to be considerate backfired on me. For example, one morning a deputy brought in a man charged with a minor offense. The prisoner was in bad shape, showing every evidence of having been on a rip-roaring drunk the night before. He was trembling and jerking all over. So I told the deputy he had better give our man a drink. I unlocked my storage cell and handed over a bottle of liquor which we had on hand for evidence in another case. The deputy gave the man a swig, which he certainly needed.

Under the influence of the draught the prisoner steadied enough to ask the jailer to telephone his lawyer. The lawyer soon showed up and asked his client what he was charged with. Whereupon the prisoner piped up: "Well, I guess it must be for being drunk; but they gave me the whisky right up there in the sheriff's office!"

Although we explained to the attorney that ours was only a humanitarian deed in his client's behalf, that lawyer—would you believe it?—left us with a devilish smile on his face.

Sometimes it took quite a bit of doing to make a case stand up in court. I remember that B. J. Lindsay came to me one day with a complaint. Lindsay was a leading insurance man of Denison and a mighty fine man. Upstairs over his place of business were a man and wife who were selling liquor. But they had been mighty hard to catch. "Lee," said Lindsay to me, "it ain't fair to send up all these people for selling hooch when you let Gus and Ada sell all they want right upstairs."

"The trouble is," I answered, "that Gus and Ada won't branch out. They won't sell to anybody except to known customers. But we'll see what we can do."

I laid for Gus and Ada. I trapped them; I make no apology about it. I figured that people who break the law and make a business of breaking the law have it coming to them. Now, as it happened, we had a one-legged lad who had also been selling liquor. We had two airtight cases against him and could have sent him up without the least bit of trouble. But he had a wife and two or three children. I got to studying about him, and I went to him and said: "Bill, you know I can send you to the pen. Would you rather stay home and make a living for your wife and children?"

"Mr. Simmons," said Bill, "you know I'd rather stay home and look after my family."

"Well, we'll see about that. If you'll help me catch Gus and bring him to trial, I give you my word that I'll speak to the county attorney and ask him to let you off light."

Bill agreed to co-operate, and I got an old country-looking boy who was to be introduced to Gus as a customer. Bill, my one-legged defendant, was to do the introducing. First we searched our witness to make sure he had no liquor on him. Then I gave him some marked money and sent him up with Pegleg to call on Gus.

"Gus," said Pegleg, "this here's a customer of mine, and I wish you would take care of him for me." Gus sold the customer a quart, and the boy came on down to the office and delivered the quart to me. Then after dinner he went back to get another quart of evidence. Gus wasn't there, but this time Ada sold our customer a quart. A little later we went in and searched Gus and Ada. We found the marked money on both of them.

We tried Ada first, and she got two years in the penitentiary. But Gus got only one year. In Texas, you know, the juries fix the sentence within the limitations set by statute; and juries vary widely in the seriousness with which they regard offenses—particularly liquor offenses.

I remember that, when I was testifying in the case against Gus, I spoke out of turn. I knew better, but the jury heard me just the same. Also, it worked. At the moment, the defense attorney was after me and whipsawing me in cross-examination: "And you knew that this witness (Pegleg) had himself violated the law, and you promised not to prosecute him, and you induced him to serve your purpose in that unlawful manner?"

"Yes, I did. I figured it would be better for him to help enforce the law and to stay home to make a living for his wife and three children than to . . ."

"Your Honor! Oh, your Honor," the lawyer was shouting in the effort to shut me off, "I didn't ask him that." But he was too late. The jury had already heard about the wife and babies.

After the jury gave Gus a year less than Ada's jury had given her, I said to her: "It ought to have been the other way round, Ada. Gus should have got two years and you but one. But when Gus has done his time, I will go to the parole board and ask them to let up on you, too." I did go to the board, and the board released them both at the end of Gus's term. They left for parts unknown, and I never heard of them again.

Some of our liquor-sellers were pretty smooth. My brethren in the Elks lodge had a pretty keen thirst in those days, and when a salesman came along with a special introductory offer of a ten-gallon keg represented to contain prime bourbon for $35, they eased the bung out of the keg, sampled the contents, found it to be prime as stated, and closed a cash deal. The only trouble about that keg was that it had a special compartment just under the bung, sealed off from the rest of the interior. So my brother Elks got one quart of liquor and nine gallons and three quarts of water.

Under the circumstances, I did not feel it my duty to take any official action in the matter of the double-bottomed, special introductory keg, particularly as the news was well noised about, and the Elk nose for a bargain became the subject of rude and repeated jest all over the county.

The boys in the lodge also got to gambling rather heavily. Now, when it was only a few of the fellows in a friendly poker game, I didn't take the trouble to bother them. But one night when I was down at the hall they had quite a dice game going. Also present was a policeman who, as I happened to know, was just aching to run against me for sheriff. Naturally, I waited around for him to get into the game. But he disappointed me; he didn't get in. I warned the boys that I couldn't have such goings on. But as I went downstairs, I said to myself: "Lee, you just can't have it said of you that you let your lodge brothers run a gambling game while you're running in all the Negro crapshooters in town."

So I went and got County Attorney Ben Gafford. Ben was a prominent Elk. I took him up to the hall and showed him what was going on. "Aw, Lee," he expostulated, "you can't do this to these fellows!"

"Ben," said I, "I simply can't afford to let this go on."

"What you aiming to do?"

"I'm going in to get them."

So I raided the game. My brother Elks, naturally, were plenty indignant about it. One of them began to get really rough. So I said: "You boys come down in the morning and pay your fines. If you don't, I'll file on the Elks lodge for running a disorderly house."

They all paid their fines the next morning. Shortly afterward I met up with one of my Negro friends on the sidewalk: "Yah, Mr. Lee, you done treat them white boys jes' lak you does the res' of us."

But there came times when my brethren had the laugh on me. For example, one time my dear friend Bill Goode, who was superintendent of the road gang of county prisoners was moving his camp from the south part of the county to up above Sherman. A heavy rain came that day, and Goode asked me to let him leave fifteen or so Negro prisoners in the jail for the night. Of course, I agreed readily enough. The jailer placed them in a row of cells which opened on an enclosed runway, and he simply locked the runway without confining the prisoners to individual cells.

He forgot that nearby was a cell which held our "evidence" in liquor cases. In fact, it was stacked up with bootleg whisky in every sort of package and container, awaiting court orders to be destroyed. Somehow, someway, a piece of baling wire showed up in that runway, and our overnight guests enthusiastically began fishing through the bars. They made a combined haul sufficient to get the whole crew horizontally drunk before morning. My friends made the most of the story of my jail refreshments for visitors. I had lots of friends, and the yarn didn't lose anything in the repetition of it. There was nothing left for me but to enjoy the joke with them.

I hold that an officer of the law is justified in treating different people differently. You don't always have to jail a neighbor in order to get the law enforced. For instance, we found out that gambling was going on in the back of a cleaning and pressing shop in town. The son of our mayor was in there a good deal. I didn't want to have to arrest the boy, so I went to His Honor and said: "Bill, I don't want to catch your boy along with the rest in that pressing-shop game, and I think maybe you'd better see about it for me."

"Leave it to me," said Bill. And I heard no more about gambling in the cleaning and pressing business.

There were times, however, when easygoing methods didn't work. We had a blacksmith named Charlie Blank. He was undoubtedly selling liquor. Charlie had two or three children, and that is why I went to him: "Look here, Charlie, I'd hate to have to send you to the pen."

He looked me in the eye and sullenly said: "You got no right to talk that way. You're sheriff. If you think I'm selling liquor, catch me. And if you don't catch me, go on about your business and let me alone!"

I got him caught and sent him to the penitentiary. But after he got down there, a baby was born to his wife. A petition was drawn up to get him out, and I was asked to sign it. "No," said I. "He hasn't been down there long enough."

But the next time I was in Austin I went around to the parole board and told them that Charlie had a big family and that I thought maybe he might go straight if they would turn him loose and give him a chance. The board told me to write them a letter, which I did.

They turned Charlie loose, and as soon as he got off the interurban at Sherman he came straight to my office to thank me. Of course I wanted no thanks, and I told him so: "All I want of you, Charlie, is for you to straighten up and take care of your little woman and children." He did it, too. We never had any more trouble out of him.

One evening, just after dark, a farmer telephoned in that a young man had stolen some stuff off his place. Two deputies went out to investigate and brought in a seventeen-year-old. They had found him in possession of the stolen goods. Although he was the son of a substantial citizen, I placed him in a cell by himself and let him spend the night there. The next morning I had him brought into my office.

I told him it would break the heart of his good mother and father if they knew what he had done. I said that the man from whom he had stolen the property did not know who he was and that I was not going to let anybody know what he had done. I was turning him loose without any charge. If he accepted my advice and went straight from then on, I would feel that I had done a kind deed. But if, on the other hand, he decided that he had been smart and had gotten by, then I would be making a big mistake. Well, in a year or so, that boy was married. He settled down and is today a law-abiding, successful farmer.

At another time, I had to go over into Arkansas to pick up a prisoner. I found him at Pine Bluff. I went out to his place with the local sheriff and the fellow's lawyer. The defendant was at home, and just outside his door sat his wife with a baby in her arms and a child of about two years at her side. I admit it sort of set me back. The sheriff said the lad had led an honest life in the community, with nothing against him.

I looked him over. He looked like the sort of man the sheriff said he was. "I've come to take you back to Texas," I told him.

"I ain't a-goin' with you," he said. "You don't know me, you don't know that I'm your man, and you don't know that I done it."

"No," I admitted, "I don't. But I'm going to take you with me just the same."

"I ain't a-goin'," he repeated. "And you cain't make me."

"Maybe not now," I conceded, "and maybe it will take a bit longer. But in the end, I'll get you and take you back. If you give me trouble, I can give you trouble—and I'll give you plenty. But if you're reasonable and come along voluntarily, I'll tell you what I'll do: You have a good record here, I find. Now, in Texas we have a suspended-sentence law. If you'll go along with me of your own accord, I'll speak to the prosecuting attorney and ask him to recommend a suspended sentence in your case. I'm not promising you a suspended sentence, mind you. I can't promise you that. But I will ask the prosecuting attorney, and I've never yet asked him for anything that he didn't give me. You make me trouble and I'll make you trouble, like I said. You come along with me, and I'll do like I'm saying now."

"I ain't a-goin'," he persisted.

About that time the lawyer spoke up: "Look here, Joe; I believe this feller from Texas means what he says and will do what he says. My advice to you is to go back to Texas and get this whole thing cleaned up."

The upshot was that Joe took the lawyer's advice and came back with me. When we got to Sherman, he stood trial, pleaded guilty, and got his suspended sentence. The windup of the story is that the fellow didn't have money enough to get back to Arkansas. I let him have it out of my own pocket, for I had sized him up, and he looked like he was good for it. He was, too; he sent my money back to me within three days after he got home.

People think of a sheriff as dealing only with men who are law-breakers, but the duties of the office often involve him with women and children as well. One of the hardest jobs I had to do while I was sheriff was to take a two-year-old child from its mother. I was proceeding under an order from the district judge to produce the child in court on Monday morning. I waited until Sunday afternoon and then went to find the mother and child. When the mother saw me coming, she grabbed her baby and ran out the back door. I had to run to overtake her.

There followed a truly tragic scene, with the mother weeping and the child screaming with terror. But I had my duty to perform, so I brought the little girl to my own home, where Mrs. Simmons bathed her and put clean clothes on her. The next morning I took her with me to court. After quite a trial the judge ruled that the mother was not a proper person to rear the little girl. He placed the child in the home of relatives, where she was well cared for. She grew into a fine young lady.

I recall a different sort of experience I had with the fair sex during my term of office. A woman from our community had been adjudged insane, and it was the duty of the sheriff's office to see that she was delivered to the proper custodians at the State Hospital for the Insane. Ordinarily I would have sent one of my deputies as her escort, but just at this time I needed to go to Austin to turn in some financial records, so I told my deputy: "Just fix up the lady's papers and I'll take her along with me and save the state an extra railroad ticket."

The next morning we rode over to Denison and caught the M.K.&T. day coach. My ward was not of the dangerous or violent type, but all these changes of scenery following upon her recent experience of a courtroom trial made her jumpy and excitable. As the "Katy" rattled southward, the woman began to prowl restlessly up and down the aisles and from one car to another. I stayed right behind her, as I had to keep her under observation, shifting my direction every time she took a different notion about where she was heading. Passengers began to stare. They figured one of the two of us was looking after the other, but it was plain they weren't sure which was which. When my ward went into the ladies' room I was still right behind her. I stood in the swaying corridor with one foot propped in the compartment door in case she might take a notion to throw herself out the window. But I heard the whisperings around me and felt my face growing redder and redder.

After two or three hours of this wandering around I thought up a way to get her to settle down. "Would you like to share some lunch with me, ma'am?" She seemed to take to the idea, so I guided her back to our seats and took down the shoe box my wife had packed for the trip. My companion and I munched fried chicken for a good many miles. I wanted to rest my feet as long as I could, so when she showed signs of starting off again I hailed a butcher's boy and bought a bunch of grapes.

I offered them to her. Some cloudy recollection of the proprieties of train travel must have crossed her troubled mind, for at this point she leaned across and looked me over carefully—the first time she had been aware of me as anything but part of the shifting scenery. "But I don't know you," she said suspiciously. "You're a stranger to me." Then the irresponsibility of her condition asserted itself. She giggled. "You're certainly the homeliest man I've ever run across. But"—and she snatched the bunch of grapes—"you're mighty good company."

If being a good sheriff required being good company to the ladies, it was the first I'd known of it. But I was willing, if it meant sitting out the rest of that trip to Austin.

CHAPTER 4

A Sheriff's Routine

MYSTERY STORIES and detective yarns make out law enforcement to be mostly gunfire and hocus-pocus with microscopes and weird clues. Crime laboratories have their place, and sometimes a man has to pull his gun. But much of a police officer's work is nothing but just that—work. Cleverness is well and good. But I claim that there is no real substitute for experience. You learn how to handle lawless men by handling them. I am thinking now of a case in point.

A country boy went into a hardware store at Whitesboro and stole a six-shooter. One of my deputies, Frank Kidd, went with me to arrest him. We stopped at the thief's home, a little farmhouse about halfway between Whitesboro and Collinsville, and took him in charge. But he asked if he might change his clothes. Of course, I said all right to that, and he went inside the house. Pretty soon he stuck his head out the door and called out: "Ma, where can I find a clean shirt?"

"Right there in the drawer, son, where it ought to be."

The next thing I knew, I looked up to see the boy tearing out through the barbwire at the back of the house. Frank and I took in after him. He crossed the railroad tracks and dropped out of sight in some timber on the other side. Frank went one way and I the other.

I kept on in the direction I thought the boy had gone until I came to an old shack of a place. Out in front was a long-haired cow pony, saddled and waiting. "Hello!" I shouted, and didn't get an answer. So

I went over to the horse and started to get on him. About that time the old man of the house came out. "Partner," said I, "I'm the sheriff, and I've got to have your horse. I'll either bring him back or pay you for him."

And away I rode, still following the line I figured my prisoner would take. But I got to thinking: "What in the world will I tell the boys at the office when they find out that Frank and I have let a country boy up and tear out on us this way?" I just naturally had to catch him. But the old horse I had commandeered wasn't much of a mount. I could hardly get him going. But at last I saw my man, lying down in a ditch, face up.

"Get up from there!" said I, and he got up. Then I took him back to the house for a drink of water. (I wanted one, myself.)

"Mr. Simmons," pleaded his mother, "we're terribly sorry about Son. Don't make it any harder on him because he run away."

"Why, of course not, ma'am," said I. "We wouldn't do that." We took the lad in, but when we got to the hardware store and talked things over with the proprietor, we fixed up a misdemeanor charge so that the boy could plead guilty and get off with a moderate fine.

Now that boy taught me a lesson. After that, I watched my prisoners. It was a good lesson to learn.

Of course, where a crime is committed openly, there is no mystery about it. But where the offense is planned and studied out by the criminal, the law-enforcement officer is put to the test. An experienced officer enjoys the game and the time and effort he puts into it. The matter of fear never enters his mind. He has the problem, and his whole mind is centered on solving it.

I early learned that information generally comes on a tip from a rounder, crook, or prostitute. Somebody from the underworld is most likely to know the facts. The law-abiding man is too busy with his own affairs. Let me give you a typical example.

While one of my deputies was down at the railroad depot about eleven o'clock one night, he was told that a drunken man was wandering around on the track just above the depot and that "somebody had better see about him." The deputy found the man staggering around and unable to talk intelligibly. He took the fellow up to the jail, where he was locked up for the night as drunk.

A Sheriff's Routine

The next morning, when the regular jailer came on duty, he recognized the prisoner as a substantial citizen who held a responsible job with the railroad in Sherman. He found that the man had received a hard blow on the head and was still in a bad way. In fact, he was unconscious and could not be roused. The jailer called me. I investigated and then summoned the county physician, who ordered the patient to the hospital, where he lay for twenty-two days before he regained consciousness. Even then, he was able to give me only a confused story of what had happened.

He had attended a meeting at Odd Fellows' Hall, had left the lodge room about eleven o'clock, and was on his way home, several blocks from the depot, when the lights went out for him. He was not drunk, had not been drinking, and was not a drinking man. And that was all he could tell me.

So there I was—a good, sober citizen had been knocked in the head, robbed of his fine gold watch, some old keepsakes, and a small amount of money, and there was nothing for me to go on to solve a crime already three weeks old.

As is usual in a case like this, the "law" is in for criticism. The victim's friends, and particularly his brethren in railroad work, were complaining about it. I had plenty to think about. One night not long after that, while I was standing on the street doing my thinking to myself, a half-drunk man wobbled into view from the shadows. He called me off to one side and said that if I could see my way clear to let him have a pint of whisky, he believed he could get me some information about who knocked the man in the head and robbed him.

I assumed that my tipsy friend merely wanted some whisky. But I was in no position to pass up any chance. Accordingly, I went to my office, unlocked my safe where I kept some contraband I had taken from bootleggers, and gave him his pint. "If you need any more, let me know," said I.

When I met him a few days later, he claimed he hadn't got me my information but thought he was making some progress. He was sober at the time, but confessed he needed another pint. I got him another pint. Then I told him there would also be a money reward in it for him if he helped me work out who had committed the crime.

Shortly thereafter, he told me that a group of Negroes knew something about the footpad job. He even named the man who, in his opinion, was guilty. We picked up five of the men in the group, jailed them in separate cells, and soon had the name of the man we wanted. This man, however, had left the state. I released the five Negroes and caught the robber in Oklahoma. He had in his wallet the pawn ticket on the watch.

When we got him safely in the Grayson County jail, our robber signed a confession before the county attorney, in the presence of the jailer and me. Later on, he hired a lawyer to defend him and, following the not unusual custom of defendants in such matters, swore that we had threatened him with a beating if he didn't sign up. The jury, however, was out only about five minutes, returning a verdict of guilty with a sentence of ten years in the penitentiary.

I give you another instance of how leads to crime detection frequently come to the sheriff's office. One day there came to me an ordinary punk and crapshooter who said he had been asked to help dispose of some counterfeit gold pieces. According to his story, a former peace officer told him that he wanted him to go to the Mexican border with another former officer. There they would pick up some five- and ten-dollar gold pieces, so called. These they were to pass in our area.

I did not believe the yarn, but I gravely thanked the fellow and asked him to keep me informed in regard to the scheme. A few nights later he came back to me with the names of others who had agreed to help dispose of the coins. Again I thanked him and encouraged him to learn all he could and keep me posted. Not long after that, a prostitute called the office about ten o'clock in the morning and asked me to come down to her place, as she wanted to see me.

For the calling of the prostitute I have no respect. But I did have respect for this woman, prostitute though she was. I knew she had something important to talk about or else she would not have called me. So I got on my horse, rode down to her house, and walked in. She handed me a counterfeit gold piece which had been passed to one of her girls the night before. She named the man who had passed it. He was the same man who had been named by my crapshooting punk. Things had opened up.

The prostitute had had the supposed five-dollar piece turned back to her by one of the banks. I took it to another bank and asked the banker to watch for counterfeit; he informed me that a suburban grocer had deposited a ten-dollar counterfeit piece the day before. By now I figured that the trail was getting really hot, so I rode out to see the grocer. He said the man who had passed the coin on him had paid him back on condition that he not tell where he got it.

"My friend," said I to the grocer, "I'm down here on business; I didn't come out just to visit around with you. It would take me only a few minutes to go get a warrant for your arrest. If you choose not to talk, I can put you in jail—which is exactly what I aim to do."

He talked. The name he gave me was that of the man whom my punk had identified as having asked him to help pass the counterfeit metal. Before I was finished with the case, I had recovered false coins in the amount of $500 and more and had sent five men to the penitentiary. And all this was on a tip from a rounder whose object, of course, was to court the favor of the law. The use of such people is recognized and practiced by all peace officers, but I never abused my powers in such cases, nor did I ever grant a favor in violation of law.

Perhaps I ought to add that one of the original group involved turned out to have more sense than the five who went to the penitentiary. This individual, a Negro, had been given $500 in counterfeit coins, which he was to take to Dallas and pass out among the Negroes there. "Mr. Simmons," he told me, "I tuck that stuff home with me, an' I got to studyin' about it, an' I nevuh slep' a wink that whole night long, an' come mornin' I tuck it back and tol' that man I wasn't goin' to have anything to do with it."

I told the Negro that he was the only smart one in the whole bunch. I told him that he didn't need a lawyer, that I would look after him, but that I would have to keep him in jail for a day or two until I got things worked out just right, and then I would let him go. That is what I did—I turned him out with no charges against him. In fact, I praised that boy for doing the right thing.

In the main, being sheriff is quite ordinary and unexciting. You tell a man he is under arrest, and he comes right along. You break up a fight, and it stays broken up. You serve a paper or carry out a court order, and that is all there is to it. But sometimes official duty calls for strong action. A sheriff never knows what will come up next; but he can expect the unexpected, when it does turn up, to come suddenly.

It was on a Sunday morning that a well-to-do farmer came into my office with the intention of swearing out a warrant against his own brother. His brother, he said, had come to his home, had stirred up trouble, and then had taken a shot at him. Now I knew this brother well and tried to argue my visitor out of the idea of swearing out a warrant, but he insisted. So I got out a warrant of arrest for assault to murder.

There had already been a good deal of trouble involving the assailant in this case. He had recently come out of a hard-fought divorce suit with his wife, had had a fight with her lawyer, and then had gone to her family and stirred up a mighty row with them. He had had a really big fight with one of the witnesses in the divorce suit. In short, although he had been a citizen of substance and standing, his family woes had got the upper hand of him. He was really sore in heart and mad at the whole world.

I called a deputy and started out to serve the warrant and pick up my man. I soon learned where he was staying and knocked on the door. A little old lady came to the door, and no sooner did I ask for the party named in my warrant than she began to wring her hands and cry.

She said the fellow was barricaded in the back room with his gun and had vowed that he would kill the first man who tried to arrest him. He was determined not to be taken by the law. I went around to the rear of the house and knocked on the door to the back room. "Who is it? "he growled.

I told him. I said I had a warrant for his arrest and I was there for that purpose. "Come on out," I told him. He proceeded to cuss me out: if I thought I was man enough to take him, I could come on in and try it. Knowing his mental stress, I tried to reason with him. I told him we had been friends and there was no use in his acting the way he was. I said I was taking no sides in the family mix-up. "Come on out!" I repeated.

He only cussed me the more. Again he invited me to take him, if I thought I could. Well, I thought I could. So I sent my deputy back to the office to bring two more officers back with him, but I told him to say nothing to anybody else. Then I went across the street and called up Frank Hamlin. Frank was chief of the fire department. "Frank," I said, telling him where I was, "I wish you would bring one of your fire trucks down here, just sort of drift it down here slowly. I'm fixing to set a house on fire."

"Set which?" yells Frank.

"Got to smoke a man out; he's acting up and I've got to smoke him out."

"Be right on up," says Frank. And up he came.

Then I went back to my man on the other side of the door. I tried to make him listen to reason, but again the only answer was to come on in and take him, if I thought I could.

By this time my three deputies had arrived. I went into the room next to the one in which the gunman was holed up. I pulled all the shades down, placed two officers in this room, and picked out a good stand for the third. I instructed them to shoot on sight of our quarry, as that was what I intended to do, unless he came out with his hands up.

Then I went outside to set fire to the corner of the room our bad man was defending. I had given him no inkling of what I intended to do. As I proceeded with my official arson, two shots rang out. It turned out that the deep silence had got on the man's nerves and he had "cracked" the door to the adjoining room to try to make out what was going on. The moment he had an eye to the crack both officers cut down on him. I rushed in. "I think I hit him, Sheriff," said one of the deputies.

I jerked open the door and held my gun on the fellow. He was barricaded behind a large box, with his hands on his weapon. "Put 'em up," said I.

He hesitated. "Put 'em up, or I'll kill you," said I. He put them up. You see, there comes a time when even a desperate man decides he doesn't want to die.

When we gathered him in, we found that the deputy was right: a bullet had creased the prisoner on the side of the head, just cutting the skin of his cheek, as he was peering through the crack in the door.

Later, while out on bond, this man was crossing a street in Sherman when a brother of his former wife took a shot at him and broke his leg. I was just across the street when it happened, and I was the first person to reach the assailant. I put the boy under arrest, but he was never tried for this shooting. The original charge of assault to murder against the offending brother was dismissed, and he moved to west Texas, to the relief, I judge, of all concerned.

One of the crimes I encountered during my experience as sheriff equals, I think, any of the dime novels of my youth. The crime occurred on March 15, 1884; the case was finally disposed of on August 11, 1914. The story runs as follows.

District Clerk Rudolph, of adjoining Cooke County, walked into my office one day on a peculiar mission. A long-time friend of his, Charlie Coe, had been indicted nearly thirty years before for assault to murder and for arson, and Rudolph was trying to find out about the matter. I went with him into the office of the district clerk of Grayson County, and there we found the worn and discolored indictment.

From Charlie Coe himself I later got the story behind the long-forgotten charge. In 1884 Coe and a neighbor named Belk were living in the Preston Bend area. One day, as their custom was, they came to Sherman in a wagon for provisions, the provisions turning out to include a jug of liquor for each of them. On the way home that night they got into a fight with local Negroes at Preston Bend, beating up some of the Negroes, taking a few shots at others, and winding up by burning the Negro schoolhouse.

Rather than go to the penitentiary for killing the Negro he had shot, Coe decided to leave the country. He begged a neighbor, who was a brother Odd Fellow, to look after the wife and five children he was leaving behind. He drifted into Indian Territory and from there to first one place and then another. He started a little store and settled down for a while. Then he happened to see a Texas newspaper in which it was said that his old neighbor, Belk, had gone to the penitentiary for murder.

Coe assumed that Belk's crime was connected with the shooting at Preston Bend. But such was not the case. For the colored man injured at the Preston Bend affray had not died; instead, he had recovered completely from his wounds. Belk had subsequently got into trouble with a neighbor, and out of this difficulty the killing arose for which he was convicted.

Coe said that when he read about Belk's sentence he didn't even stop to sell out his little shop. He simply closed the door, locked it, and departed. He never heard what became of the shop.

After a bit, Coe was in Mexico. When the gold rush began in the Klondike, Coe was there. But everywhere he went he felt that somebody's eyes were on him. The terror that he might be recognized was with him night and day. At length he decided to come home. Somehow he had learned that his family was in Abilene, Texas. So he wrote to his wife. A daughter gave the letter to the old family friend, Rudolph, and Rudolph gave it to me.

By this time the Coe family had decided that Charlie was dead. Mrs. Coe and her two sons, W. D. and Ben, had moved to Ardmore, Oklahoma, where both boys had done well and were known as good citizens.

Not long after Rudolph's visit to me in Sherman, in came Coe, with his son Ben. The district clerk issued a warrant of arrest for Coe. I served it and made my return on the back of it. Then we all went into the courtroom where Judge M. H. Garnett was presiding, and County Attorney Gafford stated to the court that after this lapse of time there were no witnesses available for the state. He moved to dismiss the case for lack of evidence.

The Judge granted the motion to dismiss, and Charlie Coe was a free man. He thanked all of us and, arm in arm with his son, walked out of the courthouse to rejoin his family.

Some time before the end of my first term as sheriff I had told my wife that I would clean up Grayson County and then refuse to run for re-election. No one else knew of my plans. I wanted to get back to my profitable livestock business. But the criminal faction kept up a persistent campaign against the new administration, and I felt bound to run again; otherwise it would appear that I was afraid to run.

In the 1914 primary my majority was 2,284, and the general election, as always in Grayson County, was a matter of course. I finished my clean-up job in this second term, and that was enough for me. I declined a third term, although there was considerable pressure brought to bear on me to extend my political career. But enough was enough.

CHAPTER 5

Private Citizen

WHEN I HAD GOT this far along into my story, I planned next to tell about the Texas Prison System, its history, and my own experience with it. But my friends have got after me to give a more detailed account of my early business career and the background of the many years of my long and active life. I suppose they are right.

I have been a banker. The Merchants and Planters National Bank of Sherman, organized in 1872, was at one time the second largest bank in Texas and was certainly one of the strongest financially. In 1910, shortly after I had moved into town from my farm, this bank organized the American Bank and Trust Company, with capital stock of $100,000, and I was urged to become a director.

At the time, all I knew about banking was borrowing money and paying it back when it was due—or going to see the banker the day before it was due, if I was not prepared to pay. Despite my lack of banking experience, I accepted the directorship of the American Bank and Trust Company. A few years afterward, there was a reorganization, with an increase of capital stock of $200,000, and I became active vice-president. They gave me the front office, and one morning after I had been there a month or so, a well-dressed man about forty years of age rushed in and said to me in an exceedingly cordial tone: "Hello, Lee! How are you? Haven't seen you for some time." (Everybody called me "Lee" in those days. I still like it.) "I've got to catch this interurban down to Dallas right quick," says he, "and I want you to cash my check for twenty-five dollars."

He seemed such a pleasant fellow and knew me so well that I couldn't refuse him. I stepped over into the teller's cage and counted out his twenty-five dollars. He thanked me and rushed out to catch the interurban.

The check followed the usual routine and came back marked "no account." Then I wrote a short letter to the bank on which the check was drawn. The reply came back that the person was unknown. I wrote my personal check reimbursing the bank for the twenty-five dollars—writing on the margin of my check the word "experience." Nobody ever "Hello-Lee'd" me in that fashion again. If I ever meet up with that fellow, I shall thank him. The lesson was worth the twenty-five dollars.

Banking didn't suit me. In the first place, it was too confining; a man needs leg room, you know. In the second place, I often had to say "No" to my friends—and I had a lot of friends. A successful banker must recognize that he is handling other people's money, not his own. It takes long years of real experience to make a real banker.

So after some four years of active service with the American Bank and Trust Company, I resigned my post and busied myself again with farming and livestock. Shortly thereafter, in 1923, I accepted the position of manager of the Sherman Chamber of Commerce, in which place I continued until I became general manager of the Texas Prison System in 1930.

My work for the Chamber of Commerce was a great pleasure to me. At the time, I had the reputation of knowing more Grayson County people than did any other man. I had not solicited the job, and it came to me as a surprise. "We want to pay you to do what you have been doing free all your life around here," said the directors when they came to me about it.

I soon found a real opportunity for service. And after I had put in a year at it, no man could have got better support or co-operation than I received. As a chamber, we were careful not to undertake too much, and we handled it so that we could do whatever we undertook. Not once during our seven years did we fail; we put over every item on our program.

Almost our first problem was to get a balanced farm economy. One-cropping, you know, comes natural in cotton country. Our slogan to counteract this was "Fifty-two Payrolls per Year per Farm." We lined up an intensive three-year campaign for farm improvement, with $1,000 in cash prizes given away each year. We persuaded the Interstate Cotton Oil Refining Company to make possible a tour for the study of the dairy industry in several states. The Meadow Lakes milk plant (later Mrs. Tucker's) was the outcome of all this—the first such plant in Texas.

Our next problem was roads. We made plans for a highway bond issue and took them to the State Highway Commission. The commission was then composed of Chairman Ross Sterling, Cone Johnson, of Tyler, and Judge W. R. Ely, of Abilene. We asked for their advice and suggestions and said we had confidence in them and in their judgment. They worked with us all the way, then and afterward. The county commissioners ordered an election for a good-sized bond issue, and we opened up in its support before the voters. County Judge R. M. Carter and I spoke at just about every town and schoolhouse in the county. We carried the bond issue by a decisive vote.

As I look back over that campaign, an amusing incident comes to mind. W. R. Brents, president of the sizable Commercial Bank of Sherman, owned a number of brick buildings in town. In all of our work in establishing small industries and aiding expansion of existing industries, we had never been able to get a dime out of Mr. Brents. He would always wind up by saying to me—or to our committee, as the case might be—that he intended to move to California some of these days. He had spent his summers there for a number of years. Well, just before the bond-election date, Brents came out with a long article in the *Sherman Democrat*. He was against the bonds.

The next night there was a rally on the courthouse lawn. We had advertised it pretty thoroughly, and we had a crowd of around a thousand people. I was among the speakers, and in the course of my remarks I said: "You saw in yesterday evening's *Democrat* where Bill Brents is opposing the bond issue for building good roads in Grayson County. He goes out to California each summer and rides around on the good roads out there. But he is not willing for you and me to have good roads here.

Private Citizen

"I have never yet gone to Bill Brents to get help for anything worth while for Sherman and Grayson County but what he has always said to me that he was going to California and wasn't interested. You know, I think the sooner Bill Brents moves to California the better off Sherman and Grayson County will be!" The crowd went wild. Of course this was political talk. He was my friend.

The next day I purposely went into the bank, and Brents said to me: "Well, Lee, they tell me you went after me pretty strong last night."

"Yes," I answered, "I thought you had it coming to you."

Brents was a regent of the University of Texas, and those were the days when Jim Ferguson and the university people were having the tail end of their long knock-down-and-drag-out fight. Governor Jim, of course, had been removed from office after impeachment and conviction in 1917. But with the election of his wife, Governor Miriam A. Ferguson, Farmer Jim was back in power, impeachment or no impeachment.

Governor Jim wanted to remove President R. E. Vinson from the university. The regents, Brents included, flatly refused to fire Vinson, and at about this time Brents was summoned to Austin to testify on a matter coming before a legislative investigating committee.

Charlie Stowe was a great Jim Ferguson man in those days. He followed Jim around on his speaking tours and supported the Fergusons in all their campaigns. Charlie wrote Brents and told him something like this: "If you come down to Austin and testify against Jim, one thing is certain: either you or I will be carried out to West Hill."

It was a straight-out threat, but I don't believe now that Charlie meant it. Brents, however, believed it then and sent two of his friends to me asking me to go to Austin with him as his bodyguard.

Now, I didn't feel under any obligation to Mr. Brents. He had supported the campaign of the man who ran against me for sheriff. But Brents was standing up for principle against Jim Ferguson on the university matter, and I figured that if Brents could stand up for the university I could stand up for Brents. So I went along as bodyguard.

When we got to Austin, Brents stuck to me closer than a cocklebur. All I did was to manage to let myself be seen around here and there at the right time. One of the Ferguson Rangers sidled up to me and said to me, out of the corner of his mouth, "Lee, what you doing here?"

"Oh, nothing at all, nothing at all. Just thought I would come down to Austin and look around a little."

That was all there was to it. Nobody offered to lay so much as a little finger on Brents. But shortly afterward, he moved out to California, just as he said he would.

Still another important project of the Sherman Chamber of Commerce was the Red River Valley Fair. The first fair was held in one of the Sherman parks. Will Leslie was the first president of the fair, and he did more for its establishment than any other one man I know. He was really interested in it and worked at it up to the time of his death in 1952.

The second fair was held on the public square and in vacant business houses. It was quite a success under the presidency of the late Rowan Mills, my very dear friend. In fact, the fair did so well that we began to get a vision of its possibilities. And it was at this time that I began to take a hand.

We formed a corporation, raised a fairly large sum of money, and began a construction program—after we came to an agreement with the trustees of the Old Settlers' Association for the use of some twenty acres owned by that organization within the city limits of Sherman.

The fair did great things in developing our farm and dairy campaign and in welding a community spirit among the smaller towns and between the farm population, on the one hand, and the business interests of Sherman and Denison, on the other.

One year Governor Neff officially opened our fair. Governor Holloway, of Oklahoma, was with us another year, and Governor Dan Moody was the guest of honor at a still later fair. I had run Moody's gubernatorial campaign in our county and had spent $200 out of my own pocket. I went over to Gainesville to see him while he was speaking there.

"How're we coming on?" he asked.

"Fine. We have it already won in Grayson County."

Then I cocked an eye at Dan and continued, "Of course, when a fellow does for you what I have done, he usually wants something for it." I could see that old Dan wasn't liking that a bit, so I hurried on:

"In this case, we want you to come over to Sherman and open our Red River Valley Fair."

"I think that can be arranged," said Dan, his face clearing up with a smile. And it was arranged; he came and opened the fair. It was quite a fair, too. Our opening parade would have done credit to anybody's fair in anybody's town.

The Chamber of Commerce completed two other important projects during my time as manager. One was the opening up of Wall Street in the main business section of the city, which necessitated tearing down several brick buildings. Of course, there was strong opposition on the part of some property-owners around the square, but we did it. The second of these projects was the building of the Grayson Hotel. That took a lot of work and a lot of co-operation, but both of these improvements to Sherman were to prove abundantly worth while.

The last and perhaps the pleasantest of my undertakings as manager of the Chamber of Commerce was the locating of the National Woodmen Circle Home. I learned that a committee had been appointed in Omaha, Nebraska, to select a permanent home for aged members and for orphans of members of this the largest, and financially the strongest, of all women's organizations of its type. I made contact with the committee members at once and invited them to visit us at Sherman.

They wrote me that they were looking for certain features, told me the amount of land they needed, and asked me to pick out a number of sites which they could inspect when they came down to see what we had to offer. They did come, and they gave us their plans, telling us just what they expected of us. For three years we dealt with the committee of five women, there being five of us also on the committee representing Sherman.

Those ladies couldn't seem to make up their minds. They would come to Sherman, and we would dine them and entertain them, show them our properties, and reduce our proposals to writing. But then they would leave and become enthusiastic about some other location.

One time I gave a dinner for them at a big round table where twenty-four people could sit down at once and look every one of the other twenty-three straight in the eye. I had the very top businessmen of Sherman around that table with my five ladies, and I gave them each two minutes to say what was on their minds.

I remember that E. T. Fant got up and told about living in other Texas cities before he moved to our town. "My years in Sherman," he went on, "have convinced me that it is the finest town that I ever saw. I aim to finish out my days right here in Sherman, and if you ladies bring your home down here, I think you will feel that way about Sherman, too."

It went on about like that all around the table, and it was pretty impressive—at least it was to me. But the ladies remained undecided. They went away, and it was quite a while before we heard from them again. Then I got a telegram announcing another inspection visit. I took it down to the *Democrat* office to show to Pat Mayes, who was on our committee. "I don't give a darn whether they come or not!" he exploded. "There's nothing further left for us to do with them."

"But, Pat," said I, as gently as I could, "they're coming, and we've got to go over to meet them at the train at Denison again." So we met them, and I arranged another dinner for them, this time at the Woodlawn Golf Club, which was about the only nice place in Sherman we hadn't already taken them to.

"There is nothing I can add," I told the ladies at that dinner, "to what has already been said. But I do want to say that we are glad to have formed the friendships which have come out of our negotiations, and these friendships, I am sure, will last a lifetime. I want you ladies to know that, wherever you decide to locate your home, you will always be remembered here in Sherman with the kindliest and warmest of feelings."

A few days later we got another telegram from Omaha, to which the ladies had returned, announcing that Sherman had been chosen and setting a date for closing the arrangements. The *Democrat* sprouted big headlines the next day celebrating the results of our three years of negotiations. Sherman was giving a tract of land of 280 acres, a mile west of town, and was granting free schooling for all children at the home. We were to pay $28,000 for the land, and I had obtained the signatures of forty-one men on a note for that amount to the bank, no one signer to be liable for more than $1,000 as his part. We felt pretty good about the whole deal.

Private Citizen

The day came for closing the negotiation, and Mrs. Mary LaRocca, president of the Supreme Forest Woodmen Circle, opened the conference: "Mr. Simmons, we have a different proposition that we wish to submit to you, if that is agreeable."

I was just about crushed with dismay. "What in thunder is coming now?" I said to myself. "I thought everything had been agreed upon."

Mrs. LaRocca went calmly on, reciting how pleasant had been our associations and recounting the friendships formed. And then she bowled us all over: "We are not coming to Sherman because you are offering us 280 acres of land. We are coming to Sherman because of your schools and your churches and the culture of your citizens. We believe you will treat our old folks and our orphans as you want your parents and your children treated. And that is the reason why we desire to make you a different proposition. We want to pay for the land ourselves. We have plenty of money, and we want to pay for it. Would that be agreeable to you?"

By that time the tears were rolling down my cheeks. I rose from my chair, but I couldn't speak a word. I sat down again as a friend came to my rescue: "Mrs. LaRocca, that's the first time I ever saw Lee when he couldn't talk!"

Three years of co-operation, mutual confidence, patience, and hard work had paid off handsomely. For the Woodmen Circle Home in Sherman, established in due time, is the best and most modern institution of its kind that I know of anywhere.

Before I quit this chapter on my life in the business world, maybe I had better add one more item chargeable to experience—account of banking.

When I was a youngster under indictment for murder, C. B. Dorchester, president of the Merchants and Planters Bank of Sherman, became my personal banker. He loaned me fifty dollars, without any security and without any endorsers, to give me the capital I needed to go into the cattle business and to get married. As years went on I borrowed as much as $20,000 from Mr. Dorchester without security. For he held that a man's moral worth was the best of securities.

I had continued my livestock operations on a modest scale even while I was manager of the Chamber of Commerce. I owed a considerable amount of money when I went down to Huntsville in 1930, but my affairs were in reasonably good condition, considering that I had a good farm and some business properties. Then the Depression fell in on me. Those who were in any kind of business at that time will remember how it was.

Many banks closed their doors. I not only lost my investments in bank stocks but also had to put up several thousand dollars to equal the amount of stock that I owned, as was the law at that time. I sold livestock and one of my farms at a tremendous loss, trying to meet those obligations.

While I was at Huntsville I sadly neglected my own interests. But I did not fail for one minute to look after the state's interests in the Texas Prison System or the welfare of the prisoners. It was about this time that Mr. Dorchester told me the bank examiners were demanding some security for my open notes. "I know the condition of Lee's affairs," he told them, "and I know that he is cashing life insurance policies and borrowing on other policies and doing all he can to take care of his obligations. He is one of this bank's best customers and has been for many years."

He suggested to the bank examiners and to me that I give the bank a mortgage on an unencumbered brick building for what the building might be worth. The bank would then charge off the rest of the note. I gladly gave them the mortgage on the building but insisted that I owed the whole amount of my note and objected to their charging any of it off. I argued that I was well over twenty-one and that I considered my obligations sacred.

But I had to let my private affairs drift until I returned to Sherman after my resignation from the prison system. Then I began to clean things up. I sold my properties at whatever I could get for them and was soon out of debt, except for that charged-off note. That kept worrying me. After another year or so I told my friend Pete Hudgins, who by this time had become a director in the bank, that I was about ready to pay that charged-off note. He didn't say much—except that he didn't think I ought to do it. In a day or so he informed me that he had talked with Sales Omohundra, president of the bank, and that Sales didn't want me to or expect me to.

A little later I went into the bank and told Omohundra to dig up

Private Citizen

that charged-off note as I was ready to pay it. He told me that he had discussed the matter with his directors, that they felt I had been a good customer of the bank, that I was getting old, and that besides the bank would have to pay 60 per cent of anything I paid them to the federal government. So they didn't want me to pay it.

"Mr. Omohundra," I said, "I didn't come here to argue with you. I want you to get me that note."

"All right," he conceded with a smile. I gave him my check for $7,769.75—the amount of the note. From that night on, I found that I rested better. It took about all the money I had, but once it was paid, all I owed then is what I owe now: a debt of gratitude to my friends and neighbors who have always been so considerate of me and to my community and state that have been so generous to me.

CHAPTER 6

Prisons and Politics

INASMUCH AS the penitentiary system of the state of Texas is going to be winding in and out of my story practically all the time from now on, I think I had better weave a few facts of history into the blood-and-thunder pattern which always develops when you try to restrain desperate criminals. If you stay with me, I promise you your blood and thunder. But I want you to see something of what has gone before your time and mine. Good and bad alike, we are all children of history.

In 1829 the Congress of the Mexican state of Coahuila and Texas adopted resolutions to set up the first prisons in Texas. These were to be of the panoptic type—that is, so built that a guard on duty was in such a position that he could see all prisoners at all times without being seen by them. Contractors were to build these prisons at their own expense, equip them with tools and machinery, and operate them with convict labor for the production of goods, which would be sold, the proceeds being used to reimburse the contractors.

It was to be the contractors' duty to teach all prisoners an honorable trade—weavers were to be furnished with looms, ceramic workers with potter's wheels, and so on. Upon release after completing his term, each prisoner was to be sent to the town of his choice, where he would be under "immediate inspection of the local authorities." He was to be entitled to thirty dollars from the contractor, plus the tools of his trade.

Prisons and Politics

No contractors ventured to build a prison on these terms, and Decree 93 of the Congreso del Estado de Coahuila y Texas thus became a dead letter.

After the "Texians" rebelled against Mexico and set up the Republic of Texas, prisoners were confined in county jails, if any existed. San Augustine built its jail by public subscription. It is to be feared that rehabilitation of the prisoner figured little either in the design of the jail or in the sheriff's conduct thereof. The latter was probably more interested in the prospect of fees, for the Congress of the infant Republic had just appropriated $15,000 to meet the obligations incurred under the statutory subtitle "Sheriffs—Fees—Keeping Prisoners." Henry M. Smith, sheriff of Galveston County, evidently did not share in this distribution, for he petitioned separately for reimbursement of $864.63, an amount he claimed to have spent on the keep of convicts. The Republic was long on justice but short on funds. The best it could do for Officer Smith was to authorize the county of Galveston to levy a tax upon its citizens for the liquidation of his claim.

The 1841 Congress of the Republic undertook to set up a national prison system, but nothing came of it. In the course of one of the reports filed with the Senate during debate on the subject there occur these rotund sentiments:

The noblest principles of enlightened morality, and the dictates of political economy indicate that the establishment of this institution will be fraught with important advantages to the Republic. As an institution which is intended to commute the barbarous punishments of whipping and branding, for the milder and useful punishment of confinement at hard labor, thus tending to reform the criminal by habits of industry, at the same time that his productive labor defrays the expenses incident to his confinement, it is in accordance with the enlightened spirit of the age and deserving of the cordial support of every humane and philosophic statesman.

I have quoted the flowery words of Senate Judiciary Committee Chairman Francis Moore (report of January 4, 1841) not so much for the flowers as for the sound idea thus wreathed in rhetoric. For it was the same general notion, presented by me on behalf of another committee eighty-odd years later, which got me into a predicament responsible for a number of things, down to and including this book. Although for the time being, the recommendations of the Senator of the Republic came to naught, I still give him credit. If later I helped realize something of the system which he had in mind, the dream was his before it was mine.

So open to criticism was the conduct of many early-day sheriffs in their treatment of prisoners that courts frequently ordered the defendant whipped and turned loose on society. In those days many outlaws from the United States and Mexico fled to Texas, where enforcement of law and order soon became a serious problem. Texas resorted to harshness of punishment in an effort to cope with the situation.

"For murder, arson, rape, robbery or burglary, on conviction thereof, he shall receive death." So ran the stern words of the statute. For taking or stealing any "goods, chattels, money or articles of value under $20," the penalty was a fine not to exceed $1,000, with or without the infliction of thirty-nine lashes. If the thief took anything of the value of $20 or more, the penalty was restoration of the full value wrongfully taken, plus thirty-nine lashes on the bare back, plus branding of the right hand with the letter "T," for thief. Cattle or horse theft in those days called for restoration of full value to the rightful owner and for thirty-nine lashes for the thief. Counterfeiting was a capital offense.

Three years after Texas entered the Union, the State Legislature established a penitentiary at Huntsville. It was opened, with 3 prisoners, in 1849. The total population of Texas was then 151,000, and, in that first year, prisoners arrived at the rate of 3 per month. Nowadays, with a state population of around 8 million, the penitentiary system receives about 250 prisoners a month. Crimes increase faster than the population.

The system was scarcely a year old when it had its first investigation, the forerunner of many others to come. The Legislature was worried about the expenses of prison operation and about getting useful work out of the prisoners. In 1854 a cotton and woolen mill was set up. It was in full operation at the onset of the Civil War and was a valuable asset to the Confederacy.

In 1863 the Legislature authorized free distribution of prison-made cloth to the needy families of Confederate soldiers. Demands on the mill outran the powers of prison labor, and for a time, free labor took over and operated the mill. But in 1864 the prison was authorized to borrow convicts from Louisiana, Arkansas, and Missouri in order to increase cloth production.

After the Civil War the Legislature decided to lease out the prison system. Abuses followed and brought on another investigation. Leasing was abandoned in 1883, when the state undertook the production of cloth and of iron. The new system was called a "contract lease." The state furnished food, clothing, bedding, medical attention, and transportation for convicts leased out to contractors operating inside or outside the prison walls. This system was also found to be bad. It was followed by a system of farming on shares with landowners who supplied the seed, tools, machinery, and mules. The state cared for the convicts and planted, tended, and harvested the crops, taking 60 per cent of the cotton and 50 per cent of the sugar cane, while the owner received the remainder of the yield. This plan was also unsatisfactory.

Next the state began to buy farm lands and to experiment with iron production. At Rusk a foundry was operated by prison labor for some fifteen or twenty years. The original "beehive" furnaces fired with charcoal were later converted to coke operation, with a final capacity of 23,000 tons annually. For a number of years iron pipe was manufactured and shipped out on the spur line also owned and operated by the prison system. In 1920 the furnace and foundry were sold for $112,000. All sorts of troubles had driven the state out of the iron business. Government ownership of railroads proved equally unprofitable and unmanageable, even on the prison's miniature railroad system. Its thirty-one miles of track, one locomotive, and one flatcar were soon taken over by the Southern Pacific on lease. It is estimated that the Rusk experiment lost over two million dollars under prison management. Investigators pronounced its history a "record of financial disaster."

Meanwhile, state ownership of farms was displacing the share-crop system in the prison agricultural experiments. Some of the state's land purchases were far from judicious. In 1908 the Ramsey Prison Farm was bought at $13.75 per acre from vendors who had bought it two years earlier at $5.00 per acre. By the following year the state owned six farms of varying size and fertility. The purchase price of this acreage provided political scandals for some time to come.

Investigation followed investigation, while graft, waste, and poor management went from bad to worse. During the first year of World War I, however, prison crops were so good—and wartime prices were so favorable—that the system reported a profit of a half-million dollars, or $400 per convict. By 1919 investigation was going full blast again. It was found that the Darrington and Retrieve farms, both subject to overflow, had been bought by the state at exorbitant prices.

For years there was controversy over the feasibility of relocating prison operations by selling all the system's farms. When 1923 rolled around, the system owed $700,000, and the prison population had increased 35 per cent in two years. The Legislature was for relocation, the Governor against. Because the Legislature could not agree on a site, it decided upon a prison "survey." The survey turned out to be anthropometric, physical, and psychiatric—in short, its assembled data proved to be highly scientific and quite useless for all practical purposes. Oh, maybe that is too harsh a judgment. Perhaps it was due to this survey that the treatment of prisoners began to improve a little, prison punishment became somewhat more humane, and some attention began to be paid to education of the inmates.

It was in 1923 that I had my first official connection with the prison system. A committee was set up composed of three private citizens who were to inspect the system and make recommendations. I declined appointment almost as soon as it was offered, but Governor Pat Neff later called me on the telephone and insisted that I come to Austin for a conference. Upon my arrival the Governor and the attorney general talked me into serving on the committee. The other committeemen were Mrs. W. C. Martin, of Marshall, and Dr. E. Blalock, of Woodlawn, a widely known country doctor, gin operator, and practical man of affairs.

One of my reasons for not wanting to be on the committee was that there was a woman on it. But when I met Mrs. Martin, I found that she was a well-to-do landowner and business woman of good sense and experience. I wrote my wife at the time, "She is all right; she wears flat-heeled shoes!"

Prisons and Politics

Lieutenant Governor T. W. Davidson (later United States district judge) was much interested in seeing that something was done for the welfare of state prisoners, as well as for the relief of the taxpayers, and he gave a great deal of time and assistance to the committee. We took our task seriously, and we really worked at the job. None of us had wanted it, for all of us were busy enough with our own affairs. But the job badly needed doing. We had seen investigation after investigation, most of them hurried affairs in the hands of people who knew little about business and too much about politics. Usually there was somebody who had to be "protected."

We began my inspecting "the Walls," the common designation of the official headquarters of the penitentiary system. At the Walls in Huntsville prisoners were received, assigned to the place of their confinement, and assigned some type of employment. Next we visited all the prison farms, two near Huntsville, two, forty miles to the north, near Crockett and Madisonville, and seven below Houston. Together they comprised some 73,000 acres.

We looked into all sorts of things. For example, I saw a bunch of mules on one of the farms. They were little Spanish mules weighing, I should judge, around 750 pounds apiece. They weren't worth $50 a head, at the very outside. I called to one of the Mexicans at hand: "There's a likely mule over there, bring him over here and let me look at him."

I opened the animal's mouth; he had teeth nearly as long as my finger. "How old is he?" I asked. Nobody knew. "Look here!" said I. "This mule has been burned."

"Burned? What is that?"

Then I told them of the old mule-traders' trick of filing down the teeth and burning the ends with a hot iron so as to make black rings. Then they would say, "See? He still has cups (cusps) coming on." The idea was to disguise the mule's true age.

"I'm showing you this," I told the committee, "because I'm going to testify that this mule is at least fifteen years old, and I want the committee to note this case. I want it to be plain that I know what I'm talking about." The man who had sold the mules to the state was standing right there when I said it. Later on I did report the mule incident.

When our committee made its final report, we did not aim criticism particularly at those in charge, nor even blame generally the Prison Commission then in office. Instead, we placed the blame on the public itself, because of its lack of interest in the welfare of human beings and because of its utter ignorance of a situation which we considered concerned the welfare of every good citizen.

Over my protest I was chosen by my fellow-committee members to make our report to the Joint Penitentiary Committee of the Senate and House of Representatives. In a plain, informal manner I told them of the dreadfully unsanitary conditions we had found, of the lack of proper food, of the idleness of the prisoners, of slipshod farming methods, of lack of co-operation. I stressed the absence of any program for the betterment of the prisoner's situation and for relief of the taxpayer's burden. In short, I told them that nobody seemed to care and nobody seemed to have any vision of what could be accomplished toward a worth-while goal. I was then asked by a senator to tell what I thought should be done about it.

As best I could, I then proceeded to outline our committee recommendations—nothing fantastic or theoretical, but all of it plain common sense and simple justice to both prisoners and public. In the course of my report I made a statement which got me into trouble personally. I think it was the direct cause of my subsequent connection with the prison system. What I said was this:

"The Texas Prison System, with 73,000 acres of land and 5,000 prisoners, not only should produce its own living but should produce much of the living of the 20,000 wards now in other state institutions and should manufacture shoes and clothing for their needs. And such a program will go a long way toward ending the alarming idleness of the prisoners."

Then the same senator asked me if I myself could take over the management and obtain these results. I answered that that was, of course, an embarrassing question. I would not say that I personally could do it; but I saw no reason why a good, experienced businessman could not do it, if he was let alone and if he was given the co-operation of the Legislature in keeping politics out of the prison system. I wound up by saying: "I still say that the Texas Prison System could be made outstanding in the United States; the possibilities are certainly there."

That really got me into trouble. For from that time on, the Governor, the Legislature, and the newspapers took in after me. They practically forced me to take over the job. But before I gave in to their insistence, there had to come the granddaddy of all Texas prison investigations.

The investigation of 1925, I can safely say, had more scandal and more politics in it than any other prison inquiry held in our state. The scandal part of it had to do chiefly with whether or not a certain prison official had improper relations with the wife of a convict. Aside from that, the evidence pointed to barbaric cruelty, theft, drunkenness, murder, and all-round loose dealing with property. Newspaper headlines were fat and black for weeks and weeks.

A physician recently freed from the Huntsville prison was called before the legislative investigating committee as a witness to conditions within the Walls. He swore that for a single attempt at escape he had been given five separate punishments, including twenty lashes. On another occasion, although ill, he had been forced to go to the cotton fields, where the attendants accused him of malingering and held him in an ant bed until he lost consciousness. There were reported to the committee other stories of mistreatment of convicts, including charges of at least three murders.

Financial accounts were said to be in disorder. A series of purchased items had been paid for twice. Drinking was common within the Walls. Prison sugar was stolen by the barrel for an illicit still operated by convicts. Unauthorized convicts were running around loose in Huntsville. A special auditor (appointed to look into things) was assaulted by three men as he emerged from the local grand-jury room, where he was supposed to have testified to irregularities he had found.

Several men connected with the prison system were shown to have conducted cattle operations of their own, sometimes buying from the system and sometimes selling to it. At that time the brand of the system was a five-pointed star. Special Auditor M. E. Bogle was questioned and testified as follows:

Q. Mr. Bogle, do you know anything . . . what does the State of Texas use for her brand to brand the livestock?

A. A five-pointed star.

Q. Did you have occasion to investigate whether or not they were using that five-pointed star?

A. Yes, sir. I inspected practically all the cattle on the whole system.

Q. I will ask you if you also had occasion to look up and see if a man by the name of G——, who has a ranch adjoining one of the prison farms, had not used and filed for record the same star that Texas uses, except adding the letter "P" inside the star?

A. Yes, sir; I looked up a dozen of them.

Q. I will ask you if you did not find the same condition with reference to a man by the name of L——, who had used the figure "12" inside the State star?

A. Yes, sir.

Q. And another one the letter "C"?

A. Yes, sir.

Q. And another with the Figure "4"?

A. Yes, sir.

Q. And another with the letter "B"?

A. Yes, sir.

Q. And another one the letter "Y"?

A. Yes, sir.

Q. Can you tell this committee how many different brands you found around there—the penitentiary—that, by making a little addition to the State star, they had their own brands?

A. About a dozen in Harris County alone. And there were some in all the other counties where the penitentiary was located with those star brands.

Q. Can you tell us any reason why right around the penitentiary these men should have a brand that looks so nearly like the State brand?

A. No, sir; I don't know any reason for it.

Q. For convenience, you suppose?

A. I suppose so.

By Senator Witt:

Q. Is there any letter still unused for the Star brand?

A. Well, I think not.

All the newspapers were filled with headlines covering the proceedings. Things were in a bad way at the penitentiary—very bad.

Prisons and Politics

The Legislature adjourned before the investigating committee could make its report. But one of the prison commissioners resigned, and in 1927 the Legislature abolished the three-man commission, set up the Board of Prison Commissioners, and wiped the slate clean.

Appointment to the new board was made as follows: Lee Simmons, Sherman; W. M. Odell, Fort Worth; Joe Wearden, Goliad; Dr. A. C. Scott, Temple; F. L. Tiller, Rosenberg; R. H. Baker, Houston; Rabbi Henry Cohen, Galveston; E. H. Astin, Bryan; Fred Horton, Greenville.

There soon arose a great division of opinion between Governor Dan Moody, who wanted the prison system relocated, and the Legislature, which couldn't agree on any place for its relocation. The trend of events is shown by the *Dallas Morning News* card-index entries of prison-system stories printed in 1929–30:

January 5, 1929.—Citizens meet with Governor; pass resolutions for better prison system.

January 6.—Sixty-five convicts escape from prison farms in one month.

February 1.—State prison board tells Legislature of great need of change; condition called rotten.

April 4.—Colonel R. H. Baker resigns.

April 4.—Find three convicts in cave dug under floor of prison.

April 15.—Warren Azbell, who escaped with Bob Silver, captured.

April 16.—Bob Silver recaptured; bribery alleged in his escape.

May 7.—Convict flees solitary cell in penitentiary; "safe as a chicken coop," declares member of prison board.

June 21.—Forty-three convicts kidnap guard; eighteen caught; others penned in bottoms of Brazos River by prison forces.

June 22.—Twenty-six convicts caught; four shot; one dead.

July 5.—Perfect plans for survey of state prisons; first leg of trip by Texas group to be along coast.

July 25.—Prison population now totals 5,035.

August 11.—Texas prison body goes on tour; penitentiaries in other states to be visited by commission.

August 12.—Texans study prison woes of Louisiana; Alabama penitentiary to be seen next.

August 15.—Florida has its convicts pay own way.

August 16.—North Carolina prison pays its way; makes profit.

August 17.—Army system aids Virginia in its prison management.

August 19.—Laud District of Columbia prison system.

August 20.—Pennsylvania's prisons draw Texans' praise.

August 23.—New York State building new prison camp.

August 27.—Texas board visits Michigan prison.

August 28.—Illinois plan to educate prisoners.

August 30.—Minnesota state prisons pay good profit; all inmates occupied and more than pay for their keep.

August 31.—Merit system for prisoners encountered; Texans find it in Kansas; also visit Leavenworth.

September 1.—Texas prison survey ends.

September 29.—Eighteen convicts dig their way out of prison farm.

October 1.—Three more convicts flee prison farm.

October 26.—Three buildings on Wynne State Penal Farm burn.

November 6.—W. H. Meade resigns as manager of prison system.

November 26.—Lee Simmons of Sherman elected manager of state prison system.

November 27.—Simmons refuses appointment.

January 12, 1930.—Rabbi Henry Cohen resigns from state prison board.

January 18.—Convicts go on hunger strike.

January 19.—Wynne Farm convicts go on hunger strike.

January 19.—Wynne Farm convicts abandon hunger strike; try to burn chapel; guards put out fire.

January 26.—Main prison inspected by 100 members of Legislature, Governor, and others.

January 30.—"Prison not fit for a dog," says Moody before House.

February 25.—Swamps of Trinity River block flight of seven convicts taken after prison break.

March 4.—No more prisoners to be admitted into main penitentiary at Huntsville or any of farms "until the normal capacity of the system is reached," says state prison board.

March 4.—Order to receive no more convicts arouses storm of indignation in Legislature: "Won't be coerced."

Prisons and Politics

March 6.—Governor Moody defends prison board.

March 24.—Tarrant County convicts refused entrance into prison walls. Is test of order.

March 25.—Lee Simmons to take helm of state prison; board pledges effort to remedy condition of system; "free of politics." New official sees heavy job ahead and asks co-operation.

CHAPTER 7

Within "the Walls"

GOVERNOR DAN MOODY deserves much of the credit for the creation of a responsible prison authority in Texas. In lieu of the old board of management composed of three coequal members, he now named a nine-man prison board who, in turn, chose a general manager of the Texas Prison System, vested with full authority for direction of prison operations and full responsibility for discipline.

It has already been indicated that the prison system was in a really horrible condition when the new board took over and selected W. H. Meade as general manager. Mr. Meade was a successful civil engineer by profession, and he worked diligently and honestly at the job. But he was inexperienced in handling prisoners and in directing extensive farm and livestock activities. Moreover, responsibility for dealing with the public, with the press, with the Legislature, and with the various state departments was too much for him. After three years, he realized he was not making a success of the job and tendered his resignation, which was accepted.

It was at this time that the post was offered to me. I refused it, but Governor Moody and my friends in the Legislature and over the state insisted that I accept. I finally agreed to do so at a meeting of the board held in Houston.

On my return to Sherman the next day, I was met by Mayor Will Leslie and a committee of my fellow-townsmen, who took me to a conference room and sat down with me. There they told me that I was not going to leave Sherman. They said I was to stay on the job as manager of the Chamber of Commerce. They claimed I had not finished my work.

These were the friends of a lifetime. I simply couldn't stand against them. So I wired Chairman Paddock of the prison board that, upon thinking things over, I found I could not take the position. Governor Moody, members of the Legislature, and even leading editorial writers across the state then began to put the heat on me.

I hope the reader will not conclude that I was playing hard to get. I honestly didn't want to leave Sherman, where I was at home with my closest friends. I was happily situated there and well content to stay. As it turned out, the very friends in Sherman who demanded that I stay at home later turned around and demanded with equal firmness that I take the job at Huntsville. They finally convinced me that it was my duty as a citizen to accept the responsibility of the job thrust upon me. But it was hard to have to pull up stakes after all those years in Sherman.

I think the incident that touched me most was the farewell of Mike Moss. He was the son-in-law of old Dick Guess, from whom I'd collected that load of *bois d'arc* posts when I was a little fellow. Mike drove his team into town after the word had gone around that I was leaving and came up to see me. "Mr. Lee, jes' come to town t' tell yuh all us cullud folks sure hates t' see yuh go. But yuh'll be doin' fer de state jes' de same as yuh've been doin' fer Grayson County, an' while yuh're down thar my wife an' Ah'll be prayin' fer yuh all de time."

I knew I was going to need those prayers to help me out in what I then thought of as the hardest job in all Texas officialdom. Six years of experience in the task left me of the same mind about it.

Well, then, on Saturday noon, April 12, 1930, I met at Huntsville with the State Prison Board, composed of Chairman W. A. Paddock, Houston; Joseph Wearden, Goliad; D. R. Nelson, Orange; Fred Horton, Greenville; Mrs. Florence Floore, Cleburne; J. B. H. Holderby, Fort Worth; Dr. Holman Taylor, Fort Worth; Frank L. Tiller, Rosenberg; and E. H. Astin, Bryan. As soon as he had administered the oath, Chairman Paddock turned to me and said: "Here it is; it's yours. Do the best you can with it."

TABLE 1

Acreage, Cultivated, Uncultivated and Value for Year Ending December 31, 1933.

	Total Acreage	Uncultivated	Cultivated	Corn	Cotton	Feed	Garden	Average Value per Acre	Total Value
Huntsville	140	140	....	....	....	....	....	$162.50	$ 22,750.00
Blue Ridge Farm	4,416	686	3,730	1,000	2,125	370	235	53.67	237,009.50
Central Farm	5,227	1,152	4,075	1,500	1,200	575	800	54.94	287,175.35
Clemens Farm	8,212	3,562	4,650	2,500	1,500	325	325	43.65	358,480.00
Darrington Farm	6,746	3,590	3,156	2,000	600	350	206	42.00	283,365.60
Eastham Farm	13,040	7,890	5,150	2,000	2,300	545	305	25.00	326,000.00
Ferguson Farm	4,320	2,225	2,095	900	....	930	265	20.00	86,400.00
Goree Farm	1,000	920	80	....	....	56	24	11.00	11,000.00
Harlem Farm	5,707	1,857	3,850	1,800	1,250	380	420	60.00	342,420.00
Ramsey Farm	15,040	7,175	7,865	4,225	2,250	655	735	36.00	541,400.00
Retrieve Farm	7,228	4,355	2,873	1,900	448	365	160	35.97	259,980.00
Shaw Farm (leased) *	4,688	4,688	....	....	....	....	....	20.00	93,760.00
Wynne Farm	1,976	1,819	157	....	....	85	72	11.00	21,736.00
Totals	77,740	40,059	37,681	17,825	11,673	4,636	3,547	$ 36.94	$2,871,476.45

* The Shaw Farm (Bowie County) was subsequently sold to Jim Smith, a banker of Paris, Texas, thus reducing the total acreage in the prison system to 73,052 acres.
SOURCE: *Annual Report of the Texas Prison Board for the Year Ending December 31, 1933.*

Within "the Walls"

I took over assets to the value of $4,627,072.25—73,000 acres of land, together with buildings, livestock, crops in the field, shop and factory equipment, tools and materials on hand (see Table 1). I also took over 4,833 prisoners. Mr. Meade had made some changes for the better, but things were run-down. Prison morale was mighty low. From every angle, there was plenty of room for improvement.

I assembled the key men, the managers of the farms and the officials of the system. Our first duty, I told them, was to hold the prisoners. We had to stop the escapes. Every key man, I reminded them, was head of his department or of his farm or of whatever was under him. I was going to hold him responsible—directly responsible to me. He could hire whomever he pleased. I wound up this way: "I never intend to make any recommendations to you on that subject. You pick your own people. I know that many guards and some of you farm managers frequently call the prisoners 'you old thing, you old son of a bitch, you.' It is a common practice around here. It is cowardly, as I see it, to talk that way to a prisoner who dare not answer back. No man in this system can work for me and talk that way. I am going to hold each manager responsible for the conduct of his guards.

"From this time on, every prisoner is some mother's son, some woman's husband, some sister's brother. I expect you to treat them as human beings.

"I am aware that occasionally convicts are whipped in the field, and I know that it has the silent approval of the manager or of his assistant. This practice has got to stop. There is a law regulating the whipping of convicts; I expect you to abide by that law."

I meant what I said. But not long afterward I learned of an assistant farm manager who had slapped a prisoner and called him a "damn son of a bitch." Although I had no "snitches" or stool pigeons (I never needed them nor believed in them), I had positive evidence in this case. I sent for the prisoner and asked him about the whipping. He earnestly denied that he had been slapped or cursed. But when I convinced him that I already knew the facts, he admitted them. Then he asked me to do nothing about it: "You know what will happen to me; I want to get along around here."

"How can I help you boys," I replied, "if you won't let me? Don't worry about what will happen to you; I'll take care of that."

Then I reported to the farm manager what had occurred and told him it was up to him to handle it. He made his own investigation, and his assistant was discharged. Of course, that got around to all the guards and to the prisoners as well. It had the desired effect.

However, I learned shortly after that of a case where a Negro prisoner had been whipped in the field. I looked into it thoroughly and found the report was true. So I went down to the farm and spent the night. Next morning I told the manager what I had found, and he admitted the facts. "But, Mr. Simmons," he argued, " a whipping in the field once in a while does a lot of good and gets more work done."

"Captain," said I, "you remember my instructions to you farm managers at our first meeting about the punishment of prisoners?"

"Yes, sir."

"You remember that I told you the law was to be observed, and that I would hold you responsible to see that it is observed?"

"Yes, sir."

"Captain, I think you are the best all-round farm manager in the system, and I like you, but if I ever hear again of a prisoner's being whipped in the field with your knowledge and consent—silent consent—I'll fire you so damn quick you won't know what happened to you. And I'll tell the public why I fired you."

You should have seen the expression on his face. He didn't even reply. The news got around: the Old Man was looking out for the welfare of the prisoners.

All this was merely in line with what I had told the prisoners themselves when I first took charge. Within a few days after I took the oath of office, I assembled a thousand or more prisoners within the Walls and made them a short talk on my duty and responsibility. I had a stenographer's transcript for the record and saved it so I could check on myself from time to time. I am sorry that I have since mislaid the transcript but in substance this is what I said:

I did not seek this job. I turned it down more than once. I was happily situated at home and wanted to stay there.

But I am a Texan, born in Texas, and I feel that the time has come when I ought to accept this call for service in this position of large responsibilities, subject though it is to severe criticism.

Within "the Walls"

I ask you to recognize that I did not put you here. I am not responsible for your being here. If you feel that you got too severe a sentence—if you feel that you have been framed—if you feel that you have been jobbed by the law, don't hold that against me. From the moment you enter the prison gate your care and your welfare become my responsibility.

I have accepted that responsibility. I never expect to try to shift it to other shoulders. I am the one to whom you have the right to look. I am the one from whom you have the right to expect fair treatment. I plan to treat you the way my father always treated me. I expect to treat you as I would expect to be treated, were I in your place.

I strongly favor a liberal parole policy based on merit alone, and not on pull or pay. And as prisoners are discharged, promotions to better jobs with greater overtime pay will go only to the next man in line, when he is deserving. No man's influence will ever get a new prisoner into a good job over a deserving prisoner already in line for it.

I accept seriously my duty to look after your health, your general welfare, and your chance at an education. But I also owe a duty to the public and to the taxpayer. And that duty requires me to control you and to get a reasonable day's work out of you.

Now, I hope you boys won't try to jump [escape], but if you do jump, boys, we will jump with you. If you will co-operate with me, I will co-operate with you. If I didn't believe that 75 to 95 per cent of you would stand for fair treatment and co-operate with me—after you see that you are getting a square deal—I wouldn't fool with this job.

Now, the small, minority per cent—you hell-raisers—I want to say to you that, if I'm not tougher than you boys, then the State of Texas has got the wrong man for this job. To you, too, I say that I expect to hold you, to control you, and to get a reasonable day's work out of you.

I say again that it is my duty and the responsibility of the State Prison Board, as the representatives of the state itself, to look after your health, your education, your general welfare, and your rehabilitation to the highest degree possible, in keeping with justice, fairness, and common sense— bearing in mind the interests both of yourselves and of the public. And I see no reason for any conflict between humane policies and good business management of the prison system.

Two years later, when I reread it carefully, I honestly believed that I stuck to my policy throughout. And the results so outran my expectations that I felt that my efforts were well repaid.

But then it was up to me to prove I meant every word of it. And that I set out to do. The conditions which confronted me were appalling. At the Walls fifteen hundred prisoners were confined in quarters designed for a maximum of twelve hundred. There was no sewerage accommodation and practically no fire protection. The three-story antiquated hospital building was infested by bedbugs and had no fire escapes. In the cell blocks men were sleeping on the floor, in the aisles—anywhere there was room for a blanket on the concrete floor. Five hundred men were idle, with absolutely nothing to do.

The accommodations for the guards were, if anything, worse than those for the prisoners. In a room used by the forty guards of the staff there were only two broken-down old chairs. At night the men had to throw their clothes on the floor under their cots. There was no other place to put them. One toilet and one lavatory served these forty men. They had to walk two blocks to take a shower.

We started a cleanup immediately, both of the prisoners' quarters and of the guards'. We built a substantial two-story frame building to house two hundred men. Then we moved out a large number of prisoners to the farms and put everybody to work at some useful employment, either inside or outside the Walls.

I immediately had two more windows cut in the guards' room, installed additional toilets and lavatories, put in two adjoining showers, and provided each man with a 24-inch clothes closet, built from prison-cut lumber. One day the hat was being passed for a guard who was sick. Of course, I kicked in, but I said, "Surely his pay goes on while he's unable to work." Upon being informed that it didn't, I immediately announced a change of policy: thereafter any guard honestly unable to perform his duties remained on full salary. That policy paid off in real co-operation from the guards.

Then came the problem of meals. The food furnished the prison system was bought from wholesalers who did not hesitate to work off their spoiled goods on the state. Even when it was good, it was pretty much the same thing every day, 90 per cent of it out of sacks or cans. The guards, who were served the same food, were in the habit of bringing in their own fresh eggs to add to the prison menu, but the prisoners had no choice but to eat what was put before them.

As soon as I took charge we started gardening on a big scale, and within sixty days we were cutting food costs and improving our menus. The number of escapes began to drop immediately. And what I saved on food I could put into further improvements, for which there was plenty of room.

Out on the farms conditions were even worse. The slave camps of olden times could not have been more unsanitary. At Camp Two, located on flat land with no drainage, the sewerage stood in the open flat. Everywhere was filth and garbage—and in consequence a set of disgruntled and rebellious prisoners. I soon put our manpower to work to clean up and remedy conditions.

I had appointed W. W. Waid, of Greenville, as my warden. He was a big, fine-looking man with a shock of heavy black hair. I had known of his past record as a peace officer and expected that what he lacked in formal education he would make up for by his intuitive knowledge of human nature. I was never disappointed in my choice. Early in the days of my administration I called in Waid and the two prison chaplains and outlined what was next: "I have a high regard for religion, but I want to give the prisoners something else, too. I want an educational program, and I want some worth-while recreation. I expect you fellows to get busy and help me put it over."

Up to this time, 136 convicts were attending a school of sorts, meeting with the chaplains at night. Little or no interest was shown. Beyond an occasional baseball game here and there and a play staged once in a while in the prison chapel, no real recreation was provided.

I couldn't have asked for more enthusiastic co-operation than I had from Warden Waid and the chaplains. Waid cleared out a large upstairs room over one of the shops and had the construction foreman, C. C. Johns, make desks and benches from lumber that had been given us in exchange for clearing wooded areas on nearby private farms.

Waid then selected as teachers a group of prisoners with fairly good educations. No sooner were they installed than attendance picked up promptly and sharply. A good baseball team was organized, and a ball park was fixed up. Waid also found a Negro who was a professional theater man. This lad was placed in charge of our show business, and things began to hum.

According to the first annual report by Warden Waid:

Movies, shows—both amateur and professional—and other clean entertainments have been provided for the men, and the prison ball team enjoyed a successful season. . . . Fifty guards are now assigned to duties that formerly required eighty-five. Every able-bodied man is now employed in useful occupation. . . . Number of inmates approved as trusties, 295. Number escaped, 3. . . . It has been my endeavor to show the prisoners that the management is willing to co-operate with them and aid them in every manner, and that "politics," as the term is understood in prison, has ceased to exist.

There was no budget provision for hiring a schoolteacher, but savings in operation costs and income from gate receipts at shows and ball games enabled us to employ L. B. Tindall, an experienced teacher and a fine old-time schoolman, at a salary of $125 a month. He certainly earned his wages.

Warden Waid had his school at the Walls going along splendidly, and Tindall began operating a school or so on each of the eleven farms. Because farm managers were slow about helping him, it was a worrisome job. But Tindall kept at it, and within ten months voluntary attendance at our schools rose from 136 to 1,242.

"Mr. Simmons," said Board Chairman Paddock, in his annual report for 1930, "has taken hold with a strong hand, and is making great progress in developing a spirit of co-operation among the personnel of the employed organization and of the prisoners as well." I guess I did use a strong hand at times, but, anyway, I appreciated the kind words of the board. Most of all, I appreciated the way everybody worked together on the thing we had to do.

In 1931 school development proceeded under handicaps. Tindall's time was taken up largely with the instruction system on the eleven farms. After the supper dishes were cleared and the tables cleaned, the dining rooms became schoolrooms. That meant short and late hours for school. Most of my farm managers simply weren't interested in the project. They required a bit of educating, themselves. But Tindall worked hard, and school attendance rose from 1,242 to 1,686.

By this time I had surveyed results from every angle, including discipline, conduct, escapes, punishments, service, and operating economy of the prison system as a whole. I was convinced that education and recreation were paying off. So I decided to open up; I em-

ployed a top vocational-agriculture teacher, J. M. Reynolds, a young
A. & M. graduate whom I had earlier lured to Sherman, to be school
supervisor and Albert Moore, to be recreation director.

The outcome was beyond all my hopes. None of the credit was
mine; I just sat on the fence and watched the boys go by! In 1933
Victor Schoffelmayer, then agricultural editor of the *Dallas Morning
News*, spent a week visiting the penitentiary system. When he saw
Red Reynolds there, he turned to me: "Red Reynolds! Red Reynolds!
Best vocational teacher in Texas. Simmons, how did you get him?"

"I just got him," said I, noncommittally. The fact was that I had
appealed to Red to come down and go over the system with me. When
he came, I said to him: "Here is the greatest opportunity for educational service to be found in all Texas. I want you; I need you; and I
will back you up to the limit."

He came, and our 1933 report was able to say:

Outstanding among our accomplishments for the year 1933 has been
the teaching of 696 men to read and write. A spelling and writing contest
was conducted during July and August, in which 2,300 prisoners participated. Four hundred and fifty-four packages of cigarettes have been
distributed as prizes. . . . Approximately 75,000 copies of good, current-
issue magazines have been distributed to the twenty-three units of the
prison system the past year. *American Magazine, Popular Mechanics,
Literary Digest, Liberty* and *Cosmopolitan* were among the majority distributed. These magazines were donated by Houston magazine agencies,
and incurred no cost to the prison system.

In the following year Reynolds gave advanced-classification tests
to 276 teachers, all prisoners, with notable improvement in the teaching work. Magazine circulation totaled 100,000 copies, all given to us
without cost. We were also able to put into the prison libraries a few
copies daily of each of the larger newspapers of the state. Library
books to the number of 10,000 had been acquired. Books were paid
for out of our welfare fund, at no cost to taxpayers, except those
books which were donated by various cities and towns throughout
the state. These came at the solicitation of Mrs. Floore, of the prison
board.

Courses of study had now been standardized throughout our twenty-two prison schools, and an exhibit of their work was produced as

TABLE 2

TEXAS PRISON SYSTEM—COMPARATIVE DATA

	1929	1930	1931	1932	1933	1934	1935
Average population....	4,868	4,998	5,550	5,535	5,362	5,359	5,623
Total punishments....	326	321	232	137	140	89	80
Total escapes	302	187	110	87	109	94	71
New prisoners received	2,543	2,592	3,189	3,300	3,118	2,953	3,165
Cost of transporting prisoners	$43,097.00	$ 41,882.82	$ 22,479.48	$ 10,976.55	$ 11,809.70	$ 13,597.59	$14,291.13
Average cost per prisoner	$ 16.95	$ 16.16	$ 7.05	$ 3.33	$ 3.78	$ 4.60	$ 4.51
Escapees recaptured...	298	233	154	125	104	98	79
Recapture expense...	$15,471.26	$ 11,743.21	$ 4,821.63	$ 3,055.02	$ 1,965.00	$ 1,795.60	$ 1,776.70
Average cost of recapture per prisoner...	$ 51.92	$ 50.40	$ 31.32	$ 19.71	$ 18.19	$ 18.32	$ 22.49
Cash expenditure for improvements	....	$107,004.87	$335,992.26	$144,093.59	$113,187.48	$148,673.09	$91,219.35
Average operating cost per prisoner	$ 393.73	$ 342.25	$ 278.44	$ 253.69	$ 224.79	$ 260.57	$ 238.29
Net operating cost per prisoner	$ 293.64	$ 174.14	$ 160.32	$ 160.29	$ 85.46	$ 76.66	$ 151.55
Barber work, laundry, meals, sales, etc......	$ 1,247.40	$ 7,082.12	$ 13,781.30	$ 12,499.44	$ 11,291.50	$ 12,363.26	$10,475.27
Total enrolled in prison schools..........	136	1,242	1,686	2,262	2,420	2,234	2,963

the result of an interschool contest. This exhibit was taken to Galveston for the annual meeting of the Texas State Teachers' Association, where it won favorable comment. The same year, 1934, I persuaded the American Prison Congress to come to Texas, and, of course, I took our prison-school exhibit to the Rice Hotel for the sessions of this body at Houston.

I admit that I was so proud of the exhibit that I hung around it quite a bit and got great pleasure out of praise given it by officials of both state and federal penitentiaries. Reynolds had provided extra copies of his prison-school instruction books, and I saw numbers of them carried away by visitors for further examination and study.

Summing up in his report for 1934, Reynolds said: "During the past four years, there have been more than 2,300 taught to read and write in the prison schools. We have the school record of men who have gone from the primer through the fourth grade while enrolled in the school the past two years."

And, though it's getting ahead of my story a little, I want to quote from the school supervisor's report on the Texas Prison System for 1935. By that time the full effect of Red Reynold's work was showing up.

The progress of the year shows an average of 2,963 inmates enrolled in the school for the year, which represents 52.8 per cent of the inmate population. However, there was a total of 4,848 different individuals enrolled during the year. The progress sheet shows an average of 334 men enrolled in vocational work and special subjects for the year; a total of 956 illiterates were received among the new prisoners for the year. An average of 785 were enrolled in the first and second grades. However, there was a total of 1,686 different individuals enrolled in the first grade for the year. Of this number, more than 1,200 have been taught to read and write and will be advanced to a higher grade. . . . The prison schools have shown a steady growth from the year 1930, when a prison school supervisor was first appointed. The total enrollment increased from an average of 47 during the year 1928 to an average of 2,963 the past year.

Education was paying off, as can be seen from the comparative data assembled in Table 2.

CHAPTER 8

Education for Reform

OUR PROGRAM of education was incomplete—education
never is finished, anyhow. In particular, Governor Moody and I found
two branches of instruction that badly needed our attention. The
Governor had as his concern the education of the people of the state
of Texas to the needs of the prisons, while I, as manager of the Texas
Prison System, had for my concern the stubborn, hell-raising minority of prisoners to whom I had given warning in my first address to
the prison inmates.

Soon after I arrived in Huntsville, Governor Moody took the de-
plorable physical conditions of the penitentiary to the people by
radio hookup. He started his school of the air at 1:00 P.M. on a Sunday, after wide advertisement of it in the press. I sat in the class myself that day, along with the people over the state.

The speech wasn't political. Governor Dan was plain, blunt, and
forceful. He said he wanted to cast reflections on nobody. But the
prison system was his responsibility, and he wanted the help of all the
people. He said he intended to put it squarely up to the Legislature.
He closed his remarks thus: "If I had a dog that I thought anything
of, I wouldn't want him kept in the Texas penitentiary under present
conditions."

In addition to being Red Reynold's right-hand "man" in the development of prison-school plans, prison board member Florence Floore was president of the Texas Federated Women's Clubs and a woman of state-wide influence. Under her leadership the women of Texas were most effective in carrying forward the Governor's campaign for prison reform.

Thus Governor Moody got the job done. From the Legislature and other bodies he got the co-operation he demanded. I thought him a great man then. I still do.

But what about me and my hell-raisers? The crisis came suddenly, as I suppose crises always do. This one presented me with my hardest assignment, for upon it depended the success or failure of prison management.

The trouble arose in the wood squad. You may remember my saying that when I first took over we had about five hundred men in the yard at the Walls with nothing to do all day. Besides these, we had some twenty prisoners confined in the cell block reserved for bad men. They were locked in cells with an extra framework of steel bars. A special guard was kept over them day and night. They were not allowed to enter the yard at any time.

I had told all these fellows that I expected a reasonable day's work out of each of them. My word was out. But no one can do a day's work while he is in a cell or in solitary confinement. As soon as Warden Waid came on the job, he and I went over the situation. I told him the bad boys had to work, too. Waid moved the hell-raisers down to the first row of cells. Then he called in Oliver Ross, and they worked out their plan. The bad boys went to work.

At this time the prison system needed both fuel and lumber. We had a small wood squad out clearing land for individual farmers. We took firewood and saw logs for our pay. Waid and Ross rigged up a big truck, picked out about forty prisoners for the wood squad, including all our hell-raisers. Ross was allowed to pick his own guards for this squad. He chose Barnes and Osborne and made ready to start out to work the next morning. "Ross," I asked him, "you think you can hold them?"

"Yes, I'll hold them, Mr. Simmons."

Those were his exact words; I have reason to remember them, as you will see. For a week, everything went well. The firewood and the timber were coming in plentifully. The saw logs were what pleased me. My bad boys were sawing wood, as ordered.

Then one afternoon at about four o'clock, I had just returned from one of the farms and was standing in Warden Waid's office when we heard a car coming up the street with its horn wide open. We rushed out to meet the trusty-driver from the wood squad. "They's made a big break in the wood squad," he shouted, "an' they's all gone!"

Waid and I gathered up guns and guards, and away we went. When we drove up the road in the woods to where the break had occurred, there was good old Oliver Ross sitting down, gun in hand. The wood squad lay on the ground in front of him, some of them dead, some of them wounded, but all of them quiet, counted, and accounted for.

"They're all here, Mr. Simmons," came his calm voice. "I'd rather you had come out and found me dead than to come out here and find one of these fellows gone."

Ross himself was shot up pretty badly. But they were all there, as he said. There were three dead and four or five wounded. Among the latter was a former town marshal and deputy sheriff—with an arm shot off.

The break had occurred this way. Just after the prisoners were loaded into the truck to be taken back to the Walls, Ross and Osborne had deposited their shotguns in the automobile with the trusty-driver and then had stepped on the running board of the truck cab from either side, armed only with their six-shooters. Just as the truck started out, two prisoners from one corner of the truck bed leaped over the top on Ross, bearing him to the ground, while two others from the other corner landed on Osborne.

Barnes, the remaining guard, had retained his shotgun, as his post was at the back of the truck while the prisoners were being loaded. Seeing two convicts on top of Ross, Barnes promptly shot them off, wounding Ross pretty badly in doing so. But another of the four escapees had got hold of Ross's gun. Using Osborne as a shield, Osborne's captors turned both guns, his and Ross's against Barnes. Barnes stood and took their fire, waiting for his chance to save the life of Osborne, who was bobbing and weaving from side to side as much as he could in the grip of the two convicts who held him.

Meanwhile, Ross, despite his wounded condition, had crawled around and up to Barnes, got Barnes's six-shooter, then crawled around and behind the two men who had Osborne, and shot one of them through the head. As the dead man fell, he pulled Osborne over to one side a little, exposing the other convict. Barnes did not miss; he dropped his man without harming Osborne.

One of the two who had been on top of Ross ran in front of the truck and took off down the road, but the Negro water boy chased him with a wrench in hand, struck him over the head, and forced him to return. (Of course we took care of that Negro trusty for his act of courage and fidelity.)

But what of the prisoners left standing in the truck? Barnes was there with his smoking shotgun—and somehow it didn't occur to any of them that it would be healthy to leave just then. They all stood fast.

Later, when the former deputy sheriff recovered from his wounds, Warden Waid said to me: "What we going to do with Old Tom?"

"Send him back to the wood squad," I answered.

"Old Tom can't cut wood with one arm!"

"No, but he can pile brush." And he did. Old Tom, the former peace officer—and the brains of the break—went back to the wood squad.

I still like to think about those guards who didn't turn tail and run at the first sign of trouble, like some others I shall tell you about. They didn't "stick 'em up" at the command of a convict with a gun, as guards have been known to do. They stood like men, real men, true to their trust. They stood every chance of being carried away feet first, but all hell couldn't run those three away.

"They're all here, Mr. Simmons!"

And so they were. I loved those old boys. I still do.

But I had more classwork ahead of me. It was pretty much of the same sort. For years and years there had been "bucks" (prison mutinies), more often on the farms than within the Walls. Prisoners would refuse to go out to work, refuse to work when they got to the field, go on a sit-down strike, or refuse to re-enter the prison barracks when they returned from the field.

Their complaint generally was that they didn't like their food or the quantity of it or that they were mistreated, whipped, or otherwise abused by the guards. I am sure that, in many cases, their complaints were justified and were never either investigated or properly dealt with. Before I became manager bucks took place frequently. During one of these mutinies while I was on the prison board, I happened to be inspecting the farm concerned, along with the manager of the farm. The balky prisoners were sitting on the ground, the armed guards holding them there. When the manager asked what was the matter, they said the ground was too wet to work. He talked to them for a while, but they refused to move.

He then asked me to speak to them. At that time, of course, I had no direct authority over them, and it was not my immediate problem. While I was clear in my own mind that I certainly was not going to attempt to handle things for him, I did agree to say a few words. And I did:

"Now boys, I know farming. The ground is not wet." I kicked up a little dirt with my boot. "I'm not running this farm, but I know what my father would have done to me, if he had sent me out to the field to work like this. He would have put me to work. And if I were manager of this farm, I know what I would do to you boys. I would put you to work."

But they refused to move out. After more talk from the manager, they got up and marched back to the building. It was then the middle of the afternoon.

After I had served out my tour as general manager and had retired, bucks again became frequent in the system; but while the responsibility for such things was mine, I gave the handling of such outbreaks my most serious attention. And the first buck under my managership was the last one. There weren't any more.

One September on the Clemens Farm there was an attempted mutiny of this sort. The weather was hot, and we were getting ready to harvest a fine cotton crop. In the course of our monthly meetings with the eleven farm managers and the Warden, we discussed our problems and program. I cautioned all concerned to take it easy with the prisoners as they started picking cotton.

"We have plenty of time," I reminded them, "and plenty of men. Look after the boys; don't crowd them. Let them go to the shade, if it's too hot. Start out a little late after dinner, if you think best."

Education for Reform

I meant what I said. To make it plain that I did, and to make it certain that everybody understood me, I called in my secretary, Clyde Watson, a day or so later, and gave him a letter to all farm managers in which I ordered extra care with cotton-picking prisoners, as the weather was then quite hot. By way of further precaution, I made the rounds of the farms personally. On the second day of this inspection, I drove into the Clemens Farm, near Brazoria, at about 4:00 P.M.

I found that two prisoners had just died, after being brought in from the cotton field. Shortly thereafter, the dog sergeant came in with a prisoner who had escaped from the field that morning. The trail had led for hours through the brush and briars and big, sharp-spined cactus. The fugitive was scratched and had cuts from the cactus as wicked-looking as if they had been done by a knife. But when I examined him for evidence of abuse, he bore no bruises whatever.

By this time all eight of the field squads had been brought in, and as soon as they heard the news of the deaths and the escaped prisoner the excitement started. They felt, I am sure, that they had cause to be disturbed. I was distrubed, myself. Captain Will Hickman, who was with me, was very much disturbed.

We began our investigation. I questioned the guard in whose squad the two men had died. This guard was a man of some fifty years, rather quiet and serious in disposition. He was positive that Captain Hickman had given all the guards instructions to be careful in looking after the men. He also said that I had myself instructed him to see that it was done—as I had.

He said he had taken his squad out a little later than usual after dinner and that he had told the men: "If any of you boys feel that you are getting too hot, come to the wagon and lie down in the shade until you cool off."

It so happened that the father of one of the dead boys was himself a prisoner. This father was in the squad next to that of his son. I took this man out that night and made him understand that I wanted the facts. He verified all that the guard had said. Then he made the statement on which I based my line of thinking:

"Nobody but the boys themselves was to blame. When the water boy came by with the water, I heard them say they were going to drink enough water to make themselves sick, so that they would have to be taken back to the barracks. Mr. Simmons, he's my boy, but it is not the guard's fault; it was his own."

I did not stop there. The guard lived in Brazoria, and I went over there and called on a banker whom I knew. I went out to his home at about eight that night. I didn't tell him what had happened, except that I said that there had been some trouble on the farm. Then I asked him about the truthfulness of this guard. My friend seemed surprised at my question. He would vouch for the man in any man-. ner on anything. He had known him for a long time and would swear by him. Assured that there had been no neglect of duty by guard or farm manager, I returned to the farm.

There I found Captain Hickman more upset than ever. "The prisoners aren't going out to work in the morning," he said, "unless I fire the dog sergeant. There's going to be an awful buck, and I dread it. Of course, I could exchange dog sergeants with Manager Kelly of Retrieve Farm, and maybe settle it that way."

I said nothing, just listened. Finally the Captain asked me what I thought about the exchange, and I merely told him that we would see about that in the morning. We retired for the night, but I didn't sleep a wink. I don't imagine that Hickman slept much more than I did. I knew I had an attempted buck on my hands. How I handled it would pretty well tell the story of Lee Simmons, general manager of the Texas Prison System. Of course I didn't sleep.

In the morning, Hickman and I ate breakfast as usual at five o'clock. He wanted to know what I thought we ought to do. I said nothing at the time; but I knew what I was going to do. He persisted with the question. "We'll see about it," I replied, "when we get over to the camp."

The camp was about a mile over in the farm. When we walked into the picket, the prisoners said they had a committee who wanted to talk to me.

"Sure," said I. "Glad to hear you."

They began by telling me how the dog sergeant mistreated prisoners and how he had whipped the escaped man all the way back to camp. They said that the two boys died because they were overworked while it was too hot. They said they were not going out to work that morning, unless Captain Hickman discharged the dog sergeant. If he did that, they said, they would come on out and pick cotton for me and give no more trouble.

As calmly as I could, I made my appeal to the prisoners. I acknowledged that it was a most unfortunate affair, and that I was truly sorry that it had happened. As I had made a thorough investigation, however, I felt that I knew the facts.

"Now, here is Davis," I said. "His son was one of the boys that died. Davis says that it was not the guard's fault. And I myself examined the escaped man who was brought in. You boys know that there are only scratches on him, no bruises or whip marks, as you claim.

"You boys know that I am doing everything I can to help you, and I'm going to keep on helping you, and I am going to see that everything is taken care of down here all right, if I have to spend half my time on this farm." Then I stepped out of the way.

"All right, Boss," said Captain Hickman, and the picket guard unlocked the door and opened it. Squad 1—not a man stirred. Squad 2—nobody moved. And so it was, on down through the entire eight squads, sixteen men to the squad. Not a word.

"They're not going to come out," said Captain Hickman, softly.

I stepped back up to the bars and again addressed the mutineers: "You boys are in the wrong about this; if you can tell the manager to fire the dog sergeant, you can tell him to fire the steward; you can tell him to fire the assistant manager, if you don't like him. We are not going to let you do that. When the gate is opened this time, you had better come on out."

I turned to the picket boss: "Open the gate." He opened it and began to call the squad numbers. He called them all; not a man moved. The stillness was full of threat.

The gate was shut again, and again I stepped up to the bars. I bore down on the investigation and what it showed. I knew I was right, and I knew they were wrong, and I told them so. I told them I was running the prison system. "When the gate is opened this time, boys, it is not to be closed until every man of you has come out of there. *Open the gate!*"

It was opened. Three seconds of silence dragged out as if they were three minutes. But my gaze didn't shift; it didn't waver. Then a big old boy up in front cried out: "Boys, I think the Colonel means what he says. I'm comin' out."

Squad 1 made a rush to get to the gate. Squad 2 followed, and, as each number was called, that squad swung into line. They marched out exactly as if nothing had happened at all. I looked around at Hickman. He was pretty pale. We got into his car to go back to head-quarters. He took a deep breath, and said to me: "I didn't think they were coming out! Tell me what you aimed to do to them, if they hadn't?"

"You heard me say that when the gate was opened this last time it wouldn't be closed until the last man came out? Well, I made my decision and planned everything out last night."

"But what did you aim to do?"

Then I told him. Had they refused that last time to go to work, I would have sent for all the pitchforks and baseball bats on the farm. Then I meant to call on his most dependable guards. The armed guards I intended to place just inside the front of the building. All the other guards I planned to arm with the pitchforks and the bats. At the head of these latter, I expected to step right in, pitchfork in hand. And I expected them to follow me in. I was going to order the armed guards to pick off any prisoner who made so much as the motion of his hand toward any of us on the inside. Then I meant to tell everybody that somebody might be carried out feet first, but that I had already made up my mind who was running the prison system.

Had it come to this last resort, according to my plan, I realize now, as I did then, that hell would have broken loose in Texas. But I knew I was right. I figured that right pretty generally prevails. Just the same, I was mighty fortunate—and mighty thankful—that there was no blood on my pitchfork and nobody to be carried out feet first.

Clemens Farm cotton was picked on schedule without any further trouble. In consequence, I had more opportunity to develop the less unpleasant phases of my program of education and rehabilitation.

Our prison school system was reaching many of our prisoners, helping them improve their condition. But there were others, the psychotics, the disturbed, who could not be helped by normal educative processes.

The unsound body is frequently the cause of an unsound mind.

Education for Reform

Physical defects play an important part in disturbing the psychic factors, unbalancing the mind and leaving a weakness such that the individual actually cannot resist temptation. And, of course, crime follows readily enough. In such cases, the pathologist and psychiatrist take over to great advantage.

Classification of incoming prisoners with scientific examination and treatment of this psychotic group has long been recognized as a must in modern prison management. Convinced of the need, I began to look around for a psychiatrist for the penitentiary. While visiting the Austin Rotary Club one day, I sat at a table with my good friend H. Y. Benedict, at that time president of the University of Texas. We had lived on the same floor in old Brackenridge Hall while I was a freshman and he was a senior at the university.

I told Dr. Benedict I wanted to employ a psychiatrist. He showed me what might be done through a foundation fund under the direction of the university. Accordingly, at the next meeting of the prison board, I reported what I had learned and recommended action along the lines set down in the minutes as follows:

Motion was made and seconded that the Chairman of the Prison Board, General Manager and Dr. S. M. Lister, together with such other members of the Board as they may choose to act with them, be authorized to make contact with the University for a psychiatrist, if they see fit. [Minutes of the Seventy-ninth Meeting of the Texas Prison Board, September 2, 1935, at Houston.]

That was the origin of the well-staffed classification system which is now in operation. It had a small beginning. But I saw that it was essential, and I am glad I had a part in it. I believe that the work of qualified scientists on the staff of a penal institution can reclaim a worth-while percentage of men who need their attention.

CHAPTER 9

Convicts at Play

ALL WORK AND NO PLAY makes Jack a dull convict. I am
a strong believer in recreation, when it is rightly handled. Of course,
you have to be reasonable about recreation, just as about everything
else. I've never been much of a believer in measuring work by the
hour. In all my varied occupations, I've never paid much attention
to hours. I favor getting the job done.

I figure that recreation can help get the job done. So we went in for
recreation in the prison system. The record will show how far we went
with it. I frankly confess that I enjoyed it myself and took part in it. I
became a part of the boys and the boys became a part of me. When it
came time to play, we all played. We wound up by having rodeos,
baseball, shows on stage and off, band practice, and band concerts
just about all over the place.

I'm telling you, it was great. Thousands of outsiders flocked in to
see and hear it. Occasionally a newspaper or a member of the Legislature complained that there was too much play in the prison system.
Whenever I heard criticism of that sort, I actually got something like
pleasure out of it.

Indeed, I grew boastful about it. I bragged that our system of recreation involved more participants than could be found similarly engaged in any half-dozen other penitentiaries in the country. I think I

was right about that. Certainly we got plenty of compliments on the size, diversity, and success of our recreation scheme.

We didn't get it all going at once. While the prison board was of a general mind to let me do as I liked, others in authority had mighty little sympathy with the notion of prisoners at play. We had to do a little educational work in high places—and in some places not so high.

For example, there was the feeling that convicts were sent to prison for punishment and ought to have it. They were there to work, and the work ought to be got out of them. Hard work, dirty work, and lots of it was considered the proper medicine, and the bigger the dose the better.

Besides all that, it is a fact that when prisoners are playing ball or pulling off a rodeo out in the open or staging a big show at night, practically all the inmates are in attendance in a body. That presents a greater opportunity for escape. There is some substance to that objection.

Now I had been bearing down on this matter of escapes. I had to keep it in mind—and keep it in the mind of the people under me. So I had to work things out gradually. Moreover, until the prisoners themselves were ready for the program, we had to feel our way along. Albert Moore, the athletic director, made a beginning with prison baseball.

His program meant that the farm managers had to prepare the playing fields. Guards had to stand watch on Saturday and Sunday afternoons, whereas they undoubtedly preferred to rest, play dominoes, or go to town. As it seemed to them, baseball was foolish business for convicts, anyhow. As a matter of fact, I had a lot of sympathy for the guards; they had a hard job, with long hours for which they got little pay and plenty of criticism.

To be sure, I am not claiming that there was no basis for criticism of the penitentiary guard. In every line of business there are always some who are not up to par. I am quite certain that among our four hundred guards there were some pretty bad eggs. In and around Houston there were many disreputable places, in the red-light district and out of it. Not infrequently Monday morning papers had big head-

lines telling everybody how some of my prison guards had got into a
brawl. I remember in particular one Sunday afternoon when one
guard shot up another in a Negro dive where neither of them had any
legitimate business.

But, good guards or bad, they preferred to spend their spare time
in the city to doing extra duty in the prison system. So we had to work
on them to get them interested in what we were trying to accomplish. This was fundamental, for our system was a sprawling affair,
and much of our program would have to take place in the open. Three-
fourths of our prisoners were on the eleven farms; and they deserved
even more attention than did the men inside the Walls.

"The more cotton we chop up," ran the saying of the field hands,
"the less we have to pick." You couldn't blame them too much for
feeling that way about it. The lads who were out in the sun and the
rain were our working prisoners. I figured they had something coming to them.

Under the old regime, which had lasted for many years, nobody
cared much about these fellows—certainly the guards didn't, for nobody cared for the guards, either. The welfare director's first problem, then, was to get the co-operation of the guards, the farm managers, and the prisoners. The guards were the key men, of course.

Now, I was proud of those guards. I still am proud of them. They
were my guards, particularly mine, and before I left the system I
came to see the time when nearly every guard who could get there
was on hand at Albert Moore's baseball games, at his shows, and especially at the rodeos. The events on the farms were Albert's doing,
but when we got to the rodeo at the Walls—the biggest exhibition of
all—that was "our" rodeo, his and mine. It was mostly his, but I always claimed a part of it as mine. I got right down in the arena and
partnered with Albert. I liked the game, I liked Albert, and I liked the
way he played the game.

From the beginning I centered upon providing entertainment for
the prisoners and the prison employees and their families. Running a
prison is a hard and serious business, dealing, for the most part, with
the unfortunates of life. Many of these men never had much of a
chance. Most of them had never had proper guidance in their youth.
Oh, some were hardened, reckless, devil-may-care criminals, such as

you always find in such a place. But I felt that all of them deserved a chance when I could offer it to them. They didn't all accept it; but you and I—the state—ought to give them the opportunity. In any prison system, morally and literally we become our brother's keeper; we can't escape the implications of that, either morally or literally. I thought we ought to accept the responsibility wholeheartedly.

Before too long, Albert had his baseball grounds in shape and began to pull off some mighty good baseball games. At first there were no grandstands. But they came later. Rivalry between prison-farm teams grew hot. The hotter the better, thought I. Indeed, the games got better than I realized, and the public on the outside wanted in to see them. "The public?" we asked ourselves. "Where do they figure? Where do they come in?"

We decided they came in at the gate. They liked our games—and we had the games. We were poor—and the public had money. So it worked out fine: they came, they paid, and they had the time of their lives. We took the gate money and paid for grandstands, equipment, band instruments, stage apparatus, and so on. We were set up in business and doing well. But public patronage was a sideline, and we kept it as a sideline. Recreation for our own people came first.

To be sure, the public were our customers, and we had to give them their money's worth. We gave them that. But they gave us more than their money; as the result of coming in to see the games, they began to see the prison with new eyes. Thus we won their sympathetic understanding and their co-operation.

As for myself, I got a heap of fun out of the Negro ball games. My problem there was that I could not be at the Walls and down on the farms on the same Sunday afternoon at the same time. Yet all over the system the boys were after me to come see their teams play. Let me tell you about a couple of games, by way of a sample.

The industrial unit of Central Farm had two large grandstands built—one for the public and one for the prisoners. Both were erected with welfare funds, not a penny of which came out of the taxpayer's pocket. The first game that I want to tell you about was between the Negroes of Central Farm (Sugar Land) and the Negroes of Clemens Farm (Brazoria). Manager Hickman, of Clemens, liked baseball, and he had the best Negro team in the system. Buck Miles, assistant manager, handled the team. Captain Buck Flanagan, of Central Farm, had two teams, one white and one Negro. As the teams shuttled from farm to farm several times during the season, the competition became quite sharp.

On this particular afternoon the crowd was roaring, and we had a game to roar about. The weather was baking hot, which seemed to steam everybody up that much more. The Clemens Farm boys were on hand to wipe up on Captain Buck Flanagan and his Negro players. Things were looking bad for Hickman's boys from the "bottoms." Flanagan's Central team was out in front in the fourth inning, and Central's pitcher was hotter than the thermometer. He was swabbing the sweat out of his eyes and fogging that ball across the plate. He was making the batters cross-eyed.

The hotter it got, the more the pitcher mopped his face on his sleeve. Miles took one startled look at that pitcher and shouted: "Flanagan, you old son of a sodalitarian, you've got your white pitcher and catcher in there! Get 'em out!"

Flanagan had had his stage-show man get out his make-up kit and blacken the two white players to match the complexion of the rest of the team. Of course, Flanagan had to take out his burnt-cork battery —and the Clemens Farm outfit went on to win handily. I don't believe that anybody who saw that game will ever forget it.

But the biggest game of all was one that wasn't seen by the prisoners because it was played in the Buff Stadium at Houston. At the Walls we had played most of the better semipro teams, but I had declined to take our teams out on the road. I felt that it was bad policy and wouldn't be well received by the public, although friends in and out of politics pressed me to take teams here and there.

However, Lloyd Gregory, of the *Houston Post*, had built up quite a circuit of semipro teams, many of which we had played at the Walls. Gregory and the *Post* were our friends when we needed friends. In particular, they had backed our recreational program. Well, the first thing I knew, the papers were saying that efforts were being made to match the Prison Tigers against the Sun Oilers of Brenham, with the game to be played at Houston. Albert Moore and his Tigers were "r'aring at the bits." "We can beat that bunch," said Albert. "The boys are begging for the game, and I'll guarantee you there won't be a bit of trouble."

I was on the spot. Albert had spoken the mind and ambition of five thousand prisoners. Now, I had asked the loyalty and co-operation of those men, and they had responded beyond my hopes, from the very bottom to the very top of the system. They had placed entire confidence in me and my plans for them. What was I to do?

I journeyed over to Houston and consulted with Board Chairman Paddock. "It's all right with me," said Paddock, "if you think you and your men can handle the situation."

That left it up to Albert, the Warden, and me. I talked it over with Waid; if anything, he was more enthusiastic than Albert. "I've talked it over with the boys on the team," the Warden said, "and they promise me they will behave in every way. And I believe them. They can beat that bunch, and I think you ought to let them go. I will guarantee you there will be no escapes."

By telephone I consulted with several other members of the board. They said do whatever I thought best. (That was a wonderful board; nobody could have asked for a better.) Now the truth was that I had as much confidence in the reliability of the men on the team as had either Waid or Moore. I had talked to all the players, and I believed in them. The upshot of all my deliberating and hesitating was that we went to Houston and played the Oilers.

We had, they told me, the second-largest crowd that had ever assembled in the ball park. I judge that just about everybody was there who could squeeze in. The best part of it for us was that the rooters were mostly for the Tigers. That helped tremendously.

Our best pitcher was a life-termer. He had been a hard case, but he had been coming around fairly well of late. When he got his dander up, or when the umpire failed to call them to his liking, he really shot that ball across. In the first part of the game, things were going pretty well for our side. In the fifth and sixth innings we were out in front—and then the Oilers tied it up. It stayed tied until the last half of the eleventh. We were at bat, score 4 to 4, two on base and two out. The Oilers had been plenty tough. As our catcher came to bat, I called out to him: "Step on it boy; you can do it!"

Ball one: it was low. Ball two: high and inside. Strike: curved in. The batter shook his head, stepped out of the box, knocked imaginary dirt out of his cleats, resumed his stance, and waggled his stick.

Wham! The Oiler lad out on the mound smoked that one in. "Stee-rike two!" says the umpire. Batter groans his unbelief, wipes his brow, digs in his toes, and waggles the stick again. The pitcher checks his bases—everybody playing safe—and hoists his left foot in the general direction of the sun. Then, with almost no windup at all, down he comes with what looks like another whizzer.

"Ball three!" rules the ump. Three and two. Business of digging in at the plate again—business of checking bases again—hurler's foot up in the air again—more windup this time—and it's an express special right through the middle. At the crack of the bat, our man on second is streaking for home.

It was a two-base hit, well placed. The crowd stood up and did things to the welkin. It seemed to me that everybody was wildly pleased except the Oilers and my friend Mayor Reece Lockett, of Brenham. Between ball games, Reece was as cordial a man as ever you saw. But before the game started, he had come to me, shaking my hand and saying, "I ain't your friend any more!"

While the rejoicing was going pretty big with the grandstands still in full eruption, two policemen came up to me and said: "What about this collection?"

"What collection?"

"There are a couple of fellows taking up a collection for the prison orchestra."

"Grab 'em and take the money away from 'em. We never allow that sort of thing. Besides, we've got plenty of money without any collection." The officers grabbed the money and arrested two ex-convicts. The money the ex-cons had collected was turned over to us—$88 it was.

But we had won only the first of a double-header. The nightcap was yet to come. We stood to win it, too, if only our pitcher could hold out. He was a former Texas Leaguer, well known and liked. Small and wiry and pleasant, his only trouble was that he liked automobiles—other people's automobiles. That was why we had his services on the Prison Tigers. He was good for five innings, but if he got

into trouble he might not last out the seven. That was our "if" as we
started play again. "I'll make it," he promised. "I've got to!" Well,
he did, 1 to 0. It was a fast game and a sweet one, if you ask me.

Now my Tiger boys and the Bob Silver Orchestra had promised
me that all would be well and that they would see to it that there was
no trouble. While I believed them, the responsibility was still on me.
There were men in the lot who would have to be classified, on the
basis of their past records, as bad "hombres," men who had committed terrible crimes. Several of them had bad records since commitment to prison. There was risk—and I recognized it. But we came
prepared for it, and the boys understood. You see, we had Bud Russell
along, Bud Russell and his "one-way bus." (Uncle Bud had delivered
over a hundred thousand prisoners from place to place, chiefly to the
penitentiary, with the loss of but one prisoner. He could easily have
killed this lone exception, an undersized Mexican, but, for reasons
best known to himself and to most peace officers in Texas, he didn't.
His vehicle was known far and wide as the "one-way bus.")

I had called in Uncle Bud before we left the Walls and told him we
were going to take forty prisoners to Houston to play ball before a
crowd of over twenty thousand. We were also to take them to a big
restaurant for their meals. "It's a risk you know better than I do,"
I said. "I'm turning the job of handling them over to you. You've
got it!"

"All right, Mr. Simmons," Uncle Bud came back cheerfully, "I'll
take 'em down and I'll bring 'em back." He did take them down and
he brought them back. But before he did either, he went down to
Houston, looked over the diamond, the restaurant, and the entire set-
up. Then he made his own plans and selected his own guards. Uncle
Bud knew his business. I made not a single suggestion.

The newspapers were kind to us. Lloyd Gregory, of the *Houston
Post,* "spread it on" liberally. After all, he had sponsored the game
and had just about worked it up singlehandedly. But the *Houston
Chronicle* was equally generous.

It was Waid's orchestra and Moore's ball club, but Albert had told
them he would take them all to Kelly's Restaurant for a big feed. Men
who had not eaten outside the Walls since commitment were to eat at
Kelly's! The boys did not miss the thrill of that.

The Buff management was big hearted in dividing gate receipts with us. For once, our welfare fund was fairly bulging. That meant more and better equipment, better libraries, more stage equipment, with surplus funds out of which to help, now and then, a needy and deserving prisoner or his family. All in all, the Houston expedition was successful.

CHAPTER 10

Texas' Fastest and Wildest Rodeo

I DON'T LIKE HOGS, though I should, for the first livestock I ever owned was a pig. When I was a small boy, Father gave me a runt pig that he thought would surely die. But I pulled the little fellow through and filled him out to where I sold him for ten dollars. To this sum I added another dollar and then paid my eleven dollars over to Jake W. Levy for a good little second-hand saddle. (Jake Levy was the fine, big-hearted mayor of Sherman. Originally he was from Lick Skillet, now more respectfully known as Pilotgrove.) The saddle was the first piece of property that I ever bought. I have told you about it to get around to this: from the days of that saddle until now, I have been interested in rodeos.

My first rodeos were on the open prairie at White Mound. There, and in many places elsewhere, I have seen boys "bust 'em and get busted." I have busted and got busted, myself. My earliest experience was at the age of eight. Late one Sunday afternoon, a big, fat bull yearling came a-bawling up to the cow lot as if he were the boss of the prairie.

"I'll string him," said old Mack Coates, our cowhand, "if you'll bust him."

"Put her on," I answered, "and I'll try him."

He strung the yearling—and the yearling busted me. He threw me over his head, and his forefeet took a lot of hide off my breast and sides as he came down. Father wouldn't have minded; he would have enjoyed it. But it was Sunday, and I didn't want Mother to know about it. I could hardly walk the next morning, however, and Mother was terribly worried about me. "What if you had been killed!" she said. Mothers always worry, God bless them.

Having told you about that one, I suppose I ought to go ahead and tell you about another memorable ride I had—this one when I was seventy years old. I was then United States district clerk under Federal Judge Randolph Bryant, of the Eastern District of Texas. The boys on my farm had spoiled a big, fine three-year-old horse to the point where they could hardly handle him. He was a good-looker and turned out well, but he was getting to be pretty mean. So, one afternoon about four o'clock, I put my spurs and my saddle into the car and went out to the farm to straighten out my young "hoss." At about the third jump, he busted me. Seeing that there was nobody around at the moment to take home the story of my downfall, I got to my feet and forked him again. He pitched all over the place, and he busted me again. Even so, I knew when I hit the ground that I had almost ridden him. I figured that things had come to a point of decision between horse and man. I just naturally had to bust him to show him who was who. So I crawled back on the critter for the third time. And that time I busted him. I rode him. I rode him good and proper.

I admit now that it was a foolish thing for a man of my age and condition to do. For I had a bad arm, still weak from a break sustained the year before while chasing jack rabbits on a Sunday morning with my greyhounds. The fracture had knit but had not ceased to bother me. (My excuse for the Sabbath-day chase was that I was trying to help my friends Pete Hudgins and Bill Hartwig "save the grass" for their cattle. I don't think Pete or Bill believed me.)

The one-man, one-armed rodeo that I pulled off that day on my farm gave me a lot of satisfaction. But two or three days later, when I showed Pete Hudgins and Randolph Bryant the black-and-blue marks on my body, they shook their heads. Judge Bryant began to cuss me out. He really said his mind. He didn't think much of my intelligence and still less of my judgment. Of course, I took it, for Bryant was my friend—my very good friend until the day he died. He was also, in my opinion, a great judge, a fair and just man to all, and an unfailing friend to the poor and unfortunate who appeared before him, even to antiquated broncbusters. So I had to take it. As for old Pete, he just stood there and grinned his enjoyment of the Judge's lurid vocabulary. "Well, Lee," said Pete, "I'd have known that, if you started a fool thing like that, you'd be bound to finish it."

That was not necessarily a compliment, but I took it kindly, under the circumstances. Anyhow, all this digression is intended, not as an old man's wandering talk, but as an explanation of how much I like rodeos and why—and how it came about that I set my heart upon establishing at the Walls "Texas' Fastest and Wildest Rodeo." For that is what I named it. (After I left the system, they changed the name of the rodeo to "World's Fastest and Wildest Rodeo." They shouldn't have done that. I kind of think that the word Texas is ample. I have always liked it for size.)

The idea of a prison rodeo grew on me. I called a conference with Warden Waid and R. O. McFarling, the livestock supervisor around the dairy and mule barns, and we began preparations for our first rodeo, to be held in October, 1931. I knew that, to be successful, our shows would have to be held on Sunday afternoons. That was the only time when the prisoners and the system employees and their families could be on hand together.

I sort of visited around with the preachers of Huntsville and explained to them the situation and what I hoped to accomplish in my school and recreation program. I told them, of course, that Sunday was the only day on which we could either play ball or hold our rodeo. I wanted their approval. They told me there would be no complaint about it from them. And there never was any complaint during the five years of Sunday rodeo under my direction.

For this first rodeo I rather looked to McFarling to take the lead, with Moore, the welfare director, to assist him, and everything worked out very well. I showed Johns, the construction foreman, what I wanted done, and well do I remember his comment: "Mr. Simmons, of course I'm going to do what you tell me; but you're throwing away your money. You can't get any crowd here. They ain't gonna come."

"They may not come the first Sunday," I replied, "but they'll be here for the rest of the rodeos."

As it turned out, however, we could not seat everybody even at the very first rodeo. Mr. Johns came out to me while I was busy in the arena and, removing his hat, said to me: "Mr. Simmons, I take off my hat to you. I'll buy the Cokes."

We rodeoed. And Mr. Johns built. Then we rodeoed some more, and Mr. Johns built some more. But we never were able to take care of all the crowds.

After this first season I turned the rodeo over to Mr. Moore and became the silent partner in the firm. But there never was a rodeo staged at Huntsville while I was general manager but what I was right in there on Old Dan, backing Albert in every way possible. And when the last event (bull-riding) started, I always changed to Rabbit, a younger and faster horse, so that I could knock the steers or bulls off the boys, if it became necessary. There was no fence-sitting for me. I was one of the boys down in the arena.

Albert was putting on a show. By this time this rodeo was in fact and in truth the fastest and wildest in Texas. And it was drawing the largest attendance of any sporting spectacle in the state.

But crowds were not what we were aiming at. We figured the rodeo as entertainment for the prisoners and for the prison employees and their families. I always stuck to that. On some one Sunday in October, every prisoner who had a clear record was permitted to go to the Walls, if he so desired, to see his rodeo. Truckload after truckload, from all the prison farms in the system—they piled in every Sunday of the season. And, of course, the officials and the employees came, too, bringing their families with them. There was no charge, except to the outside public.

I passed the word on to the farm managers: "You've got some good neighbors; they have endured a lot on account of our prison farms, with escaping prisoners, and so on. Your dog man has cut their fences; your prisoners have stolen their horses and their cars; their families have had to live in more or less constant fear. They are real neighbors, for they have been for you right down the line. Let me know how many free passes to the rodeo you will need for them. Watson will send them to you."

And to Warden Waid I said: "The peace officers of the state are our friends. Don't ask me for passes; see Watson, and he'll give you as many as you need."

And so we built our rodeo. Albert? No. Albert and I? No. Albert, Waid, and I? No, it was bigger than that. The prison board, the five hundred employees, and the five thousand prisoners built and staged this largest and best rodeo of its kind. And that is why it served so well the purpose for which it was founded.

At the Prison Congress in Indianapolis, held October 3 to 7, 1933, I extended an invitation that the meeting for the following year be held in Houston, Texas. Houston was growing rapidly at the time and was attracting a lot of attention. Texas was big, and people were curious about it; many had never seen any part of it. There was also some curiosity about a prison system of 73,000 acres of land with thousands of head of livestock. So they voted to come on down. Of course I knew they weren't coming to see a rodeo, but I promised them one, anyhow. I told them it would be good and fast and wild. It was.

Moore was called in, and then Waid, to discuss plans. We decided to stage this rodeo at the industrial unit on Central Farm, near Houston. We would show our visitors through our modern packing and canning plant, give them a big noonday meal (entirely prison-produced), and follow with the rodeo at two o'clock.

This meant that Manager Buck Flanagan had to be called in, as it was Buck's industrial unit. Captain Buck liked nothing better than to be summoned for such a project. From that time on, our rodeo firm was Moore, Flanagan, Waid, and Simmons—with Albert and Buck doing the heavy work.

Our regular rodeos were held at Huntsville each Sunday in October, so the local preparation for this event at Houston had to be from the ground up. We did have grandstands at the Central Farm, however—one for the prisoners and one for the general public who came in to see the interfarm baseball games. We felt that it wasn't practical to have prisoner spectators at this rodeo, so we made ready to have only the Prison Congress visitors plus the general public from nearby points in the state.

We felt that the coming of several hundred prison officials and educators from all over the country was an important occasion, and we drew up our plans accordingly. It cost money. But everybody co-operated, including Houston newspapers and businessmen. Bill Blanton, the manager of the Houston Chamber of Commerce, and Haygood Ashburn escorted hundreds of visitors to the various farms to see our livestock, our industries, our dairies—and our rodeo. Everybody helped us, and I think everybody had a good time.

It soon reached the point where thousands of visitors were coming to the Walls for the rodeo. Sometimes all standing room was taken and we had to turn people away. Two o'clock was starting time, but on one Sunday just about every seat was occupied by 12:30. Space was reserved for the employees and their families, while the prisoners occupied all of one side of the arena next to the east wall, with Bud Russell and a large number of guards on hand.

Many prominent citizens were invited and came; many came who were not invited. But all were welcome. Senator Tom Connally and all the governors under whom I served attended at one time or another. Governor and Mrs. Hobby came a number of times. Then came Speaker of the House Coke Stevenson, J. E. Josey, of the *Houston Post,* and many others. Mr. Josey, by the way, was a wonderful friend of the system and was very kind to Mrs. Simmons and me.

Among celebrities who came was Tom Mix, at that time the idol of the young folks of the nation. I had long admired Mix and had entertained him in my home. I liked him for his showmanship, to be sure, but especially for his character. I recognized his wide influence upon the millions of his juvenile devotees. He was conscious of this and told me that it was the reason he never smoked.

We let the prisoners know that Tom Mix was coming, and it seemed to me that everybody within the Walls was thrilled about it. Mix spent the night with me, and we showed him about the penitentiary. The general public didn't know he was to be on hand. In fact, we didn't want it known; for by this time the large crowds had become a great problem, not only for us but also for the town of Huntsville and for the State Highway Patrol.

From our welfare fund we had financed the purchase of a handsome palomino horse for our prominent visitors to ride while being introduced to the spectators. I myself also rode him at times, although not in the arena. Tom Connally and Coke Stevenson had both been so introduced. But Tom Mix was not content simply to take his introduction and then dismount for a seat in the grandstand. Instead, Tom stayed on in the arena with Albert and me. And what a rodeo those prison cowboys gave him!

We were no longer concerned about the public—we knew they were getting their money's worth. We were thinking about Tom. The judges that day were Ranger Captain Tom Hickman, Reese Lockett, and Paul Waggoner. My boys put on a show. Luther Berwick, my prisoner-driver, roped and tied a goat in twelve seconds and a wild Brahma calf in sixteen seconds—a good record in any man's rodeo. Many of the other boys also made fine records, and I was proud of them all.

On this occasion there occurred—instinctively so far as I was involved—one of the most satisfying incidents in all my work at Huntsville. You will remember that I have already told how I have seen broncbusters, all the way from neighbor lads of my prairie boyhood on up to the top riders at the biggest events, and that I have always enjoyed seeing the horses "rid."

Well, one of my boys came out of the chute on an outlaw, and he "hooked him front and behind," with hat and hand high in the air all the way until the whistle blew. I have seen a lot of them go high and handsome, but I believe this old hoss topped them all. The crowd stood up, yelling deliriously. The pickup man took the rider off his mount. By that time I was down there myself on Old Dan. I shook my foot out of the left stirrup and gave the rider a hand. Up he came behind me, and we galloped to the front of the grandstand. The crowd caught the spirit of it instantly and broke into thunderous applause. It was the most wonderful mass display of appreciation that I have ever witnessed. As for my part of it, I vow I did not stage it deliberately. It was but a spontaneous recognition of as good a bronc-rider and of as fine a ride as ever I saw. And I think the prisoners, even more than the public, sensed the situation, as prison manager and convict-rider came in on the same horse.

After a fashion, that was one way to look at it. But then again, that was scarcely the way of it at all. The way of it really was that the state of Texas owned the ranch. Governor Ross Sterling was ranch manager, Albert Moore was foreman, Walter Waid was wagon boss and cook—and that old boy and I who were a-riding the same hoss together were just two of the hands with the outfit. I was kind of "pointing the lead," so to speak, but the other cow hand wasn't "following the drags," for he was right up in the lead with me.

Yes, we rodeoed that day. Tom Mix had a great time. Everybody, I think, had a great time. As I write these words, on the wall of my office there is a picture of Tom riding that handsome palomino of ours.

The West Texas Cowboys' Reunion at Stamford was originally a community affair organized by the Swenson boys of the famous SMS ranches. It began about two years before we started our prison rodeo. At the time it was unique in that only active and bona fide ranchers and ranch hands could participate—no professionals allowed.

At Stamford, Bill Swenson was the leader. He worked, directed, and developed the West Texas Cowboys' Reunion into what I think is the greatest of all rodeos. As a home affair—and you might call it that—it is unsurpassed, either for pride of accomplishment or for community entertainment. But that community is west Texas–wide. It grew and expanded, and the thousands came. It drew prominent visitors, too—more than we did at Huntsville.

Almost all the governors and prominent officials attended at Stamford. Ranchers brought their chuck wagons, and they ate "sure-nough" beef and red beans, with onions and sour-dough biscuits and black coffee. The big boys really milled around. You see, this rodeo vote could vote, did vote, and influenced plenty of other votes. Down at Huntsville, you understand, our top rodeo hands counted for zero at election time. Even so, the Cowboys' Reunion was never intended as a political roundup. It was a west Texas get-together for the best time of the whole year.

Well, one morning about ten o'clock, while contestants and officials were getting ready for the show and onlookers were beginning to gather around, somebody noticed a slim fellow sitting on the ground talking to two or three cowmen. Excitement jumped when it was learned that he was Will Rogers, unexpected and unannounced. Will himself was top of all cow hands, of course; and when he heard of the west Texas rodeo, he simply couldn't stay away.

I was down around the chute at the time, helping get the roping calves penned up. Will recognized me and pulled a fast one on me. When it came to pulling fast ones, I reckon Will was the best in the country. They told me about it later. Shortly after he had been identified and had been surrounded by a crowd, he turned to a bystander: "Ain't that Lee Simmons down there at the chute?"

"Yep, that's Lee."

"He's the fellow who turns 'em out over in Huntsville, ain't he?"

It had been only a few months before, as I shall shortly explain, that we had had the most daring escape in prison history—three prisoners had escaped from the death cell while we were having a prison ball game. Well, the boys got the point, and the *Fort Worth Star-Telegram* carried the story so that everybody got the point. Will enjoyed it. So did I.

When chuck time came, Will, Tom Hickman, and a few other fellows fell in line and went after the red beans, onions, and all the rest of it, returning for seconds before everybody got ready for the rodeo. I took the chance to tell Will about our prison rodeo, and Tom Hickman and the Swenson boys praised it pretty highly. So I said to Will: "I believe you will see the best bunch of rodeo cattle you ever saw put together, if you will come down and look us over."

"Where do you get them?"

"Raise 'em," I replied. "We've got six thousand head to pick from."

That statement seemed to astonish him. He showed his interest at once and asked me many questions. Finally, I put it to him this way: "Will, I don't want you to draw a crowd down there. We have never been able to take care of the crowds that come, anyhow. And I don't want you to come to help us raise money; we've got all the money we need in our prison welfare fund. I want you to come because you will see a different rodeo from anything of the sort ever staged elsewhere. But the main reason I want you to come is so that fifteen hundred prisoners will see you in action and write home and tell the folks they saw Will Rogers and that he made them a talk."

By that time he was paying close attention to what I was saying. I went on: "If you will come down some Sunday, I'll give you my word that nobody but Tom and me will know it—and the newspapers can report it after you come, instead of before."

"I tell you what I'll do, Simmons," he said, "I'll fly down one Sunday and be with you. I'll wire you."

It was not long after this that I was back on Retrieve Farm, where I had just spent the night. Manager Kelly and I had ridden out early to the pastures and did not get back to camp until about ten o'clock. When we went in to get a cup of coffee, the steward said: "The report came in over the radio that Will Rogers and Wiley Post have been killed in an airplane accident in Alaska."

I had my driver, Luther, ready to leave as soon as I could get back from the camp to farm headquarters, and we promptly got on the road. At Angleton, the news of Will's death was confirmed. Will Rogers! Surely he was the best, the cleanest, the humblest, and the most unselfish entertainer known to America. And I shall always believe him the greatest folk-philosopher of all time. That he failed to get to our Huntsville rodeo was the bitterest of all my disappointments in the years of my prison management.

CHAPTER 11

The Deadlier Sex

DURING MY ENTIRE administration I replaced only two farm managers out of the eleven I found in the system when I took charge. The first of these was at the Eastham Farm and the other was at Goree. Goree Farm was managed by a fine old couple when I took over, but the general appearance of the prisoners (Goree was for women convicts), as well as of the buildings and grounds, convinced me that a change was necessary. It took only about thirty days of observation to bring me to this decision.

M. V. Heath was the assistant manager of Goree. He and his wife lived in a cottage near the main building. In Huntsville I made a quiet investigation of the Heaths, and, upon inquiry of a number of businessmen including a banker friend of mine, I found that they had a good reputation. Then I went out to the farm and asked Mr. Heath to come to the office, where I explained that I was making a change—which I had not even mentioned to Heath previously. If Heath would accept the job, I said, I was ready to turn the place over to him and Mrs. Heath. They did take over, and everything worked out satisfactorily.

At the time, a small garment factory was in operation at Goree making white duck uniforms. The cloth was cut with butcher knives which followed the pattern through slots sawed in tables. I told Captain Heath that I planned to make all the underwear and work clothes for the five thousand prisoners. We had the labor and the "market"—all we needed was the product.

The Pool Manufacturing Company of Sherman was one of the largest garment factories in the South, and the Pools were good friends of mine. I told my troubles to Carl Pool, and he came down to help me. Without any charge whatever, he lined things up for us and helped us to buy some electric cloth-cutters and a few more sewing machines. Then he sent his foreman down—and Captain and Mrs. Heath were on the road to production. They produced.

We were out almost no expense and were soon making all the sheets, pillow slips, and garments used by the prisoners. Thereupon I decided we would also make the discharge suits given to the three thousand prisoners who left the system each year. For this purpose various patterns of cloth were chosen, light-weight for summer and heavier for winter. Women prisoners were busy now, and Goree Farm was saving the taxpayers' money. The net profit for the garment factory in 1935 was $26,251.73.

After Warden Stone and his wife, of the New Jersey penitentiary, had spent a week with me, he told me that his greatest surprise was in Goree Farm: "In New Jersey my biggest headache is in controlling women prisoners. They are far more troublesome than the men."

"Well," I replied, "if I didn't visit Goree Farm occasionally, I wouldn't know we had any women prisoners."

And that was pretty nearly a fact, too. When I first took charge, the women of Goree were not allowed to smoke. Although I had some difficulty about it, I finally persuaded the prison board to allow the women to smoke. I knew perfectly well that most of the women in prison were smokers, for they had tobacco-stained fingers when they were received. When I announced at Goree that we were going to let them smoke and would furnish them cigarettes and tobacco, just as we supplied the men prisoners, you should have heard those hundred women shout.

The Heaths put on shows and dances each Saturday night, and before long we had built a regular stage and dance room for the women convicts. Trouble? We never had any at Goree. All we did was keep the prisoners busy, allow them overtime credit when it was deserved, and give them an all-round square deal.

The Deadlier Sex

Carl Pool steered us right in the garment factory, as I knew nothing of such operations, and he was of great help to us with his practical suggestions. Similarly, the Justin boys of Fort Worth came down on another occasion at their own expense to start us off with our prison shoe factory. The state and I owed the success of the enterprises to the capable assistance of these fine friends.

We had some rather interesting women prisoners. I happened to be in the Warden's office one afternoon when Uncle Bud came in with a fairly good-looking woman and delivered her transfer papers to Waid. She was sent inside the Walls to have her picture made and her record completed, including fingerprints and so on. Then she was taken out to Goree Farm.

For a long time this woman had been bursar of a prominent religious college in Texas. Then one day she checked out several thousand dollars short. As reported to us, it was the exact opposite of most embezzlement cases. These usually involve a man's spending too much money on some woman. This time it was the man who was spending the stolen money and the woman who was doing the embezzling.

"What did you do with your good-looking prisoner?" I asked Captain Heath one day.

"Come let me show you," he replied. We went into the garment factory, where some sixty women were running sewing machines and making uniforms, suits, and the like. There she was, running her machine, mixed right in with all classes of criminals—from prostitutes of the the lowest type to professional criminals and murderers.

When the Captain told her what her task was to be, she said she had never run a sewing machine and couldn't do it. The Captain told her she would soon learn; many of the girls had had to learn on the job, and she could do the same.

"She won't be at that machine very long," said I to Heath.

"Well, no," he conceded. "I really need her somewhere else right now. I'm glad to get her, in fact. But you know, if you want a prisoner to do a job well, just start her at the bottom." The Captain was right. The theory works as well inside a prison as it does outside. Anyway, it wasn't long until Heath had a very efficient secretary and bookkeeper to handle his growing manufacturing business.

An amusing character at Goree was Captain Heath's "stockman," Mary Jane. Mary Jane was a Negro woman with whom I became pretty well acquainted. I learned to like her for two reasons. In the first place, she was industrious and she always had a smile. In the second place, because I was a lifelong stockman myself, we understood each other. It is an old, old tradition, you know, that stockmen stand together.

Mary Jane didn't have much of an "outfit" when I first took charge; in fact, few people then connected with the system were well equipped. It was not long, however, until Goree's "stockman" had a good horse and a saddle. I think that horse and saddle helped Mary Jane to think well of me. "Colonel," Mary Jane would say to me, "I wants to show you somethin', if you'll go wid me." Then I would go along with her and she would show me all the things she was having the Captain do for her. Now get that: putting the farm manager to work to fix up things for prisoner Mary Jane!

Occasionally I would borrow Captain Heath's horse to ride with Mary Jane to look over the cattle in the pasture. She was mighty proud of her job—as proud as a grandmother of her first grandchild. And I was rather proud of Mary Jane.

I have said that Mary Jane always had a smile. However, I remember one time when she lost it. I had purchased five horses for the system, and when they were received at the Walls barn, I rather liked the looks of a buckskin among them and thought that, if he suited, I might keep him for my own use. I had the barn man saddle him up and I got on him there in front of the barn—on the hard, rock-paved roadway. I took him down below the barn a little way to where the ground was soft and worked him out a little. There I saw that he did not suit me.

Captain Heath was wanting to change horses for some reason, so I told Captain McFarling to send this horse on out to Goree Farm. He loaded the animal in a trailer and sent him right out.

The next morning when I was around the barn McFarling greeted me: "Captain Heath's mad as hell."

"What's the trouble?"

"He called me over the phone and started cussing me out. He said he didn't appreciate me sending him that bronc out there for him to ride. Said he threw him twice, said for me to send for him and get him out of there."

"What did you tell him?"

"I told him to hold on to that hoss. Told him not to go cussing me out; he would have to go higher up than me, I says. Told him I had nothing to do with it. If he wanted to cuss anybody out, I says, he could just up and see the big boss."

It was getting around almost to the time for the rodeo, and I had been planning to have Goree represented at this next one. So I drove out to Goree and visited around with Heath for a while. The horse incident wasn't mentioned. Finally I said to him: "Captain, the rodeo is coming on pretty soon and Albert Moore told me he was short on bronc-riders, and I kind of thought maybe you could help us out."

Heath saw the joke and took it in good humor. Then he told me how it happened. He said that after the horse threw him the first time, he went to the house, took off his low-quartered shoes, put on his boots and spurs, and told his wife and Mary Jane that he was going to show them—and the horse—how he could ride him. The buckskin threw him again, and then it was that he called McFarling and told him to come and get his horse.

I managed to get close up to Mary Jane and out of the corner of my mouth I said: "Mary Jane, I sure wish I had been here when you put them sandburs under the Captain's saddle blanket to make that old hoss buck the way he did. Sure would have enjoyed the fun if I had been here."

Mary Jane clouded up, with distress spread all over her face: "Colonel, I didn't put no sandburs under the blanket. You tell the Captain that, and he'll rank me and put me in the garden squad. Please don't. Please! Colonel, I don't want to lose my job. I jes' saddle that hoss lak I always does."

"Don't blame you a bit," I went on, with a straight face. "Don't blame you. I know it was all in fun. I just wish I had been here. I ain't going to tell him about it. Of course not!" By this time Mary Jane was crying, and I had to confess that I was joking.

When I got back to the Walls, I told Albert about my scheme to have Mary Jane ride a bronc at the rodeo. I knew how the Negro prisoner-spectators would take that. Albert agreed with me. I cautioned him, however, not to breathe it to a soul; I wanted it to be a complete surprise. Naturally, we made certain that she was not to get a very bad horse.

I mentioned the plan to Captain Heath, and he, too, was highly pleased with the idea. As a matter of fact, the Captain liked Mary Jane as well as I did. She did her work well and earned the good will she got. Next I had to tell Mary Jane about it. I never saw a happier woman.

Rodeo day came around, and presently here came Mary Jane out of the chute, with hat in hand, fanning that old bronc to a fare-ye-well. The crowd pretty nearly tore down the stands. All the Negro prisoners on hand—five hundred of them in all—stood in their seats and yelled their heads off. Goree Farm's stockman, our stockman, your stockman, friend taxpayer, rode that bronc and rode him to a frazzle.

There was no end to the talk about Mary Jane and the ride she put on. Nothing could have been finer in its effect on the Negro prisoners. After that, Mary Jane and I were pretty firm partners. As stockmen we understood one another.

I regret to admit that some stockmen will steal. Not many of them will, I like to think. But Mary Jane did. Captain Heath had gone down to Yoakum to buy a new saddle and had taken Mrs. Heath and Mary Jane along. He paid for the saddle, and while they were on the way back Mary Jane spoke up from the back seat: "Looky here, Captain, what I got for us."

She displayed a really fine cow whip which she had stolen while the Captain was picking out his saddle. He told me about it, and I had him write to Yoakum for the price of the whip and have it paid for, as I wanted Mary Jane to keep the whip.

Then we both bore down on Mary Jane and gave her an old-fashioned lecture. She promised us everything if the Captain would only not "rank" her. He didn't. But neither he nor I could ever understand how she managed to conceal that long blacksnake so that nobody saw it. She never told us how she did it; she merely smiled and said: "I got it, all right."

Among our prisoners we had a woman who had been given the death penalty. She had been convicted as accomplice and codefendant under charges of killing her invalid husband. It seemed that she and her boy friend had framed it up to put her husband out of the way, and they did it in an exceptionally brutal manner. The newspapers printed a lot about it, and when her conviction was confirmed by the Court of Criminal Appeals, Warden Waid came into my office considerably disturbed. "What're we going to do with that woman when we get her over here? We've got no place to put her except in the death cell, and we can't afford to put her in there."

"We?" said I, "*We* haven't got anything to do with it. This isn't *my* unit; this is *your* responsibility!" But I smiled when I said it.

"She'll never come here," I ventured. "In my judgment, you'll never have to bother with her. The misdirected-sympathy people will work on the parole board and the Governor for a pardon. But if she does come, just put her in the death cell, the same as all the others sentenced to the chair. And each morning, when the others are taken out in the death-house run-around to get to their bath, just hang a heavy curtain over her door."

"We can do that," said Waid with obvious relief, "can't we?"

Incidentally, I managed to use the case of this murderess to prove that the weaker sex is also the more sympathetic. You see, we had a lot of visitors, and of course most of the women wanted to see Goree Farm. They always asked about the different prisoners and why they were there. Especially they would ask about a nice-looking, gray-haired woman of about seventy, as she sat in a chair plaiting rag rugs. "Oh, she didn't do very much," I would say, "just poisoned four stepchildren to get them out of the way."

Next they would inquire about the woman who had helped kill off her husband; and then I would explain my theory about how women were more tenderhearted than men. This woman, I would say, was a living example of the softheartedness of women folk. To prove it, I would relate how she had gone to bed with her husband and how, when her friend came in to do the killing, she had turned her face to the wall so as not to have to watch her friend hit her husband with the ax. This, I argued, proved that women are instinctively more tender in their sensibilities.

Practically without exception, the verdict from my feminine guests was that she should have been knocked in the head with the ax herself.

CHAPTER 12

The Cotton Pickers' Glee Club

ONE ELEMENT was lacking in our recreation program. In the main, it was quite satisfactory, and I was proud of its success. But we had a wealth of dormant material, and I was not content to let it stay dormant. I could not forget that we had 2,200 Negro prisoners. I kept thinking about that.

As a farm lad, I had picked cotton with Negroes, and many a night have I sat and listened to Old Harve and John as they picked the "juice-harp" and played on the "mouf organ." It was great music to a country lad.

Twenty-two hundred Negroes meant talent. I knew it was there, and I meant to see it developed. Now, as it happened, my accountant, Ray Chapman, was a fine song leader. He liked to sing, liked folks— and he always managed to break out with a wonderful smile. He was my man.

I talked the thing over with Chapman and with Red Reynolds, but I took my time about issuing any orders. On Saturday nights and Sundays, however, when I happened to be on the lower farms, the "Bottoms," I made it a point not to miss the meetings conducted by Elder J. G. Griffin, our Negro chaplain.

Elder Griffin was a fine, sincere preacher, an old-timer interested in his work. I have heard him preach and pray; I have heard him soar into the very clouds as he warmed up. And I have seen his congregation warm up with him. Such singing! No white-skinned folks can equal it.

I liked Elder Griffin. He made me think of the great Negro orator, Sin-Killer Griffin, who used to warm 'em up among his people when I was a boy. I decided the prison system should have its own music of its own making.

I called in Chapman and Reynolds and told them about it. I put the direct responsibility on Chapman and told Reynolds to back him to the limit. Hitherto, Reynolds had all but lived on the farms, whereas Chapman's work was wholly within the Walls. But from now on, they went together to all the farms, one after another, for Saturday night and Sunday singings. In this way they picked out the best singers. These Waid would transfer to the Walls and assign them to some job there.

At length we had assembled forty Negroes in the chapel, where I made them a pep talk, coach-fashion: "Boys, when we work, we work; when we farm, we farm; when we play ball, we play ball; when we rodeo, we rodeo. And if you boys will pitch in and do your best, we'll have the finest glee club in Texas. What do you say? You boys like to get in the game with us on that?"

"Yassah, Boss! Yassah, Cap'n! We's wid you!" they shouted with a mighty shout. The glee club was on its way. From time to time, as rehearsals were necessary, Waid brought the singers into the chapel, and Chapman took charge. He reduced the squad of forty to thirty, picking four of the latter group for his quartet.

I didn't want any hifalutin' music; I wanted it just as it came naturally from these boys in their natural voices. I had an end in view. The American Prison Congress was coming to Texas, and I had told them at Indianapolis that if they came to Houston for the next meeting I would give them some real entertainment. When they came, Chapman was ready. His club was all dressed up. I had arranged for that out of the welfare fund. They were ready to perform.

Waid and Chapman took the Cotton Pickers' Glee Club to the Rice Hotel in Houston for a special program. Officials from practically every state and federal prison in the country were there. So were prominent educators, clergymen, and others. Former Governor Pat Neff was there—Pat Neff, who in 1923 had persuaded me to assist in making a prison survey. When the concert was over, everybody was satisfied except Neff: "Lee, you've got to bring your glee club to Baylor University." At this time, Neff was president of Baylor University, in Waco.

I was on the spot. But Pat kept right on; he promised that if I would bring the club to his campus he would provide an audience of fifteen hundred students and five hundred Waco citizens.

Of course, I told him I would consider it. But I put the problem squarely in the lap of Prison Board Chairman Paddock. He said it would be all right; he thought we ought to go and said we owed it to Neff. By that time my problem had got around to figuring how to get the club to Waco and back with all my singers on hand throughout and no bad luck going or coming. Somebody would have to—why, Bud Russell was the man! Uncle Bud could do it. "What say, Bud?" I asked him.

"Took 'em to Houston and brought 'em back, didn't I? 'Tsall right with me."

I put it up to Warden Waid. The men were a part of his unit. I always considered that I myself had no unit, no farm. I never assumed the responsibility that belonged to another man. I made that a rule. "Let's go, Colonel!" Waid said. Waid was like that—always ready to go along on any worth-while idea.

I have seen a good deal in my time. But I never saw another reception such as ours at Baylor. The big new auditorium on the campus was crowded. Pat Neff introduced me, I introduced Ray Chapman, and Ray introduced the Texas Prison System Cotton Pickers' Glee Club. Ray had arranged a carefully selected forty-minute program. But by the time that audience had all the encores it demanded, our forty minutes had stretched to an hour and forty.

In the course of proceedings, I presented one of the singers as the best crapshooter and cotton-picker in the system. He had picked 720 pounds in one day in a squad of Negroes who averaged 500 pounds per man per day for a week. On Sunday, as their reward, each man among them was served with a complete fried chicken all to himself (to less celebrated prisoners, Farm Manager Hickman served only a half-chicken per man on Sunday).

The Cotton Pickers' Glee Club

We came back, as we went, without losing a man and without mis-adventure of any kind. Bud Russell saw to that. I still like to think of Ray Chapman and his singers. I have their pictures on the wall of my office now, alongside the Prison Tigers.

Waco newspapers were kind in their write-up of the two programs by the glee club, one at Baylor and one at the downtown Rotary Club. My friend Frank Baldwin said it was "by far the best entertainment brought to Waco in years."

At the 1934 annual rodeo, and again in 1935, the glee club sang from the deck of a large flat truck for the benefit of thousands in at-tendance in the grandstands. The crowd liked it. We had one 385-pound singer who had an unusually powerful voice of wonderful quality. As stage props for his entry, I had the boys rig up an old one-horse wagon, to which we hitched a large and angular mule that had not been sheared in some time. Under the wagon we tethered an old hound. The wagon contained a few old quilts and like plunder, while on the side next the grandstand we hung a skillet, a coffee pot, and a lantern.

The instructions to our big singer were to drive into the arena about midway of the grounds without looking up until he got oppo-site the grandstand. Then he was to halt his equipage, stand up in the wagon and sing "Goin' Down Dat Lonesome Road." He knocked them over—he really did. And I got as big a kick out of it as any-body.

About this time there happened into our prison world a man whose coming later caught the attention of millions of people. But, whatever the consequences turned out to be, the way of it at the time was simple enough. This man walked into my office one day; I had never laid eyes on him before, although I had heard of him. He was John A. Lomax, the ballad man. He explained that he had a recording ma-chine and he was taking down the folk songs of the people—songs of every description. He wanted to visit the prison farms and see what he could find. I fell in with his program. I told him there were more than two thousand Negroes in the prison system and that we had the material—more of it than he was likely to find anywhere else.

I gave Lomax a letter to several of the farm managers, with instructions to lend him every aid in his work and to co-operate with him and his son Alan in every reasonable manner. Living quarters were to be provided for both of them.

The Lomaxes found what they were looking for. It was on our farms that John found Iron Head and Clear Rock, about whom he writes in his *Adventures of a Ballad Hunter*.*

Iron Head got his name because he had been struck by a felled tree; when the limb hit him on the head, the limb broke off, but Iron Head kept on working as if nothing had happened. Clear Rock explained his name by recounting how he had "throwed three Nigguhs wid rocks," meaning that he had slain all three of them with rocks—three rocks, three dead men. "Dat's how come dey calls me Clear Rock."

Clear Rock had a patter song:

> Way up yonder, Darlin', 'bove de sun, Sugar,
> Gals all call me Honey, Sugar Plum. Sho' 'nuff!
> Got a horse, Sugar; buggy, too, Baby.
> Horse's black, Darlin'; buggy's blue. Sho' 'nuff!
> Dat's all right, Honey; dat's all right, Baby.

Lomax said he never heard it elsewhere, either words or tune.

Iron Head was partial to "Ol' Hannah." Hannah was the sun, and the convicts in the field used to raise their voices together:

> Been a great long time since Hannah went down;
> Oh, Hannah, go down!
> Been a great long time since Hannah went down;
> Oh, Hannah, go down!
>
> She's goin' down behin' dem western hills.
> Oh, Hannah, go down!
> She's goin' down behin' dem western hills.
> Oh, Hannah, go down!
>
> Bullies, if yo' wuk, I'm gwine trust yo' well.
> Oh, Hannah, go down!
> An' if yo' don't, I'm gwine give yo' hell!
> Oh, Hannah, go down!

---

* The Macmillan Company, New York, 1947.

Tom Brown, the man who saved my life

Lee, Nola, and Vernon Simmons. Our finest and most enjoyable trip, Medicine Creek, I.T.

Main Prison Building, Huntsville, Texas

First Vocational Training Class, 1933. Industrial Unit, Central Prison
Farm, Huntsville, Texas

Books purchased with proceeds of recreational program

"The Prison Tigers" with Welfare Director ALBERT MOORE

The Cotton Pickers' Glee Club

LEE SIMMONS (third from left), Warden WAID (fifth from left), and the eleven farm managers

At the Rodeo

Prison Rodeo, 1935 (Lee Simmons on "Rabbit" in front of bull)

"Old Sherman," the steer they couldn't ride

Elder JERRY GRIFFIN, Prison Chaplain (second from left)

Workers at Goree Farm

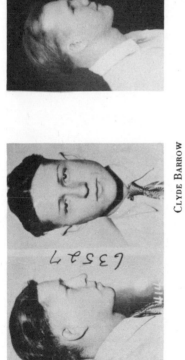
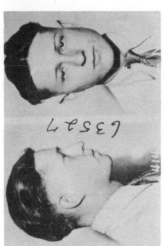

CLYDE BARROW

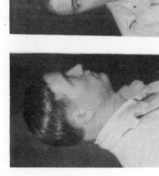
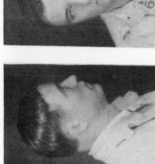
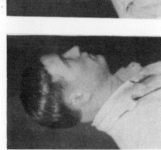
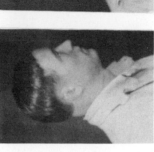

RAYMOND HAMILTON

HENRY METHVIN

JOE PALMER

The Barrow Gang

CLYDE BARROW and BONNIE PARKER. A widely publicized picture of the '30's

CLYDE and "BUCK" BARROW BONNIE PARKER

The Barrow Death Car

Rock-crushing Plant, "the Walls," Huntsville, Texas

Captain FRANK HAMER (left front) with officers who handled the Barrow case

Captain FRANK HAMER

> Y'oughta come on dis rivuh in Nineteen-Fo';
> Oh, Hannah, go down!
> You'd find a daid Nigguh on ev'y turnrow.
> Oh, Hannah, go down!

There were many more similar verses. Lomax obtained a parole for Iron Head and took the man with him on a tour of the country. The full story of that tour and of other vicissitudes of Iron Head is told in John's book, to which I have already referred.

CHAPTER 13

Clyde Barrow's Raid

WHILE THE TEXAS prison population had been steadily increasing, the number of escapees had steadily decreased. During the four years preceding my administration, the escape record averaged 12 per cent of the convict population per year. During my first four years as manager, escapes were cut to 3 per cent per year. In 1929, 302 men "jumped"; in 1931, 110; and in 1932, only 87. Then in 1933 the number rose to 109, an increase which gave me great concern.

In this year a fine old prison guard, Jim Sneed, was killed in an attempted prison break on Retrieve Farm. At eleven o'clock one night, as Sneed sat in his chair at his picket post, two prisoners shot him with guns smuggled in to them by the sister of a convict. The assailants, one a lifer and the other a fifty-year man, intended to get Sneed's keys and release no one knows how many of the inmates. But the guard, mortally wounded though he was, ran to fall outside the door of his picket and died with the keys beyond the convicts' reach. Captain Kelly, who lived close by, rushed over, gun in hand, and ordered the convicts to give up their pistols. At his second demand the weapons came to him—butts first. The prison break was stopped, but that didn't bring Jim Sneed back to life.

At about nine o'clock on the morning of January 16, 1934, Captain B. B. Monzingo, manager of the Eastham Farm, called me at

Clyde Barrow's Raid

Huntsville with more bad news. There had been a raid on the farm, and a number of prisoners had escaped in an automobile provided by an outsider.

Warden Waid and I left hurriedly for Eastham, some forty miles north of Huntsville and about midway between Trinity and Crockett. On arrival we found that the raiders had opened up with a machine gun, critically wounding a guard, Major Crowson. During the confusion of the attack, several desperate prisoners had escaped: Raymond Hamilton, Joe Palmer, Henry Methvin, and Hilton Bybee. Beyond that, our definite information played out.

I returned to Huntsville, notified the radio stations and the peace officers of the Southwest—first of all those of Dallas and Fort Worth, for I judged that the fugitives had gone north.

I make no excuses for the loss of these four prisoners. But I believe you will understand the situation better if I make an explanation of my system of handling the more dangerous of my prison charges. I had singled out especially for this class of prisoners Eastham and Retrieve farms, principally because of their remote location, each being some five miles from any main highway.

My instructions to Captain Monzingo, at Eastham, and to Captain I. K. Kelly, at Retrieve (both of whom were dependable managers, good farmers, and experienced men in handling prisoners), were for each of them to select a highly trustworthy guard and make him what I called a "long-arm man," or "backfield man." This guard was to be picked for his marksmanship as well as for his discretion and courage. It was to be his business to be around on the edges of the area where convicts were working, especially when the group was near standing timber or when opportunity for escape was better than common.

The backfield man was not assigned to guard any particular squad. He had no duty except to stay well clear of the convicts and to be in the background ready with his Winchester in case of any excitement. The prisoners seldom knew precisely where he was, and this uncertainty had its value in keeping the bad men under effective control. Such, then, was my arrangement for guarding the more desperate criminals consigned to my safekeeping.

On the morning of the Eastham escape, about two hundred prisoners were cutting timber near a country road some two miles from camp. On this morning Raymond Hamilton had "jumped his squad," that is, he had come out not with the squad to which he belonged but with another squad, which included Joe Palmer. Before the prisoners got to the woodlands, the guard of the Joe Palmer squad noticed that he had Raymond, who didn't belong with him. That fact in itself should have put him on the alert, but it didn't.

When the guard brought the squad down to the woods, he called Major Crowson over to him. As Crowson rode up on his horse, Raymond Hamilton and Joe Palmer came around a brush pile, each of them armed with a .45 automatic and each of them pouring lead into the mounted guards. The horses wheeled and reared at the gunfire. At that moment a machine gun began to chatter. Under the whine and zing of direct and ricocheting fire some of the prisoners dropped to the ground. Others broke and ran.

Two of the guards lost their nerve and fled. But guard Bullard stood fast, shotgun at the ready, roaring out to the squad men to the right and left of him to lie down in their tracks. The first man to raise his head, he shouted, would have it blown clear off his shoulders. The heads stayed down. Had it not been for Bullard, there is no telling what might have happened.

By this time, however, four prisoners were already gone—Hamilton, Palmer, and Methvin, as we later learned, as part of a previously arranged plan, with Bybee a last-minute addition to the party. As soon as order was restored among our prisoners, the entire gang—less the four escaped men—was marched back to camp and confined in a large, secure concrete building. Crowson, the wounded backfield man, was taken promptly to the Huntsville hospital.

That night I went by to see how he was doing. As I walked in he looked at me earnestly and held out his hand: "Mr. Simmons," he said, "don't think hard of me. I know I didn't carry out your instructions. I'm sorry."

"Don't bother about it," I said. "I'm for you. Those fellows had their day; we'll have ours. I promise you I won't let them get away with it."

Crowson died the next day. At the funeral his father told me that his son believed I would make good on that promise. I fully intended to. Several times before Crowson died, so his nurse told me, he stated:

Clyde Barrow's Raid

"I know I did wrong. I hope Mr. Simmons won't think hard of me." Of course I didn't. Every man makes mistakes. Crowson had simply made his last one.

I stop to tell you all this to show how the top man in a prison system may plan and plan, lying awake nights to figure things out. But no matter how he plans, he has to rely on somebody down below to carry out that plan. Crowson's duty was to stay away from the prison gang at work and never to go near them at any time. He was a crack shot with both revolver and Winchester. Had he kept his post on the edge of the timber, things would have turned out differently, I have no doubt.

To be sure, no matter where Crowson might have stationed himself, there would have been a break some time in the course of that morning, for it had all been arranged. There is no way for guards or officials to know of such attempts in advance. You can judge pretty well what is going on inside a prison, but you can't be expected to guess what is due from the outside. If Crowson had been where he belonged when the break occurred, however, some men might have been killed, but I don't believe any of them would have got away. At least the probabilities would have leaned to such an outcome. On just such probabilities I had planned my defense. My strategy of the "long-arm man" was to offset the surprise element in attacks from the outside. But that strategy was nullified by the disobedience of one man.

What with the killing of Jim Sneed, followed now by the death of Crowson, I felt strongly that the time had come to demonstrate to the underworld and to the public that the life of a guard was as valuable as the life of any other citizen. Up to this time none of the long-term convicts who had killed a guard—and there had been many—had paid the death penalty for a crime which was certainly murder. Juries had usually just tacked on another life sentence to the one the defendant already had, so that for the killing of a guard the convict received actually no punishment at all.

The death of Crowson put my duty in a new light and left me in a sterner mood. The killings of our guards involved a fundamental principle of justice. Also they constituted a fundamental hazard to our whole system of prison management. If such murders could be committed with impunity, we would have to change our whole manner of handling convicts in the field. A prison guard is responsible for sixteen to twenty men while they are at work in the open. Generally, eighteen whites and perhaps twenty Negroes can be handled by a single guard who carries a revolver and a shotgun. But if such a guard must anticipate raids from ex-convicts on the outside his morale will be gone, and the safekeeping of prisoners will be at an end.

This Eastham Farm raid was the first of its kind. I figured we had to make an example of some people if we were ever to put a stop to this sort of thing. No guard could be expected to prevent wholesale escape under such conditions. It is true that the fortitude of guard Bullard did keep nearby prisoners from getting away, but that couldn't be hoped for in the future, if machine-gun raids became common affairs. So I made my plans for retribution on those responsible for the Eastham affair.

The first step was to deal with my own two guards who had run away. I discharged them and put them on the black list so that they could never be employed by any other prison farm.

A few weeks later State Senator Nat Patton, who was a good friend of the Texas Prison System as well as a good friend of mine, called me by telephone to make an appointment. The next day, accompanied by Representative Albert K. Daniel, of Crockett, he brought the two discharged guards into my office, and spoke in their behalf, claiming they were family men and good fellows and shouldn't be blacklisted.

I let the Senator talk and, when he had finished, I took over. I told the boys that they had taken a sacred oath to do their duty as guards and that every guard had a heavy responsibility to protect the public. Then I turned to the gentlemen of the Legislature and said:

"Now, Senator, let us say that you and I are going out of here tonight to raid a house, and say that we know we have a rather dangerous character to pick up. Say that I go to the front door and you go to the back door. All at once I hear some shooting at the back door and I just turn and run off, leaving everything for you to handle. Now, tomorrow night, we will say, you're going to make another raid. Would you take me on that raid? You know you wouldn't!" I paused, and then I said, "I have nothing against these fellows personally; but as long as I am general manager, their names will never be taken off the black list."

Senator Patton threw up his hands and said good-naturedly, "You know we are behind you a hundred per cent, Lee, but we just felt we ought to come down and talk to you about it."

With the affairs of my official household thus put in order, I could turn my attention to the long fight to settle up scores with the Eastham Farm raiders. I was determined to see Raymond Hamilton and Joe Palmer electrocuted for the slaying of Crowson. And I wanted their accomplice of the machine gun likewise captured and condemned. By this time we were convinced that the man who had wielded the machine gun and engineered the entire escape had been none other than Clyde Barrow.

Those of you who were reading the newspapers through the nineteen thirties need no introduction to that notorious outlaw of the Southwest, Clyde Barrow, nor to the woman who joined him in rebellion against society, Bonnie Parker. But for the benefit of a later generation of readers let me summarize their gun-blazing careers up to that eventful day of January 16, 1934.

Clyde Champion Barrow was born at Ennis, Texas, in 1910. He grew up in west Dallas, where he was first arrested at the age of sixteen for auto theft. During the next three years he was arrested four times in connection with various burglaries in Fort Worth, Dallas, and Waco (the last time under the name of Elvin Williams). But in each case he was released for lack of evidence sufficient to convict.

Then in March, 1930, he slipped in his career of crime. The District Court of McLennan County sentenced Barrow for burglary of two business houses and for theft of five cars, giving him two years in each case. He was placed in the county jail at Waco on March 4. Exactly a week later he escaped, reputedly with a gun smuggled to him by Bonnie Parker. When he was recaptured a few days later in Middleton, Ohio, the same District Court added fourteen years to his sentences and sent him down to Huntsville for safekeeping.

I had no personal contact with Clyde Barrow while he was serving this term. He was just a convict number to me, one of the anonymous men assigned to Eastham Farm, one of those who early in my administration appeared in the records as a victim of self-mutilation.

For Barrow had cut off a toe in hopes of being transferred to the Walls. He stayed on Eastham Farm, however, until, after serving twenty-three months of his original two-year sentence, he was paroled by Governor Ross Sterling.

Seldom has an act of clemency been so unfortunate in its results. Immediately the posters flared in public places. "WANTED: For burglary and robbery with firearms, in Dallas—Clyde Barrow." "WANTED—$250 REWARD: For robbery and the slaying of J. N. Fulcher in Hillsboro—Clyde Barrow and another" (who later proved to be Raymond Hamilton). "WANTED: For robbery with firearms and for robbery of the Neuhoff Packing Company, in Dallas—Clyde Barrow." Thus ran the record of Clyde's activities in the first six months following his release from prison.

He was a youth of slender build and refined features, a nice-looking chap whose appearance belied his criminal record. But he had taken the wrong turning and become a killer. The next circular that described Clyde Barrow did so in connection with the murder of a sheriff and assault to murder a deputy in Atoka, Oklahoma. Raymond Hamilton was also involved in this case. The outlaws were cornered in a dance hall but shot their way out. Bonnie Parker, who had grown up in the same section of Dallas to become Barrow's sweetheart, was now also in the picture. She weighed ninety pounds and was red-haired, and freckle-faced. I never saw her alive, but her description was familiar to me as it was to all the peace officers of the Southwest, as the "Barrow Gang" stole and shot its way across the country.

In August of 1932, with the chase becoming hotter, Barrow, Hamilton, and Bonnie got the drop on a deputy sheriff at Carlsbad, New Mexico. They forced him into the car with them and took him on a wild ride across country, releasing him at San Antonio, Texas, the next day, after a thousand-mile drive in something like thirteen hours. Clyde was an expert driver and often covered such distances in a single day, much of it at seventy miles an hour over unpaved country lanes, as he doubled and twisted to throw off pursuit.

Next the gang stole a second car at Victoria, Texas, and the same night robbed the Cedar Hill Bank in Dallas, three hundred miles away. Two weeks later they were seen again in south Texas, where they engaged in a gunfight with a deputy sheriff of Wharton County.

Clyde Barrow's Raid

Soon thereafter, Barrow and Hamilton went in different directions. Hamilton engaged in a series of bank robberies with other accomplices and was finally captured in Bay City, Michigan, in December of 1932. He was brought back to Dallas for trial and was received at the Walls on August 8, 1933, with sentences totaling 263 years.

Hamilton was a different type from Barrow. There was nothing of cold calculation in his make-up. On the contrary, he was restless and excitable, talkative and quick-acting, more like the popular conception of a gangster. With his past record I was justified in holding him on Eastham Farm with others of my more desperate charges.

Joe Palmer was still another kind of individual. I came to know Joe rather well later on when he was in the death cell, and if there is such a thing as feeling admiration for a criminal, I felt it for Joe Palmer. He had nerve and ability. He talked only when he chose, but when he talked he told the truth explicitly. Nothing Joe Palmer ever told me checked out differently.

When Joe first came to Huntsville I was impressed with him and made him a trusty at the Walls. He drove a pickup truck belonging to the system, delivering various products from Huntsville to the nearby farms and getting shipments from the railroad depot for delivery to the prison warehouse and store. For this job he was receiving thirty days' overtime credit on his sentence. He had, in fact, a preferred trusty job. Then the assistant farm manager at Eastham needed a houseboy, and Warden Waid sent Palmer to that assignment. He was still a trusty and still earning overtime. Nonetheless, he stole a car and ran off, picking up two school children as hostages. He was recaptured and brought back. No longer a trusty, he was serving his time in the fields—while Barrow remained a parolee, eluding capture.

The "wanted" posters continued to display Clyde's portrait across the country. The rewards for his capture mounted. A two-hundred-dollar reward was posted for Barrow as the murderer of Howard Hall, in my home town of Sherman, on October 11, 1932. On January 7, 1933, Deputy Malcolm Davis, of Dallas, attempted to trap Clyde and Bonnie on one of their frequent visits to their folks. He was shot in the attempt. For some months thereafter the Barrow Gang gave Dallas a wide berth. Buck Barrow, Clyde's older brother, who had also been serving time at Huntsville, was pardoned on March 23, 1933, and with his wife promptly joined Clyde and Bonnie in Missouri. The two couples were holed up in a rented garage apartment in Joplin when officers of the law again struck their trail. A blazing gunfight ensued. When the smoke cleared, the four criminals had escaped, leaving behind them the corpse of another officer. Another reward for Clyde Barrow, this one for one thousand dollars, was posted.

The trail of the Barrow Gang crossed and crisscrossed eastern Oklahoma, eastern Kansas, southwest Missouri, most of Texas, and parts of Louisiana. In Ruston, Louisiana, they were wanted for kidnapping a man and a woman. Clyde Barrow was wanted in Lucerne, Indiana, for a bank robbery involving the wounding of two women, and for transporting a stolen automobile from Dallas to Pawhuska, Oklahoma.

On June 11, 1933, Clyde was driving at his usual breakneck speed with Buck and Bonnie in the car when he missed a detour sign north of Wellington, Oklahoma. The car plunged over an embankment into the Salt Fork of the Red River. Bonnie was burned and badly injured. When neighboring farmers came to the scene of the accident, the Barrows forced these good Samaritans at gun point to give them shelter in their home, a favor they later repaid by shooting in the hand the woman who had nursed Bonnie. One of the farmers escaped their vigilance and alerted officers in nearby Wellington. Sheriff George Corry and City Marshal Paul Hardy drove to the outlaws' refuge, only to be captured themselves. In their own car the officers were taken for another of the breath-taking Barrow rides and left handcuffed together and bound to trees with barbed wire near Erick, Oklahoma.

On July 28, 1933, Buck Barrow was killed in a running gun fight with thirteen officers of the law, near Platte City, Iowa. Clyde and Bonnie eluded capture, but from that night on they never again slept in a bed. They were forced as fugitives to snatch whatever rest they could by the roadside, to eat their food in their car with pistols at the ready, afraid to patronize a tourist court or a public restaurant in any corner of the land. Peace officers all over the West and Middle West had sworn to get them, and the May, 1933, issue of a nationally known detective magazine had published their pictures, posting an additional reward for the capture of Clyde Barrow.

Clyde Barrow's Raid

But Clyde and Bonnie continued their surreptitious visits to their families in Dallas, and in November again shot their way through a posse of officers posted by Sheriff R. A. (Smoot) Schmid to trap them. And on January 16, 1934, they engineered the release from Eastham Prison Farm of Hamilton, Palmer, Methvin, and Bybee.

Henry Methvin was under ten-year sentence and had, of course, known Clyde Barrow when Barrow was himself a prisoner at Eastham. That was why Methvin was invited to join the escape. Hilton Bybee merely took advantage of the confusion to join the party. He separated from the others at Vernon, Texas, the night of the escape, and plays no further part in this story. I was interested in Methvin and Bybee only as escapees who must be recaptured.

With Hamilton and Palmer, and with Clyde Barrow, I had more serious business—the avenging of the murder of my guard, Major Crowson.

CHAPTER 14

An Ambush in Arcadia .

IT WAS NOT too difficult to reconstruct what had actually happened on that morning of January 16, 1934. Most of the details of the escape plot were obtained from information given by an ex-convict, James Mullin, alias Jimmie Lamont. Mullin had been released recently from Eastham Farm. But he had served time in eight different penitentiaries, and we were so sure that he was somehow mixed up in the break that we promptly had him picked up.

Mullin was already in trouble again, having stolen some guns and ammunition from a federal armory. Thus he was sure of imprisonment again, either by Uncle Sam or by the state of Texas. Mullin didn't like to work, and he had already had a taste of labor as it is required on Eastham Farm. Accordingly he struck a bargain with us: if we would let him serve his next term at the federal prison, instead of at Eastham Farm, he would tell us what he knew about the break. We figured we needed help in the form of information more than Mullin needed a choice of prisons, so we agreed. His story was substantially as follows.

Upon being discharged from Eastham, Mullin had agreed to go to Dallas on behalf of Hamilton and Palmer to tell Floyd Hamilton, Raymond's brother, to get in touch with Clyde Barrow and ask him for help in the break, which had already been planned in detail. Barrow at once fell in with the plan, and further details were worked out.

An Ambush in Arcadia

Clyde and Raymond had a west Dallas pal in Fred Yost, then a trusty around the yard at Eastham Farm, who helped with their arrangements.

On the Sunday afternoon before the Tuesday break, Floyd Hamilton came down to the farm to visit Raymond and confirmed the plan in detail. The next morning around two o'clock Floyd and Mullin placed two loaded automatics under a small culvert near the woodyard. On Monday, the trusty, Yost, picked up the guns and smuggled them into the building where the convicts slept. On Tuesday, Hamilton and Palmer came out to work with the guns concealed in their clothing, a safe procedure as convicts are not ordinarily searched when they leave a building.

Hamilton jumped his squad to be with Joe. Clyde and Bonnie were waiting down by the timber, guided by Mullin, who knew the exact place where work would be going on. The break worked out exactly as planned, with the exception of Bybee's joining the party. Palmer vouched for Bybee to Clyde as being safe, since he was a life-termer. Three of the four fugitives crawled into the turtleback of the car. Clyde, Bonnie, and Mullin rode in the seat, and Raymond Hamilton rode in Mullin's lap.

A Negro near the farm saw them climb into the car and head north. Another witness near Hillsboro saw them throw striped prison clothing into the creek. A service-station attendant on a country road filled Clyde's car with gas and oil, chattering excitedly about the news that had just come over the radio. There had been a big break over at Eastham Farm, he reported, and Clyde Barrow had done it.

"Are you going to give me some gas," Clyde demanded, "or are you not going to give me some gas?" This was the first news the fugitives had had of the excitement caused by their raid. With the broadcast out, they stole another car, and Hamilton and Palmer separated from the Barrows with plans to meet in Missouri.

Henry Bybee, whom they considered excess baggage, was left to hitchhike. Bybee stopped a young woman and took her car at the point of a gun, telling her that he was an escaped convict. He had to stop at a service station and forgot to take the car keys when he went in. The young lady noticed this oversight, leaped into the car, started it, and roared away full throttle to the nearest town, where she notified officers. Bybee was soon picked up and returned to Huntsville. There he landed in the death cell for safekeeping.

Meanwhile, Clyde and Bonnie, Joe and Raymond went their ways, robbing and shooting. And I went on thinking and planning ways to bring all four to justice. I lay awake nights until I worked out what I felt to be a feasible plan. It involved a great deal of detail and would require the fullest confidence to be reposed in me by my superiors. In particular it had to have the fullest assistance of the Governor.

First I requested the prison board to create a new position, Special Investigator for the Texas Prison System. This could be done, under the law, with the approval of the Governor, the chairman of the State Board of Control, and the comptroller of accounts. After I had explained my plan, the board and the other necessary officials granted my request.

I told the board that I wanted to hire an experienced and dependable person to put on the trail of Clyde and Bonnie to stay on it until they were either captured or put out of business. Board members asked me who this person would be, and I answered that I did not yet know but that when I had made up my mind I did not intend that they or anybody else should know who he was.

I had my eye on one or two former Ranger captains. I weighed my choice strictly on the basis of who would be the best man for the job. Barrow was a desperado with no regard for human life, a man who despised the law and hated all peace officers. Whoever stopped Clyde Barrow would do so at the risk of his life. I knew from what Bybee and James Mullin (and, after his capture, Palmer) told me that Barrow had made up his mind never to be taken alive and that Bonnie Parker was determined to go down with Clyde. That was the kind of game we had to hunt; it was my task to find a hunter of the kind to handle it.

My decision was for Frank Hamer. I talked to nobody about it, but my own mind kept telling me that Hamer was the man. I had known him and his career for thirty-odd years. But I also knew that there was bad feeling politically between Hamer and the Governor. So before discussing the matter with Hamer or anyone else, I went to Governor Miriam A. Ferguson and former Governor Jim Ferguson. (You will remember that Jim Ferguson, after being impeached and convicted, had campaigned for his wife's election on the promise of "Two Governors for the Price of One" and that she had been elected in 1932.)

The Fergusons agreed to help me in any way that was right and proper. They had already assigned certain Rangers to the job and were going to offer a one-thousand-dollar reward for Clyde Barrow, alive or dead. I told them of my need for a special investigator and that I was considering Frank Hamer. Did they have any objections?

"Frank is all right with us," spoke up Governor Miriam. "We don't hold anything against him."

Hamer would need help from the underworld, and I was being approached by several of Barrow's former associates, both in the penitentiary and on the outside, who were offering to help put Clyde and Bonnie on the spot. "I might want to put somebody on the ground," I told the governors, meaning that I might want to promise someone clemency. "But that would have to be after he made good, and not before. You will have me between you and the public; it will be on my recommendation that you grant clemency, if my man makes good."

"Go ahead," said former Governor Jim, speaking first. "Go ahead. I told you we would do anything you want to assist you."

"Is that all right with you, Governor?" I asked, turning to Governor Miriam. After all, she was the one legally empowered to act.

"Yes, that is all right with me," she answered.

From the gubernatorial office I went straight to Hamer. I told him what I had in mind—to take Clyde and Bonnie off the road. I needed his help, and I told him why. I told him that his name had been mentioned only to the Fergusons and that they were agreeable to the assignment. I said I would put him completely in charge and back him to the limit.

"How long do you think it will take to do the job?" he asked. That was his way of indicating that he had no intention of jumping into something that might peter out under him. He knew that the FBI, the Texas Rangers, and a great many peace officers had been trying unsuccessfully for years to run down, capture, or kill Clyde Barrow. Hamer was not about to accept an arrangement whereby after a few months I might say, "Well, it looks like we are not getting anywhere, so we might as well call it off."

"That's something no man can guess," said I. "It might be six months; it might be longer. Probably it will take you thirty days to get your feet on the ground before you start to work. No matter how long it takes, I'll back you to the limit."

"Well," he replied, "if that's the way you feel about it, I'll take the job."

I made a suggestion to Hamer at this point, one of the two I made during the time of his employment as special investigator. "Captain, it is foolish for me to try to tell you anything; but in my judgment, the thing for you to do is put them on the spot, know you are right—and then shoot everybody in sight."

Hamer made no comment at the time, but later, at Arcadia, Louisiana, he was to refer to my remark. We went ahead with our plans, observing the utmost secrecy—for a very good reason. Barrow had radios in all his stolen cars and kept informed of what was being done against him and by whom. We never gave him any occasion to suppose that Frank Hamer was after him. When Frank wanted to talk to me, he would call me to meet him in some hotel room in Austin or in Dallas, never in Huntsville, where our meeting would call for comment. He made no important move without discussing it with me, and he never discussed any phase of the pursuit with me but what I said, "Go ahead. You're running it." After the job was all over, Hamer told me that it was the only job of its kind where he had been his own boss and had felt at liberty to do just as he thought best.

Meanwhile, the Barrow Gang went their way, robbing and shooting. Joe Palmer and Henry Methvin played only minor parts in their doings. Joe had both heart and stomach trouble and could not keep up with the others on their long drives. But Clyde kept Methvin, over whom he had complete domination, with him at all times, so that Henry was an accomplice, although not a principal, in the crimes. Raymond Hamilton went it alone part of the time, as I shall recount.

Up until this point I have given you the facts about these criminals in exactly the sequence they came to me. But the rest of their story came to me in fragmentary form as it was being acted out. Information trickled in, bit by bit, from various sources. And the picture did not take clear shape until after we had dealt with Clyde and Bonnie and had had time to talk it over with some of our prisoners whom we rounded up thereafter, and with others whose lips were unsealed by the realization that what they told us would no longer be "squealing." I must tell you the story as it actually happened, although many of the details were not reconstructed until later on.

In February, 1934, the Barrow Gang robbed a bank at Lancaster, Texas, of more than four thousand dollars. There the thieves fell out. According to the story later told me by Joe Palmer, Hamilton tried to hold out part of the stolen money. He also objected to cutting Bonnie in for her part of the loot. But the decisive break between Hamilton and Barrow came when Hamilton tried to get Bonnie to leave Clyde and team up with him instead. After that episode Hamilton was being hunted not only by the law but also by Clyde Barrow.

After the Lancaster holdup, Clyde, Bonnie, Joe, and Henry went back into hiding in Missouri. But Raymond Hamilton and his brother Floyd continued to operate in Texas, robbing banks at West and at Grand Prairie. Barrow sent Joe Palmer to Texas to try to make connections with Hamilton. The first time Palmer didn't suspect Clyde's intentions. He merely thought Raymond was needed to help on another robbery. He was unable to locate Raymond, who had quit the highways, giving up automobiles in favor of riding freight trains.

A second time, on February 28, Barrow sent Palmer to Texas to look for Hamilton. By this time Palmer was suspicious of Clyde's intentions. On a third occasion when he was sent on the same mission, Clyde told him frankly that he wanted to locate Hamilton to kill him. But Hamilton could not be located.

On April 1 the radio broadcast went out reporting Hamilton's robbery of a bank near West. Barrow was sure that he could anticipate his former partner's next move. For it was Hamilton's established practice, after having pulled a job, to head as directly as possible for the area of unpaved country lanes north of Grapevine, in the vicinity of Roanoke, there to lie up while pursuit swept by. This time Clyde and Bonnie reached the area ahead of him and parked their Ford a short distance off the Grapevine highway at a point which Hamilton was expected to pass. It was a bright, clear Easter morning.

State Patrolmen E. B. Wheeler and W. D. Murphy passed the spot and noticed the parked car with several people in it. At the end of their run the patrolmen wheeled and returned. The Ford was still there, so they racked their motorcycles and walked over to see if there was any trouble and to offer assistance. Just before they reached the car Barrow stepped out on one side and Bonnie on the other. Without any warning whatever they shot and killed the two officers.

William Schieffer, the farmer near whose home this killing took place, told me that he had been watching the car for some time because it had stayed there so long. He saw the entire occurrence. Bonnie's victim fell and was lying on his side. She walked over to the prostrate patrolman, put her foot on his body, and pushed him over so that he lay on his back. Then cold-bloodedly she stepped back a few feet, fired another shot into the body, turned, and ran to the Ford. The car drove off at high speed.

Hamilton, who was indeed proceeding toward the place where Barrow waited in ambush, had bogged down on a country road, a delay which undoubtedly saved his life. Unable to get out of the mud, he kidnaped a farm woman, Mrs. Cam Gunters, leaving her four-year-old son in the road. The next morning he released her in Houston. He left her afoot but did give her thirty dollars to get home on.

After killing the two highway patrolmen, Clyde, Bonnie, and Henry Methvin sped north. Near Miami, Oklahoma, they skidded into a ditch. As they were pushing the car back on the highway, two officers came to investigate, and in a matter of moments Constable Cal Campbell lay dead. Police Chief Percy Boyd, who had been wounded, was forced into the car in the kidnaping pattern that was becoming Barrow's trademark.

I happened to be in Dallas in the office of Detective Will Fritz, a long-time member of the Dallas police force, the day of this Oklahoma killing, and we listened over the radio to the chase that was then going on in Kansas. Clyde was staying on country roads and plowing through the mud. He spent the night in a haystack, stole a new Pontiac the following day, and threw off pursuit. Boyd, who had been shot in the forehead and was in serious condition, was left by the roadside. Henry Methvin later told me that Barrow claimed Boyd had more nerve than any other man he had ever seen. Although he was badly wounded, Boyd made no complaint and showed no fear. Yet he must have known that he stood a close chance of being shot again and killed at almost any moment.

An Ambush in Arcadia

The entire Southwest was on edge at the hell-roaring, gun-blazing swath cut by Clyde and Bonnie. Those two were out-dime-noveling the wildest paperback of them all. Meanwhile, the public was doing a little roaring of its own—and with good reason. The Barrow Gang, along with "Pretty Boy" Floyd and number one criminal Dillinger, were making almost daily headlines with their activities.

The Easter-morning shooting of the two patrolmen had underlined the fact that nobody in Texas was safe, not even on the "big road," as long as Clyde and Bonnie were loose. Chief Phares, of the Highway Patrol, was so aroused by the slaughter of his men that he began to move heaven and earth to get something done about it. How he learned that Hamer was representing me, I don't know. But he did learn it, and he summoned Hamer to meet him in Austin.

Phares should have called me, of course. But he called Hamer, and Hamer then called me. So I met Frank at his hotel room. He told me that Phares wanted to place one of his own men in the position of Frank's assistant. It was understandable that Phares would want to put a man on the trail of Clyde and Bonnie, after the unprovoked murder of two of his officers. But his offer did not appeal to me very much. Too many cooks spoil the broth for the law as in other affairs. I wanted secrecy maintained for Hamer's protection as well as for the success of his undertaking. I told Frank, however: "It's your job. I'm going to back up everything you do. Whatever you do about this is all right with me. Only I am depending upon you to run the show."

"I'll damn sure run it," he said.

"Whom does Phares have in mind?"

"Manny Gault." M. B. Gault, then with the Highway Department, has previously been with the Texas Rangers, where his judgment and reliability had been tested. He had served in the same company with Hamer and was a good man. I knew Gault fairly well and was pleased myself with his selection.

"You want him?"

"Yes, I'd really like to have him."

"Well, you're running things," I said. And Manny Gault it was.

On April 1, Deputy Sheriffs Ted Hinton and Bob Alcorn, of the Dallas sheriff's force, were also detailed to work with Captain Hamer, by order of Judge Noland G. Williams of Dallas County's District

Court 2 (Criminal). The judge had also found out by this time of Hamer's assignment. Both these deputies had been with Sheriff Schmid when Clyde and Bonnie had shot their way out of a trap laid for them on November 23, 1933, on the North Fort Worth Road. Thus they knew both of our criminals by sight, a fact which Hamer thought would be a help to him, as he had never seen either Clyde or Bonnie.

From this time on, then, Hamer was no longer working alone but had the assistance of Gault, Hinton, and Alcorn. He was soon to add to his team Sheriff Henderson Jordan and Deputy Sheriff P. M. Calley, of Louisiana.

For it was about this time that I made the second of my two suggestions to Hamer about the method of his pursuit. (The first, you remember, was when I told him to put Clyde and Bonnie on the spot and then shoot everyone in sight.) I had knowledge now that Henry Methvin's parents lived over in Louisiana, and I had a hunch it might be a good idea to drop in on them and see what could be learned. I said so to Frank. He replied that he was already planning to do that soon. In other words, my suggestion hadn't been needed, after all.

Frank did go to Louisiana, and he reported his findings to me when next I met him in Dallas. He came to me of his own accord, as I did not expect him to make any reports to me, although he frequently did. He said that in Louisiana he had encountered a free-talking sheriff with whom he was hesitant to work, and so he had returned to Texas without revealing his mission.

In a few days Hamer made another trip to Louisiana. This time he met Sheriff Henderson Jordan, of Bienville Parish, whom he found to be highly co-operative. Together they got things working favorably. It was going to take a full pardon for Henry Methvin, Frank reported, to get help from that direction.

I went at once to Austin, where I reminded Governors Miriam and Jim Ferguson of our former conversation, and I arranged with them that Methvin would be "put on the ground," if he came through with the information that we needed. When next I saw Captain Hamer, I gave him a letter setting forth that, upon certain conditions involving certain assistance to the law, Henry Methvin would be granted a full pardon. Then I waited, expecting something would happen shortly.

An Ambush in Arcadia

About eight o'clock on the night of April 22 Hamer telephoned me: "The old hen is about ready to hatch; I think the chickens will come off tomorrow."

The morning of the next day I got the word, and in ten minutes I was on the road to Arcadia, Louisiana, with Luther Berwick, my convict-driver. Luther was stepping down hard on the gas. As we drove along, radio reports came rolling in which I pieced together with my knowledge of Hamer's plans for an ambush into something like this:

On the afternoon of April 22, Clyde and Bonnie stopped with Henry Methvin at a restaurant. Henry went in to get some sandwiches for them. He didn't come back. Clyde waited for some time, and then concluded that Henry "got hot" and had been "jumped." Clyde drove over to the house of Henry's father and told the old man that he was sure Henry would come home during the night. He left word that he would meet Henry on the road between Gibsland and Arcadia at about nine o'clock the next morning.

Henry did come home. His father got in touch with the "proper parties." During the night the officers of the law made their plans. On the morning of April 23 old Mr. Methvin was on the road with his logging truck. He stopped at a rise of a hill and drove a little to one side. He was removing a tire when Clyde and Bonnie came along in a brown Ford which they had stolen in Kansas. Just as they slowed down, Hamer, who had his men concealed on the other side of the road, gave the order to fire. Guns roared. Clyde and Bonnie had come to the end of the trail.

A large crowd had gathered at the parish jail by the time I reached Arcadia. Many newspaper reporters had flown in at the first flash on the radio. As I walked up and shook hands with Captain Hamer and his fellow-officers, Hamer turned to the newsmen: "Now, here's the boss. I've been acting on his instructions. If any statement is to be given out, he is the one to make it."

Actually, of course, Hamer was his own boss. He deserved to be. But he was carrying out his lifetime policy of taking small credit for his accomplishments. As the newspaper people grabbed me and peppered me with questions, I realized that they were entitled to some information, so I went as far as I felt I could in giving them the story.

I told them of the employment of Captain Hamer and of the subsequent assignment of Gault, Hinton, and Alcorn to the job. The reporters already knew something of this, but they had known nothing of the important part played by Sheriff Henderson Jordan, which I now revealed to them. But the Methvins? How about them?

"There are some things," I finally said, "which the public is not entitled to know." Would I state that the Methvins had had nothing to do with the ambush? I stood pat on my statement and refused further comment. As a matter of fact, Henry Methvin had known nothing of the deal made with his father until the morning of April 22, when Clyde and Bonnie made their last call at Mr. Methvin's house in the woods.

From the date of Hamer's appointment by me until the accomplishment of his mission, exactly 102 days had elapsed. With the loyal and intelligent aid of the fine peace officers I have named as assisting him, Hamer did a job that had baffled the FBI, the Texas Ranger force, and a great number of capable officers of the law who had been hunting Clyde and Bonnie through four or five states for one to three years. He told me as we walked away from the reporters that he had hoped he would never have to "bust a cap" on a woman, but when the time came that he had to do it he had simply remembered Patrolmen Wheeler and Murphy and what had happened to them on Easter morning.

We walked over to the Barrow car, and Hamer unlocked it. "Here is what's in it," he said. "It's up to you to say what's to be done with it."

"No," said I. "You take what you want and then divide the souvenirs with the boys who did the job. I'm not entitled to anything. You take charge of it and handle it."

And he did. The car, which had been riddled until it looked like an oversized pepperbox, was an arsenal on wheels. It contained submachine guns, automatic shotguns, .45 automatic pistols (fourteen of them in all), and a thousand rounds of ammunition. When Clyde's body was removed from the car, the officers found $506.32 in his pockets, mostly in ten- and twenty-dollar bills. I went to the morgue to view the bodies. I turned back the sheet covering Clyde's feet and saw that one toe was missing. And I recalled that Clyde had cut off that toe so as to get out of working on Eastham Farm.

I couldn't help thinking about the reward of these two. I wondered if it might have turned out otherwise for both of them if they had had better childhood surroundings and training.

Clyde and Bonnie were put on the spot. I make no apology for that. I never have, and I never will. Their mothers said that their children had been shot from ambush without ever having a chance. That was true. But none of the victims of Clyde and Bonnie ever had a chance for his life. The criminals' mothers had plenty of other things to say, all of which I have long since excused. Fathers sometimes forsake their offspring when they get into trouble; mothers never do.

As Clyde and Bonnie had dealt, so had they received. As they had sowed, so also had they reaped.

CHAPTER 15

Settling Accounts

H̲ARDLY HAD THE CURTAIN rung down on the criminal careers of Clyde Barrow and Bonnie Parker when their histories began to be softened by legend. Already this outlaw and his woman have become semifictional characters, the Robin Hood and Maid Marian of the Southwest. Only those of us who keep yellowed scrapbook clippings pasted away can recapture the feeling that the Barrow Gang was part of legitimate history. This story from the *Austin American* of Thursday, April 24, 1934, represents contemporary comment upon their slaying.

Justice travels with a leaden heel, but it strikes mighty hard.

Clyde Barrow and Bonnie Parker made their last stand in Louisiana. They were trailed by a highway patrolman, two Deputy Sheriffs and Frank Hamer, who had been given orders to "get their man."

Well, they were trailed to their hideout. They reached for their guns. They were shot into the world of oblivion. They will sleep in dishonored graves.

Congratulations to the fearless officers of the law who trailed these enemies of the social order.

Clyde Barrow was one of the most desperate criminals. Bonnie Parker was said to have been the trigger expert of Barrow and his pals.

According to gathered evidence, Barrow was the author of 100 crimes. He had robbed with impunity and slain without mercy. He had been paroled by a Texas Governor on "good behavior." For two years he has been the terror of Texas and, with his pals, the terror of law-abiding people of Oklahoma, Arkansas, Missouri and Kansas.

The murder of the two highway patrolmen in North Texas was by Barrow and members of his gang, one of the most dastardly killings in Texas history. Those servants of the State were shot down without warning. Their slayers stood over them and pumped lead into their shivering corpses.

Well, let the curtain fall. Killer Dillinger will be the next to go. A thousand Federal agents are on his trail. They have orders, "get your man." They will "get their man."

Wherever the forces of law and order organize, the finish of the criminal terrorists in Texas and elsewhere is in sight.

"Ever the law is uppermost" is the demand of the vast majority of the American people.

I suspect that the author of that article fancied he had written himself quite a piece. At least he managed to put into words something of the exultation and something of the relief that came to tens of thousands of Southwesterners at the news that Clyde and Bonnie were through.

Now for the other side. Bonnie Parker, in her spare time between escapes from custody, occasionally wrote verse. One of her last compositions ran as follows:

THE STORY OF BONNIE AND CLYDE

By BONNIE PARKER

You have read the story of Jesse James,
Of how he lived and died.
  If you still are in need
  Of something to read,
Here is the story of Bonnie and Clyde.

Now, Bonnie and Clyde are the Barrow Gang;
I'm sure you all have read
  How they rob and steal
  And those who squeal
Are usually found lying dead.

There are lots of untruths in their write-ups—
They are not so merciless as that.
    But not without cause
    They hate all the laws,
The stool pigeon, spotter and rat.

They class them as cold-blooded killers,
They say they are heartless and mean;
    But I say this with pride,
    That I once knew Clyde
When he was honest and upright and clean.

But the law fooled around,
Kept tracking him down
    And locking him up in a cell,
    'Til he said to me:
    "I will never be free;
So I will meet a few of them in hell!"

This road was so dimly lighted
There were no highway signs to guide;
    But they made up their mind,
    If the roads were all blind,
They wouldn't give up till they died.

The road gets dimmer and dimmer;
Sometimes you can hardly see.
    Still it's fight like a man
    And do all you can—
For they know they can never be free.

If they try to act like citizens
And rent them a nice little flat,
    About the third night
    They are invited to fight
By a machine gun, rat-tat-tat!

If a policeman is killed in Dallas
And they have no clues to guide—
    If they can't find a fiend,
    They just wipe the slate clean,
And hang it on Bonnie and Clyde.

Settling Accounts

Two crimes have been done in America
Not credited to the Barrow Mob;
   For they had no hand
   In the kidnaping demand
Or the Kansas City Depot job.

A newsboy once said to his buddy:
I wish old Clyde would get jumped.
   In these awful hard times
   We might make a few dimes,
If five or six laws got bumped.

The police haven't got the report yet;
Clyde sent in a wireless today,
   Saying, "We have a peace flag of white
   We stretched out tonight;
We have joined the NRA!"

They don't think they are so tough or so desperate;
They know that the law always wins.
   They've been shot at before,
   But they do not ignore
That death is the wages of sin.

From heartbreaks some people have suffered,
From weariness some people have died;
   But, take it all in all,
   Our troubles are small
Till we get like Bonnie and Clyde.

Some day they will go down together,
And they will bury them side by side.
   To a few it means grief;
   To the law it's relief;
But it is death to Bonnie and Clyde.

Personally, I felt that Clyde and Bonnie should have been buried side by side. That was their wish, and that was their request made to those who were closely associated with them. Clyde never expected to be taken alive; he knew that he would go to the chair if captured. But on several occasions he urged Bonnie to give herself up, saying that she was young and could within a few years expect clemency.

She would not hear to surrender. They would go down together, she said, and together they would lie in their graves.

But the mothers of the two decided the matter otherwise, and the wishes of the mothers were carried out. Morbid curiosity-seekers thronged by the thousands to the funeral homes. Thousands more were present at the cemeteries. Clyde Barrow was buried on Friday. Most remarkable of the mourners at his grave was Joe Palmer.

Joe had been sitting in the lobby of the Huckins Hotel in Oklahoma City listening to the radio when the broadcaster interrupted his newscast: "Just a minute. Word has just been received that Clyde Barrow and Bonnie Parker have been killed near Gibsland, Louisiana." Joe Palmer had the electric chair staring him in the face, but he moved about openly. He told me later: "I used always to walk down the main street in a town. I spoke to many officers of the law, for I knew the officers would be looking for me in some more quiet and out-of-the-way place."

Accordingly, Joe Palmer felt that it would be safe to go to Clyde Barrow's funeral. And he did. He said the only fear he had was that Warden Waid or I would be there and recognize him. But we weren't. Joe believed in Clyde and Bonnie. The last time they had parted in Joplin, Missouri, Bonnie had given him fifty dollars and a new suit of clothes. And he was the only man that Clyde Barrow had fully trusted. I guess it was appropriate that he was at Clyde's funeral.

Raymond Hamilton was not in a position to attend the funerals, even if he wanted to—which I'm sure he didn't. The day of Clyde's burial he robbed the First National Bank of Lewisville, Texas, fled to Grayson County, and was there blocked off and arrested. He was received at Huntsville again on May 25, this time under a ninety-nine–year sentence for the Lewisville bank robbery.

Joe Palmer did not remain long at large. In Missouri he kidnaped a doctor, a citizen, and a police officer and forced them into the turtleback of his car, where they remained for twenty-four hours before being released. Shortly thereafter, Palmer was captured, and Bud Russell went to Missouri to bring him back to Huntsville in the "one-way bus."

The killing of Clyde and Bonnie was partial payment on the score I had to settle. But Hamilton and Palmer had merely been given additional prison sentences. I was determined that they should get the chair, as an example to others.

Sometime previously, when the killers of Guard Sneed had been tried, I had taken no part in the prosecution, feeling that it was my particular duty to manage the Texas Prison System and not to enforce the law in the courtroom. An able district attorney handled that case and handled it well, only to hear a jury solemnly award a life sentence, on top of a previous life sentence, for each of the bloody-handed slayers. I was determined to do all in my power to see that this same thing did not happen in the cases of Hamilton and Palmer.

The killing of Crowson in the Eastham Farm break had occurred in Houston County, but District Attorney Max Rogers agreed with me that, because of conditions in that county, it was doubtful whether the state could get a fair trial there. So we asked and obtained a change of venue by order of the district judge, with the district attorney's acquiescence. The cases were transferred to Walker County, where Hamilton, although represented by capable and experienced counsel, was tried and given the death penalty.

Hamilton's trial got a great deal of play in the newspapers, and Judge S. W. Dean therefore granted a change of venue in Palmer's case from Walker to Grimes County, both counties in the Twelfth Judicial District under Judge Dean. Palmer also received the death penalty. I worked closely with the prosecution on both these cases and now have in my possession a letter from District Judge Max Rogers (then the district attorney) stating that without my help in these two cases there would have been no death penalties.

Before Judge Dean pronounced sentence upon Joe Palmer, he asked if there was any statement Palmer wanted to make. Joe said he wanted to make one, and after rambling on quite a bit he wound up by saying: "I can take the hot seat over at Huntsville with pleasure. I'd rather take the hot seat than to spend five more years in the most damnable prison system that ever existed."

Now, as I told you before, when Joe Palmer was at Huntsville he had preferred treatment and was given a trusty job with overtime credit, until he betrayed our trust by escaping. This time Bud Russell, Albert Moore, and I took Palmer to the courthouse for his trial, and when he stood up for his sentence, I stood up right behind him. At this remark of his I boiled. I spoke up: "Judge, we can give him the hot seat with about as much pleasure as he says he can take it."

I was entirely out of order, and the judge would have been entirely justified in reprimanding me, or even in fining me. But His Honor made no comment on my interruption. He proceeded instead to pass sentence upon Joe Palmer. The newspaper boys had plenty to say, however, about my outburst, and District Attorney Max Rogers enjoyed it immensely.

Later on in the death house both Hamilton and Palmer told me more than once that I was the cause of the death penalties assessed against them. To each of them I replied: "Yes, I did everything I could to give you the chair. But I did it honestly and honorably, and I have no apologies to make. You played a rough game, and you lost."

Raymond and Joe had taken one life. They had been sentenced to pay two for that crime. That didn't restore a son to Crowson's aged father and mother as a stay and support in their last years. I could only hope it would help to save the lives of other guards. And I like to think it has had influence down to the present day. At the time—with Clyde and Bonnie dead and Raymond and Joe in the death house—I felt that I had made good on my promise to Major Crowson on his deathbed. As things turned out, my sense of satisfaction was somewhat premature.

Meanwhile, however, there were accounts to be settled with our friends as well as with our enemies. Some sixty days after the death of Bonnie and Clyde, Sheriff Jordan telephoned me for an appointment and came to Huntsville to see me about a pardon or parole for Henry Methvin. I thought it too soon and advised against it. Henry was not being bothered but was staying quietly at home away from the public, under orders of Sheriff Jordan.

The sheriff agreed with me on the time element but said that the Methvins were insisting on something being done immediately. He asked me if I thought clemency could be obtained right away. I told him I was sure it could. "You folks made good over in Louisiana," said I, "and we'll make good in Texas."

So I went to Austin and saw the two Governors. The nature of my business with them is shown in the following letters.

Settling Accounts

TEXAS PRISON SYSTEM
W. A. Paddock, Chairman, Houston, Texas
[Seal of the State of Texas]

Lee Simmons, General Manager
Clyde Watson, Secretary

Huntsville, Texas
Aug. 11, 1934

Governor Miriam Ferguson,
Austin, Texas

Dear Governor:

You recall that on Jan 16, 1934, Clyde Barrow and associates raided the Eastham Prison Farm and delivered therefrom Raymond Hamilton, Joe Palmer, Hilton Bybee, Henry Methvin and other prisoners. At that time Clyde Barrow was on parole granted by Governor Sterling, but said parole had been revoked and the officers of the entire Southwest were endeavoring to capture Clyde Barrow.

With your approval, I employed Mr. Frank Hamer on February 10 as special escape investigator for the Texas Prison System. After several months' work, it developed that perhaps Barrow and associates could be trapped with the assistance of relatives and friends of Henry Methvin, who lived in Louisiana.

Through Henderson Jordan of Arcadia, and with close friends of the Methvin family whereby, if aid was given to the prison officials, it was agreed that if Clyde Barrow were captured or killed, clemency could be obtained for Henry Methvin; and, after conference with Governor Jim Ferguson and yourself, my letter of April 24, 1934, to Captain Hamer was delivered to the friends of Henry Methvin, this letter being submitted to you, same meeting with your approval.

It was through this arrangement that Clyde Barrow and Bonnie Parker were taken and, therefore, Captain Hamer and myself are now recommending and asking that pardon be granted to Henry Methvin in order that the contract made by us be carried out. In my judgment, Henry Methvin knew nothing of this arrangement, and had nothing to do with the same, but same was made by his father and friends, in order to save the life of said Henry Methvin. We believe that the extermination of Clyde Barrow was entirely justified, as he had shown an utter disregard for the lives of citizens and peace officers of the country, and there is no question that he murdered many good peace officers ruthlessly without any cause and that he had an utter disregard for human life. Therefore, as stated, we recommend to you and ask that full pardon be granted to Henry Methvin.

This, of course, in no way has anything to do with any other crimes committed by Henry Methvin, as in my letter I made the statement that this refers only to his crime that he is now serving time on.

Thanking you for your co-operation in this regard, I am,

Respectfully

[signed] LEE SIMMONS
General Manager
Texas Prison System

[signed] FRANK HAMER
Special Escape Investigator
Texas Prison System

EXECUTIVE DEPARTMENT
[Seal of State of Texas]
Austin, Texas

August 13, 1934

Honorable Miriam A. Ferguson
Governor of Texas
Austin, Texas

Dear Governor:

We recommend that a conditional pardon be issued to Convict No. 65949, Henry Methvin, sent from Refugio County at the October, A.D. 1930, term thereof for theft and assault with intent to murder and given a ten-year sentence in the State Penitentiary.

In addition to having served three years, two months and twenty-nine days, he gave to the authorities in Louisiana valuable information that led to the apprehension and capture of one Clyde Barrow and one Bonnie Parker who murdered two State Highway Patrolmen, E. B. Wheeler and W. D. Murphy on April 1, 1934, in Tarrant County, Texas.

We further recommend that a reward of $500 offered by you for the apprehension of these murderers, dead or alive, be paid.

Yours truly,
LEE SIMMONS
By
[signed] T. L. TENNISON
[signed] FRANK HAMER

Settling Accounts

The second letter was dictated in the Governor's office at the request of the Fergusons.

Henry was pardoned for the crime for which he had been serving time when he escaped from Eastham. But others had an interest in Henry Methvin. He was arrested and taken to Oklahoma to answer as Barrow's accomplice in the murder of Constable Cal Campbell at Commerce, Oklahoma, on April 6, 1934. For this killing Methvin received a death sentence.

He wrote to me for assistance, but I refused to aid him. I had kept my promise to his father in obtaining the exact clemency set out in my letter of negotiations. While, to the best of my information, Methvin did not participate actively in any of the crimes of the Barrow Gang after his escape from Eastham Farm, he was present in the car when all those crimes were committed. In the light of that, I had no sympathy for him.

His death sentence, however, was commuted to life imprisonment on the grounds of his father's assistance to the officers in Louisiana. He was put to work in the office of Deputy Warden Jesse Dunn, an old-time sheriff and a friend of mine. After I had left the Texas Prison System and returned to private life at Sherman, I visited with Henry twice in Warden Dunn's office at the Oklahoma State Penitentiary, at McAlester, and talked with him quite a lot about what had happened while he was with Clyde and Bonnie. Here is a letter Henry wrote me from McAlester:

OKLAHOMA STATE PENITENTIARY

R. W. Kenny, Warden   J. F. Dunn, Warden   John Russell
Asst. Deputy Warden

Censored by No. 5

Prisoner No. 32834
To: Mr. Lee Simmons
Street:
Box No.:
City: Sherman
State: Texas

Rules for Writing and Receiving Mail

All mail must pass through the office of mail clerk to be opened, examined and placed on record before mailing or delivery. All officers forbidden to handle prisoner's mail. Write plainly on business or family matters—nothing else. Put your number on this sheet. Prisoner's mail must be delivered to Box 398, McAlester, Oklahoma.

If sending money, send P.O. Money Order. Currency barred. Checks will be destroyed. Prisoner's funds are deposited to prisoner's credit with Warden.

Admissible: Newspapers direct from publisher; books of proper character, shoes, underwear, handkerchiefs and socks—nothing else. Packages containing articles other than those mentioned will be destroyed.

First-class prisoners permitted to write one letter per week at the State's expense, two letters per month at own expense. Write only to relatives or friends whose names are of record in office of mail clerk. Permitted to receive letters of same character and source, if decent and proper.

Visiting: Father, Mother, Sister, Brother, Wife, Husband, Son or Daughter permitted to visit prisoners one hour once a month, any day; hours 9 a.m. to 11 a.m., 1 p.m. to 4 p.m. No exceptions without permission from Warden or Deputy Warden. Arrangements will be made for prisoners to confer with attorneys at all times. LETTERS INCOMING OR OUTGOING MUST BE SIGNED WITH FULL NAME.

P.O. Box 398, McAlester, Oklahoma
Oct. 12, 1936

Dear Sir:

My Mother was telling me in a letter last week that she and Dad was by to see you. Since they seen you, the Court of Appeals has commuted the death sentence, which I was under, to life imprisonment. I am tickle to know that I am no longer facing the chair. I had all the hopes in the world and was sure I would be given a new trial. But instead of granting a new trial the court gave me a life sentence.

Mother was telling me that you would do ever thing you could for me. With your help I know I will be given freedom in a short while so I can go home and take care of my dear Mother & Dad. And I want to prove to the world that I'm not a killer. I have several good jobs to go to when I get out, the people I was working for at the time of my arrest tells me I can go to work for them the day I get out. After Barrow & Parker were killed I went to work and worked nearly every day until I was arrested and brought to Oklahoma to stand trial for murder. I am not guilty of murder and I know you and others will help me gain freedom. I would like to see you and talk to you and if possible please visit me. I will appreciate it very much.

From the bottom of my heart I want to thank you for what you have allready done for me and am thanking you in advance for all.

Settling Accounts

Hoping to hear from you soon. Trusting this fines you in the best of health.

Respectufll

[signed] HENRY METHVIN #32834, Box 398

Put Prisoner's Number on Outside of Envelope or the Letter Will Be Returned.

Although in this letter Henry thanks me for what I had done for him and says his mother reported that I was going to help him, I never did recommend clemency in Oklahoma, although my friend Dunn asked me to do so. I did tell Dunn that I was glad he had given Henry a good job in the office.

Henry Methvin was later pardoned by the Governor of Oklahoma. I received a letter from him after his release saying that he was back home and had a job with a large firm engaged in road construction. He said he was getting along all right. I hope he still is. I don't know.

CHAPTER 16

The Death-Cell Break

THE HARDEST JOLT I received during my administration of the Texas Prison System was the death-cell break of July 22, 1934. Three prisoners under sentence to be electrocuted escaped from the Huntsville death cell and went over the wall to be spirited away by outside accomplices. Two of these men were Raymond Hamilton and Joe Palmer—which is why I said my satisfaction at their conviction proved a little premature. The third was Blackie Thompson, an Oklahoma ex-convict, then under death sentence for a Marlin bank robbery. Involved with them in the break were three life-termers, one of them Charlie Frazier, by far the hardest and most desperate criminal with whom I ever had to deal.

Frazier was a habitual criminal if there ever was one. He first came to Huntsville on January 13, 1917, when he was twenty years old, with a three-year sentence for burglary from Red River County. That year he escaped but was immediately recaptured. The next year he escaped and remained at large for six months before he was recaptured at Hugo, Oklahoma. On the very day he was returned to Huntsville he escaped again.

On February 23, 1920, he completed his term and was discharged. In June of that year he was arrested at Arcadia, Louisiana, and sent to the Louisiana State Penitentiary under the name R. E. Johnson to serve an eight-to-ten-year sentence. Paroled in 1922, he was convicted again for burglary in Louisiana, this time under the name A. W. Adams. In 1925 he escaped.

In 1926 he was sent up from Marion County, Texas, for robbery with firearms, burglary, and theft. He soon escaped from the Texas Prison System. About a week later, at eleven o'clock at night he returned. Slipping up to the prison barracks, which held 150 convicts, he shot and killed the picket guard, Will Roder. He released six convicts, including a former partner of his, but for this crime he was never convicted as there was only convict testimony to be brought against him.

He was recaptured four months later and returned to Huntsville. He escaped twice in the next year. Then he was reported to be a bootleg-runner in eastern Arkansas, where he killed Officer Roy Salmon, of Foreman. For this crime Frazier received a life sentence in the Arkansas State Penitentiary. There I first met Charlie Frazier.

Soon after I was appointed to the management of the Texas Prison System, I went over to see S. L. Todhunter, warden of the Arkansas Penitentiary, whom I had heard of as experienced in the business of handling prisoners. He and his fine wife were more than gracious to me and later returned my visit by spending a week with us at Huntsville. My consultation with Todhunter proved most profitable. While I was inspecting Tucker Farm, a number of "alumni" of the Texas Prison System gathered around us. Among them was Charlie Frazier.

In 1932 Frazier was given a fifteen-day Christmas furlough from which he failed to return. The next year he was sent back to the Louisiana Prison System with multiple sentences, including one new life term for robbery and shooting with intent to murder. On September 10, 1933, he engineered a break from Angola State Prison Farm, in which eleven convicts fled.

This break occurred during a Sunday afternoon baseball game. Frazier and another convict leveled guns, which had been smuggled in, upon the farm manager and ordered him to have the prison gates opened. When the manager refused, they shot him to death. As the prisoners shot their way out, several of their fellow-inmates were killed. Of the eleven who escaped, seven were later killed, either in attempted escapes or in resisting arrest or recapture. Of the four still alive, one is in the Arkansas State Penitentiary and two are in the Louisiana State Penitentiary.

Of these latter two, one is Charlie Frazier. In the interim he and I have had considerable dealings. Two months after his daring escape from Angola he was brought to Huntsville with four new sentences, one of two to ten years, another of five to ten years, still another of five to twenty-five years, and the fourth, a life term.

I ventured a talk with Frazier. My only object was to see whether I might in any manner influence him to change his criminal slant. I started off by saying: "Charlie, we are not responsible for your being here; but we are responsible for you and your welfare as a prisoner, now that you are here. You have quite a record; but, so far as we are concerned, that is all behind you. You will receive every consideration that you are entitled to. You will be treated no better, and no worse, than the others. Your record will make no difference to us.

"You are getting on in years and in experience. By this time you should know that you can't beat the law. I hope you realize this and that you will go ahead and behave. If you do that, I'm sure you will get along all right. And if you do that, I'll see that you get a square deal here in every way."

Charlie was as pleasant as could be. He said he realized that he should change his ways and that he intended to change them. He said we would have no trouble with him.

A few months later he attempted to escape. With a handmade key he unlocked his cell, broke the bars of the window of the run-around, and got into the prison yard; but he was stopped before he got over the prison wall. Another night he escaped from the main prison but was wounded by a guard as he was attempting to place a ladder against the wall. No, we had no trouble with Charlie.

Then came the death-cell break. On Saturday morning, July 21, as I was walking through the prison yard, a convict sidled up to me and said: "Mr. Simmons, keep walking, don't stop. They are tunneling out through the floor of the print shop. They are working on Sundays while the ball game is going on. You know what will happen to me if it gets out that I'm giving you a tip. Don't give my name."

The Death-Cell Break

I thanked him and assured him that I would not betray his confidence. I did indeed know what would happen to him if he was discovered to be a squealer. According to the underworld code, the penalty was death. I reported the conversation to Warden Waid but told him to go to the ball game Sunday as usual, for we never knew what might happen at a ball game or a rodeo. I would see about the tunnel myself, I said.

S. E. Barnett was in charge of the print shop. I told him what I suspected was going on under his shop and instructed him to meet me at my office at half-past two in the afternoon. Then about one o'clock my good friend Lewis Ball, a prominent merchant of Huntsville, telephoned that he and his wife and two friends from Ardmore, Oklahoma, would like to come over for a look around the prison. Even though visitors were not ordinarily permitted on Sunday, he wondered if I could accommodate him. I told him to bring his friends over, and I would be glad to show them around.

When these guests arrived, most of the prisoners within the Walls, at least a thousand of them, had been taken outside to the ball park. But on my tour with the visitors I noticed that Charlie Frazier was sitting by himself in the chapel and that Whitey Walker and Roy Johnson, two others of my toughest customers, were sitting on the steps of the school building. That those three would skip a big ball game aroused my suspicions. I sent my guests on to the ball park and went back to my residence and got my gun.

Then I met Barnett in my office. I told him I had a gun, although prison regulations forbade the carrying of guns at any time within the Walls. That is a good rule generally, but this time I broke it, for I felt sure that trouble was about to start. And I told Barnett that if anything happened I would take care of Frazier in case he was in on the deal.

At three o'clock Barnett and I walked over to the printshop at a leisurely pace. He unlocked the door quickly and in we went. We found a large opening in the concrete floor, with a convict hard at work underneath. He was using an electric light and a fan to aid him. We also found another prisoner hiding in the building. Both of them were naked. We made them dress and marched them back to the cell house, where we locked them in. They tried to rig up a story to the effect that they were behind with their printing work and had been in the shop trying to earn overtime. Barnett was unimpressed.

As we were walking these two boys through the prison yard, we met Charlie Frazier face to face. He gave no sign of comprehending what was up, although, as a matter of fact, he had been invited to join in the tunnel attempt. He had refused, having, as later became apparent, bigger fish to fry.

When we had our two tunnel moles safely stowed away, I went outside and over to the ball game, where our guests were sitting with Mrs. Simmons in the stands. Mrs. Ball glanced up at me with a smile and asked, "What are you doing with a coat on this hot day?"

"Oh," I replied, "I had on a dirty shirt and a coat was easier than changing shirts." She didn't guess that I was armed and had just come—as I in my own ignorance supposed—from nipping a prison break just in time.

The Prison Tigers and the Humble Oilers from Brenham were rounding into the ninth inning, with the score at five to one, our favor. The Oiler batter had three balls and two strikes on him as the Tiger pitcher wound up. Before he could let go the ball, three rapid shots came from within the Walls.

The crowd foamed to its feet like soda pop out of a hot bottle. I was going down the grandstand steps two at a time. By the time I reached the street all hell seemed to have sprouted. Thirty to forty shots crackled on the west side of the prison. I raced for my car, with my driver, Luther Berwick, and Tom Tennison, the cashier, hard on my heels.

As we came to the scene of the break, someone called out to me: "A bunch of men went over the wall and some men and women hauled them off in two automobiles." Just then Warden Waid and Night Warden T. T. Easley ran up. I clambered up the long flight of steps outside the wall to the picket stand of the guard C. E. Burdeaux to find out what had happened. I looked below and saw Whitey Walker lying dead. Burdeaux told me that several other prisoners had escaped, taking his .45 pistol, his shotgun, and his Winchester. I didn't tarry with him; I gave him my gun and ran back down the steps to rejoin Waid.

The Death-Cell Break

The two of us rushed inside the Walls to investigate. We found the door of the death house standing wide open. But inside the death house, one of the guards, Lee Brazil, and two Negroes, convict waiters, were locked in cells. Two prisoners, Pete McKenzie and Ira Rector, were still in their cells. But Raymond Hamilton, Joe Palmer, and Blackie Thompson were gone.

More investigation cleared up the story. Brazil had gone through three prison gates, each of them locked, and got the death-cell keys. He returned, unlocking the doors so as to let the cooks bring in the prisoners' food. Just as he opened the death-cell door Charlie Frazier stuck a gun in his back, warned him not to touch the alarm button, and told him to give up the keys without making any trouble. Brazil obeyed.

Frazier then unlocked Thompson's cell, forced Brazil and the two Negro waiters inside, locked the three of them in, and gave a .45 automatic to Thompson. Next he freed Hamilton and Palmer. He asked Pete McKenzie (the killer of Detective Chief Sam Street, of San Antonio) and Ira Rector if they wanted to go along, but both declined.

Frazier, Hamilton, Thompson, and Palmer came out of the death house, marched quietly through the prison yard until they met Whitey Walker, who was also armed with a .45 automatic, and Roy Johnson and Hub Stanley, both of the latter unarmed. In the lower yard they surprised Guard McConnell, marched him around to the machine shop to get a pair of steel nippers. With these they proceeded to the fire-department quarters, where they cut the chain securing one of the fire ladders. Carrying the ladder with them, they advanced on the west-wall picket manned by Burdeaux.

Using McConnell as a shield, they called upon Burdeaux to stick up his hands, which he promptly did. Had Burdeaux simply dropped to his knees to fire a single shot in the air, all would have been different. But as it was, the ladder was put against the wall and Frazier gave the order: "Death-cell men first." Hamilton and Palmer climbed over.

About this time Guard Roberts on the picket just north of Burdeaux saw a man going up the ladder. He opened fire. It was then that the battle started. Raymond Hamilton, who had already gone over the wall and reached the escape cars, was calling back, "Come on, boys! Come on!"

Thompson, Walker, Frazier, and Johnson were all blazing away at Guard Roberts, but he never wavered or slackened fire. With four men shooting at him he just stood there knocking them off as they climbed the ladder. Just as Walker started up the ladder he cried out to Johnson: "God! It looks like we are gone!" In a minute or less he *was* gone—killed by Guard Roberts' fire.

Johnson had been slightly wounded. Hub Stanley had run for cover. Frazier started back up the ladder for the second time, and for the second time was shot off. I instructed Dr. Anderson, our medical supervisor, to look after Frazier's wounds as though the break had never happened. That was our duty.

Although Frazier had handled the gun details, the death-cell break had been planned by Whitey Walker, a member of the Kimes-Ace-Pendelton gang of bank robbers formerly operating in Oklahoma and Texas. This gang had killed District Attorney Holmes, of Borger, for which crime Walker had received a life sentence. His sole objective in the break had been to save his friend and partner, Blackie Thompson, from the chair. He succeeded, though it cost him his life. And Thompson was soon to fall by gunfire. Sheriff Adams, assisted by the Amarillo chief of police and by their deputies, killed him in a running gun fight near Amarillo on December 16, 1934.

Frazier tried to smuggle some letters from the prison hospital in which he bragged that he had done something never done before in releasing three men from the death house. He was correct; he had something to boast about. And the public had something to complain about. Texas had hardly recovered from the days of Clyde Barrow and Bonnie Parker, and now three desperate convicts were at large again.

I could just hear the people saying, "Here we go again!" My newspaper friends, however, rallied to my support. They pointed out the low escape record I had maintained this far and asked the public to withhold judgment on Lee Simmons until I had time to plug up the hole in prison security. Well, I got busy. I had to.

What the newspaper boys kept asking Warden Waid and me was

this: How did three loaded .45 automatics get inside the Walls? How did they? We had no clue. Waid could only guess that they had been thrown over the wall during the baseball game. I refused to guess, although I had my private theory. On the preceding night there had been a prison show, with the public admitted at a charge of twenty-five cents, the proceeds to go to the prison welfare fund. I reasoned that some of our women visitors could have brought in the guns without much fear of being searched, and then at one moment when all the lights except the stage lights were turned off they could have planted the guns in the theater. I even thought I knew who these hypothetical lady gunrunners might have been: the notorious Davis sisters. Dorothy and Estelle Davis had been involved in a number of crimes, and one of them was the friend of Charlie Frazier. I spent a lot of time trying to work out this theory and to connect our prison break with the Davis sisters, but I was completely on the wrong track.

About this time a friend telephoned to tell me that one of our Huntsville guards had been spending money rather freely in Paris, Texas, just a few days after the break. The name of the guard was Jim. I did not know him personally, as I never dealt with guards or other employees except through their superiors. I found out that Jim was in charge of a sawmill operation down in the lower yard near the east gate, where trucks went in and out.

On the basis of this tip I sent for Jim, and with only the two of us in the room tried to impress upon him the seriousness of the break and of its effect upon the prison management's standing with the public. The public, I told him, were wondering whether Warden Waid or Lee Simmons was crooked.

Since Jim had left for Paris the day before the break, I assured him that I felt he had nothing to do with it, and began to question him just to try him out. I soon saw that he was evading me, and I went straight to the point by asking him if he hadn't been pretty free with his money in Paris.

He answered, "Yes, I borrowed $500 from my Uncle John, and I paid the bank $100 and paid $50 on a grocery bill that I owed."

I pretended to believe him and dismissed him to go back to his work. Immediately I called my friend in Paris and asked him to inquire of Jim's Uncle John, a well-to-do farmer, if this was the truth. "Don't do this in the next thirty minutes," I urged, "but do it right now."

In half an hour I had my return call: "Lee, that's a fine old man. He told me that he had heard his nephew was up here, but that he didn't see him or let him have any money."

Things were getting hot. I sent Albert Moore to check up confidentially on Jim. He returned with a full report on my man, including a detailed list of Jim's expenditures. Again I summoned Jim. He was nowhere to be found. Later I found that he had taken time off to go to Madisonville, thirty miles from Huntsville, there to call a lawyer friend who was supposed to see Uncle John and have him confirm the story of a loan. In the first place, the old gentleman was an honorable man and would have no part in the deception. In the second place, it was too late.

When Jim came back, about six o'clock that evening, I was waiting for him with my secretary, W. C. Watson. By now I also had a note written by Jim to Roy Johnson, one of the conspirators. It said: "I'm hot. They think I had something to do with it. Tell the officials the guns came through the ball park. Tell them there is still another gun hid in the ball park. Tell them anything to take the heat off me, and I may be able to help later on."

Without mentioning the note I quietly reassured Jim, saying that perhaps he knew nothing of the break. But I wanted to get all the facts. I handed him a tablet and suggested that he write down the answers as I asked the questions.

He wrote out a story about staying at the Scott Hotel in Dallas Saturday night, going over to Paris Sunday morning, borrowing $500 from his Uncle John. He detailed how he had spent it, without, however, mentioning the $100 he had given a little prostitute in Paris to get her husband a pardon from the penitentiary. When he was done, I said, "Just sign your name to it." He signed.

Then I took from my desk the note he had written to his confederate. The handwriting on the two was the same. I studied Jim's face for a minute; then I opened up on him. All of the contempt and physical revulsion possible rose up in me. Notwithstanding my feelings, I began rather quietly, reminding him that he and I had taken the same oath to do our duty by the state and that under that oath our first duty was to protect the public. This was the great responsibility which he and I had assumed. Then I let loose:

"Three desperate men have gained their freedom, and you helped to free them. I have your note here that you tried to smuggle in. Any ten-year-old child can see that the handwriting is the same. You've double-crossed Warden Waid who gave you a job when you wanted it. The only reason I won't shoot you right now is that I'm not coward enough to do it. You've sat there telling me one lie after another. Your Uncle John never lent you a cent. What have you got to say about it?"

Jim raised both hands. "Mr. Simmons, don't talk to me that way. I'd go out and rob a bank before I'd do a thing like that."

"Rob a bank, hell! Robbing a bank would be honorable alongside what you've done. What have you got to say about it?"

"All I've got to say," he answered, "is I know nothing about it and had nothing to do with it."

"All right," said I. "You go your route and I'll go mine."

I stepped into my secretary's office and told him to get Sheriff Harrington of Grimes County, at Anderson. When the connection was made I told the sheriff that I was bringing a man over to be put in jail and that I didn't want anyone to know who he was. Luther Berwick and I drove our guard over to Anderson and left him in the dingy county jail to think things over.

The next night he weakened in his story. He admitted that for $500 he had smuggled letters into and out of the prison for some unknown parties whom he had met in a beer joint in Madisonville. I got a notary public and for what it was worth had Jim's story taken down and sworn to. But I was sure that it was only part of the story.

The next night Warden Waid and I drove over to Anderson again. Jim had had some more time to think things over. When I appealed to him to come clean, since we had plenty of evidence to convict him anyway, he gave us the whole story.

On the previous Friday night he had received the three guns from persons whom he still claimed he didn't know. On Saturday he had carried the guns to the east gate, riding in on the local wood wagon. He hid the weapons in the office from which he supervised the woodyard and the sawmill. That afternoon Hub Stanley took the pistols to the upper yard to hide them where they would be available on Sunday after the lower yard was closed. Charlie Frazier picked up the three automatics there—fully loaded. And that was how the weapons had been supplied for the death-cell break.

Jim pleaded guilty to the charge of aiding prisoners to escape. He received three five-year sentences from the District Court of Walker County, the sentences to run consecutively for a total of fifteen years in all. He was checked into Huntsville Prison as a convict on August 13, 1934, and served eight years, nine months, and twenty-nine days in prison, with the remainder of his time taken off for good behavior.

CHAPTER 17

Resettling Accounts

Peace officers will never forget the year 1934. I know I never shall. The country was combed for the numerous criminals who were at large. In that year "Pretty Boy" Floyd was finally cornered and killed and John Dillinger was shot as he came out of a Chicago motion-picture theater. I can claim no part in these events, nor in the recapture of Joe Palmer and Raymond Hamilton, in which I was so vitally interested. The credit belongs to the many fine peace officers over the country who participated in the various pursuits.

Joe Palmer was recaptured in Paducah, Kentucky. He had gone to sleep on a railroad embankment, a loaded .45 by his side. Two officers came up and disarmed him by simply kicking his pistol aside. "The Lord had his arm around those two cops," Joe was quoted as saying. "If I hadn't been dead tired for sleep, you'd have to bury them."

Raymond Hamilton went back to his old game of bank-robbing. After he had taken several hundred dollars from a Continental Oil station near Dallas and robbed the First National Bank of Carthage of one thousand dollars, city police and federal officers laid a trap for him in a south Dallas apartment house. He arrived with his brother Floyd at half-past ten one night but escaped amid heavy gunfire.

Two weeks later he and an accomplice broke into the National

Guard Armory at Beaumont and stole eight automatic rifles. The next week Constable John Record and some highway patrolmen engaged Hamilton in a gun battle at McKinney, from which he escaped again. We received a postal card from McKinney canceled the following day. It read: "You be good to L. C. Barrow, Joe Palmer and Jim ————. Jim is not to blame for himself. I could live in Dallas always and not be bothered. Here is hoping Warden Waid and old Lee Simmons never see me again in that damnable place. Have plenty of Whiskey, jack and women. Dam Huntsville.——Raymond Hamilton."

Before this greeting—or this threat—was in the mails, Hamilton was at it again. Fleeing from McKinney, he and his accomplice abandoned their car, kidnaped a farm boy, took his car, and then entered the farmhouse of Will Mays, near Celina, Texas, where they stood guard over the family throughout the night; in the morning they stole another car and proceeded with their three hostages to Fort Worth, where they released the captives.

On March 28, 1935, Hamilton and Ralph Fults robbed a bank at Prentiss, Mississippi, locking five persons in the vault, and taking $1,100.00. A woman was waiting outside in the car for them; a short distance out of town they changed into a second car, provided by two other women who were waiting for them. These were the Davis sisters, of whom I have spoken. The party then separated, the women being subsequently captured by Sheriff Mathison, of Jefferson County, Mississippi. Hamilton and Fults shot their way out of several traps. They kidnaped Sheriff Ennis Crawford, of Covington County, and two of his deputies. As other members of the pursuit posse arrived on the scene they were in turn disarmed and carried along. Later in the day all were released except County Agent M. E. Smith and Ralph Bayliss, a merchant of Prentiss, who were not released until the following day, by which time the fugitives were in Memphis, Tennessee. Hamilton and Fults left the stolen car in Memphis, registered at a hotel, and changed clothes. The National Guard and hundreds of local officers were guarding all highways in the vicinity, but the fugitives eluded them all and returned to Texas, although Fults carried with him a load of shot in his back.

In the railroad yards in Fort Worth, Hamilton fell in with a drifter by the name of Nolan Alred. He sent his new acquaintance to Dallas with a note to a friend. The note was intercepted, and on April 25, 1935, Sheriff Smoot Schmid, of Dallas, who himself had scores to settle with Hamilton, led his deputy Bill Decker and Fort Worth detectives against Hamilton. The criminal was at last cornered and surrendered. He had two automatics on him when he was taken.

And so Raymond Hamilton and Joe Palmer came back to the death house at Huntsville. Their escape had cut off any hope of appeal. Now their only hope was for action by the parole board and the Governor. Palmer seemed to accept his fate without fear or worry, but, as the time of execution drew near, Hamilton became nervous and restless. Palmer tried to quiet him, telling him that he might just as well take the situation as it was and prepare for the ordeal which was to follow.

Newspapermen were eager for an interview with Palmer, but he would not hear of it. He said that he wouldn't believe a newspaperman on oath and that he didn't want them to know anything about his life or family. He said that he had fully intended to be killed rather than captured and electrocuted, for his little sister would have a hard enough time without having it advertised that her brother had been put to death in the electric chair. He finally agreed to talk to reporters, but only after I had given my word that they would protect his family in their stories. The reporters agreed to this, and Palmer was interviewed.

Up to a few hours before his death Hamilton was still hopeful that his lawyers would be able to get his death sentence commuted. Indeed, at four o'clock on execution day he became almost wild, insisting that I call Austin to see what had been done. Taking the prison chaplain, the Reverend Hugh Finnegan, with me for confirmation, I carried out this request. As the chaplain and I left the death house to make the call to Austin, Hamilton called out: "I'm not in the chair yet!"

"No, Raymond," I replied, "but you're mighty close to it, and I think you'd better recognize the fact." Palmer expressed his agreement with this.

When the chaplain and I returned to tell Hamilton that no action had been taken in his behalf by the Governor, he seemed to realize for the first time that he was actually going to the electric chair. Then he settled down and became serious. It was about five o'clock, and he and Palmer, who had been placed in the same cell next to the execution chamber, began to talk things over.

Hamilton's nerve failed him absolutely. Fear took complete charge of him. Only Palmer's exhortations and example brought him at last the courage to adjust himself to what he had to face. He listened to Joe's talk about death and about faith in the future, and Joe really proved himself a father confessor, chaplain, friend, and Good Samaritan to Raymond in his last hour. In that hour Joe showed himself without complaint, rather penitent and forgiving in spirit.

During their trials Joe had tried to take all the blame for killing Guard Crowson in order to save Raymond from the chair. In the finale of their lives he left to Raymond the choice of which of them should go into the execution chamber first. When Raymond would not choose, Joe elected to go last, for he was afraid that Raymond would break down were he to go first. But Warden Waid thought it best to send Joe first, and so it was done.

Before Joe left his cell he took Raymond by the hand, placed his arm around his shoulder, and said: "Good-by, old pal. We're going to be happy in a few minutes. We'll meet on the other side."

Then the steel door was opened, and Warden Waid and I accompanied Joe to the chair. Waid asked Joe if he wanted to make a statement, and he read a paper prepared by him late that afternoon:

Father Finnegan, I have many things to thank you for—chiefly for introducing me to our God. You have always been very patient and kind, and I am well aware I would have exhausted one with less patience.

I have enjoyed your acquaintance for a number of years, and each year I have found something more to admire in you.

I hope I may embrace death as willingly as any of the seventy-five or eighty men you have prepared.

If anyone has injured me, I forgive them whole-heartedly, and ask the pardon of those whom I have injured.

I ask God to accept my ignoble death [here Palmer interpolated: "Let's get that word right, boys; that is 'ignoble' and not 'noble'."] in atonement for my sins.

So far as my death is acceptable to God, I unite it to the sorrows and death of Jesus Christ.

My friends in Christ, I bid you good-by.

Joe then thanked the three newspapermen present for withholding from publication the names of his relatives, saying: "My stock in newspapermen has gone up two or three hundred per cent since you boys didn't mention the names of my relatives and thereby bring disgrace on them."

Somewhere on a foregoing page I have said that if there be such a thing as admiration for a criminal, I had it for Joe Palmer. Yet neither admiration nor misguided sympathy stayed my hand or aroused regret in carrying out what I conceived to be my duty.

Within five minutes after the electrocution of Palmer we took Hamilton into the death chamber. He was an entirely changed person. Crossing himself, he told those in the death cells good-by and said: "Poor Joe! I won't forget his good-by. He told me he would meet me on the other side."

He told Chaplain Finnegan: "I hope somebody will let Mama and Katie (Katie Jenkins, his girl) know how I feel about this. I am happy to die this way, Father. I'm glad to pay my debt in the chair and atone for my sins. I know Katie and Mama will be happy that I feel this way. I hope somebody will get word to them."

Warden Waid told him to take all the time he wanted with the chaplain in getting ready. But he said, "I don't need any more time; I'm ready to go now." And in a few minutes he was gone.

At Hamilton's trial in 1934 he had been asked if he had anything to say before sentence was pronounced. He was moved to say, among other things, "If there's anything to this haunting business, I'm coming back and kick Max Rogers and Lee Simmons clean out of bed." Despite this threat, neither Rogers nor I have yet heard from Hamilton's ghost.

Clyde Barrow and Bonnie Parker had met death at Arcadia on April 23, 1934. Joe Palmer and Raymond Hamilton had been electrocuted on May 10, 1935. I could sleep at nights—for I am not afraid of ghosts—secure in the knowledge that my promise to Guard Crowson had been redeemed in full.

So many conflicting reports have been spread about the activities of Clyde and Bonnie—so much have they become a part of legend—that I want to put into the record the things told me by Joe Palmer while he was in the death cell.

During my tenure as general manager of the prison system, it was my practice about once a week to visit the death cell in the evening and talk with the men about to be electrocuted. I felt that it helped them for me just to come and go, up and down, in front of the seven cells, which were usually all occupied. I would talk with the occupants about different things—never, however, about their individual cases, except as they would ask me questions about their situations or tell me interesting incidents out of their lives.

Never once did I ask any of them why he committed crime or seek information about other crimes attributed to them, although sometimes other officers wanted help in clearing up cases and had asked my help in getting information for them. The prisoners appreciated my attitude and soon found out that I was visiting them solely to see if they were getting along all right, to see if they needed me to do anything for them. I got a real pleasure out of complying with any reasonable request.

If the condemned men wanted to talk, that was their affair. They could do as they chose. Usually prisoners would tell nothing against their partners in crime. Occasionally, however, one would talk, hoping to get help for himself in return. But I stayed free of all this.

A few nights before Palmer and Hamilton were to be executed, I turned to Joe and said, "Joe, you've had quite a varied career; tell me of your experiences." Well, on this particular evening Joe started talking. I saw it was going to be interesting, so I said, "Wait a minute, Joe, if you don't mind; I'd like to write some of this down."

"All right," said Joe, "I don't care."

So I got pencil and paper, and recorded his story, just as I took it down in hurried notes. It is a garbled record, but the interesting part about it is that wherever I tried to check it, it stood up. For example, Joe spoke of being at the Conner Hotel in Joplin, Missouri. He said he had left a grip there with some clothes in it. I later wrote to that hotel, and the clerk replied, verifying Joe's story. He gave me the same list of articles that Joe had given in describing the contents of his luggage. (Oddly enough, the clerk said that he knew me, that his name was Belden, that he had been reared in Sherman, and that his father, O. J. Belden, was an old and dear friend of mine. That also was true.)

The following is an exact transcript of the notes I took of that conversation in the death cell. The sections in quotation marks are Joe's own words.

Platte City, Iowa where Buck Barrow was killed; last time Clyde and Bonnie slept in bed.

Joe quit Clyde and Bonnie at Wichita, Kan., May 4 or 5, 1934; never saw them after. Clyde furnished Joe money at Joplin to pay doctors, etc. Clyde sent Joe on March 28th to see Raymond; needed him to help do a job. This was the second time; then came the third time. Clyde told Joe he meant to kill Raymond.

Henry would not think of trying to play Bonnie any more than he would his sister.

They robbed bank 1st or 2nd of May. Got $700 apiece. Robbed one in Iowa about five or six days after they left there. Just robbed two banks—first one for $3,800; second one about fifty miles from the first one.

Joe and Clyde robbed the last one and Raymond and Bybee the first one.

All four that left Eastham Farm gave $250 each to Mullin for bringing in the guns; Floyd was to give $500 to Yost or to his lawyer; but Floyd beat him out of it. Money ($3,800) split six ways and Joe had given $250 to Mullin; "and then I was sick at the Conner Hotel, Joplin, and was robbed of all of my money but $20.

"Clyde maybe was a murderer and killed folks; but he sure was good to me and the boys, and he toted fair. I was asleep in the bottom of the car when the bank was robbed, but he split the money six ways with us all.

"I was at Methvin's last April, last of April. I would not come south and tried to get them not to come back south. They intended to go over there and do a little hunting and fishing on Black (or Bass) Lake. Talked about bathing suits.

"Bonnie was a fairly good shot—got off in swamps, mostly in Louisiana, and practiced. Clyde gave me two guns 28th and 29th of April, just before we robbed the last bank. One came out of the Eastland Armory, other out of the north.

"Clyde didn't depend on his fighting as much as he did on his driving to escape. He knew he would get killed and couldn't go much longer; figured he would be put on the spot sometime.

"Raymond stole all the cars; best car thief I ever saw. He was fast. Stole Dodge at Vernon; black sedan at DeQueen, Ark.; then next at Fayetteville, a light brown. This one had some dolls hanging in it. Bonnie gave the dolls to two little girls at a filling station around Joplin, Mo. Next stole car at Terrell; and Clyde went in that night to see his mother.

"Clyde figured, after Smoot Schmid shot them up, he would put them on the spot, as he knew he was put on the spot there. Clyde wanted Bonnie to come in, give up; said she wouldn't get the chair. Wanted her to write a letter offering to surrender. Bonnie said she was going to die with him. Wanted to quit at the start, then she couldn't.

"I don't believe Henry [Methvin] gave them away, for he knew where I was—and he would have told on me before he would have on Clyde. His father may have given them away to save Henry.

"I told the guards just to sit still. [Joe had gone back here to the Eastham Farm break]. 'Don't move and there won't be no shooting.' I backed up with my gun in hand till I got close up; then turned and Hamilton was close behind. Methvin was close over to one side, and he was to take the guns, if the guards stuck their hands up. I really thought the guards would stick their hands up. We figured Captain or Dog Sergeant would come up to put Raymond back in squad and they had authority and wouldn't let guards get killed to hold me and they would put them up and let us go.

"Clyde and Bonnie came to Joplin and gave me $150. They didn't have much themselves the day they stole the car in Topeka. Then, April 29th, Bonnie gave me this gray suit; bought it in Memphis, Tenn. They would come out on Junction C, Highway 66, and leave note under bridge; left money there for me twice; same place; prearranged. Left my grip at Joplin; ammunition, lace-leg trousers, leather leggings, pair of shoes, box of old-time .45 caliber."

Bonnie's gun was bought by Clyde to give to Leroy Boyd, chief at Commerce, Okla., as he lost his in the scramble. Clyde and Bonnie said Boyd had more real guts than any man they ever saw.

Never go in a restaurant and sit down and eat; go in and buy hot lunch; had someone always at wheel. And in case they did not get to car, had another place to get to always.

Joe saw picture show at Joplin. Attended Clyde's funeral in Dallas. Saw vandals tear flowers off grave, and "that made me wish I hadn't gone to the funeral. I was watching for you and Frank Hamer, as I thought you might be there. Clyde thought two Rangers were working on him, but he didn't know you was working on him.

Resettling Accounts

"We never saw nor heard of Dillinger or Pretty Boy Floyd and cared nothing about them. I know Tommy Carol, but have not seen him for years.

"When we went running up to the car [Joe was back again on the Eastham Farm break], Mullin said, 'Nobody but Raymond and Palmer going.' Clyde said, 'Shut your damn mouth, Mullin; this is my car—I'm handling this. Three of you can ride back there; guess four of us can make it up here.'

"Left with Clyde, Bonnie—and Raymond in Mullin's lap. Only reason Mullin was there was that Clyde was afraid to turn him loose; afraid Mullin might be putting Clyde on the spot.

"Rembrant, Iowa, where first bank was robbed, little town, 500 population; good farming country. Got all these little banks on time locks now.

"I bought automatic .45 at Shreveport for $20, and Bybee automatic shotgun, $40; and we bought our clothes there."

Clyde, Bonnie and Henry hated Mary O'Dair [Mary O'Dare, *alias* Mary Pitts, Mary Campbell, was Hamilton's girl friend; at the time of his capture at Lewisville, she was under arrest at Amarillo for her part in one of his bank robberies] and called her the "Washerwoman." Mary would get all over Henry—and he wouldn't fool with her at all. The three talked about getting Mary and bumping her off after Raymond got caught, as they thought the law would get Raymond.

"I had been in misery most of the time, especially since Clyde and Bonnie got killed. I knew the law of averages would catch up with me and get me caught.

"Of course I hated it [the death of Clyde and Bonnie] as they had been so good to me—and saved my life once—when they kept Raymond from killing me, about the 1st of February.

"I was asleep in the blankets in the bottom of the car, and Raymond was going to kill me because I had called him a punk blabbermouth braggart, and he had to take it. So Clyde slapped him and cursed him, and went into the ditch and broke the left wheel—near Joplin, about the 1st of February.

"I was in Oklahoma City in the Lee Huckins Hotel—not registered, just sitting in the lobby—and heard over the radio about 10 o'clock about Clyde and Bonnie being killed. I never will forget it. The radio announcer said:

" 'Pardon me, ladies and gentlemen. I have authentic information that Clyde Barrow and Bonnie Parker have just been killed at Arcadia, La., by Captain Hamer of the prison system and others.'

"I had my ticket while in the hotel, and took bus about 1:30 for Tulsa. Stayed in Tulsa day or so, and then came to Dallas on bus for funeral. After the funeral, I went on train out of Dallas to Chicago by way of St. Louis. Came back Wednesday night from Chicago, and that's where I got jumped up. Had spent week at the Fair (the Chicago Century of Progress) and left because there were too many Texas cars there."

Palmer went on to talk to me of Henry Methvin:

He carried me four miles on his back in Iowa when I was shot. He had one shell in his gun and I had two in mine. He said: "If they get us, I will use this one on them and you hold your two—and shoot me with one, and do what you please with the other one."

If a fellow were to sell my father out, like Old Man Methvin did Clyde and Bonnie, I would hunt him up, kill him and carry him over and dump him on their doorstep.

He thought a minute about that, and then:

Don't you know Old Lady Barrow and Mrs. Parker won't stand for that? They will have Henry either killed or put in the electric chair. I know where Henry either killed or helped kill four different people. But I believe in Henry, for he could have turned on me, as he knew exactly where I was. And I think he thought more of Clyde than he did me.

Rambling and incoherent as it was, Joe Palmer's death-cell statement may help some future historian track down the doings of the infamous Barrow Gang.

The Barrow Gang was out of the picture—"liquidated," one would say now. Of those others who had participated in the death-cell break I have already given the score. Whitey Walker was killed in the attempt. Blackie Thompson was shot down at Amarillo on December 16, 1934. The others, Stanley, Johnson, and Frazier were beaten back in the attempt, and Frazier was seriously wounded.

When Frazier recovered I had him put in the death house—not for punishment but for safekeeping, and there he was held until just a day or so before I turned over the management of the system to my successor, Dave Nelson.

Many false reports were sent out by convicts and ex-convicts about how Frazier was being treated. The *Houston Press* got some horrible accounts, involving the fact that all prison officials were afraid of

Charlie Frazier. As a matter of fact, the death cells were more sanitary than most of the others. The prisoners in the death house were fed the best of food and were all allowed to bathe regularly. But they were, undoubtedly, more closely supervised. My sole purpose in keeping Charlie there was to prevent him from escaping. His record, as I have outlined it, abundantly justifies my having him put where he could be kept most safely.

I instructed Warden Waid to give Charlie the same treatment that death-sentence prisoners got, except that Charlie was not to be shaved. His hair was cut regularly, but he soon had a long, flowing beard. If he managed to escape again, I figured that that beard would make him a marked man and that he would quickly be picked up. One night while I was visiting in the death house Charlie asked me if he could talk to me, and I said, "Certainly."

"Mr. Simmons, do you think I'm getting a square deal?"

"What do you mean?"

"Well, other prisoners have escaped and tried to escape, and you never put any of them in the death cell like you have me."

"Charlie," I said, "do you remember the conversation you and I had the night you returned to the penitentiary?"

"Yes."

"Charlie, since that time you've done everything except what you said you were going to do. Now then, it is your privilege to escape, if you can. It is my duty to hold you, if I can!" That ended the conversation.

Some time after that, Warden Waid asked me about taking Charlie out of the death house, saying that he would place him in the cell next to Pete McKenzie and put an extra lock and chain on the door, as he had on Pete's door.

"Frazier is getting along all right," I told Waid. "Just leave him where he is."

"Old Charlie has been begging me to take him out," said Waid with a smile. "And I think he will be perfectly safe with the extra locks."

"No," said I. "Leave him where he is."

Within a few days Waid learned of a tunnel some fifty yards long which had been dug from under a place where more than fifty cords of wood were stacked. It led to the wall right under the picket guard on the south. Waid came to me with a grin. "I see now why old Charlie was feeling so bad and was so anxious to get out of the death cell."

After I had announced my resignation as general manager of the prison system, Waid asked me several times to let him have Charlie shaved. He did not want a new manager coming in and ordering him to do so. But I said, "No, just wait a while and I'll take care of Charlie."

The day before I was to leave, I wrote a letter clearing Charlie's record and had the record clerk furnish me with a copy. I went down to Waid's office and told him to get the barber. We went to Charlie's cell, and Waid had the barber put Charlie in the chair and go to work. He waded in with his scissors and mowed off the long beard to a stubble. Then he proceeded with his razor. When he had finished the job I said to Frazier: "Charlie, I'm leaving tomorrow. Without a request from anyone I have cleared your record—and here it is. I hope you keep it clear and get along all right."

Then I handed him the copy of the clearance. Charlie never said a word. He looked me through and through. As we were leaving the death house, I heard the Warden swear for the first time in all our association: "Did you see how that damned son of a bitch looked at you?" he said. "Wouldn't he have liked to stick a knife into you?"

"Yes, I saw it," I answered. And that was the last of my dealings with Charlie Frazier.

But the law had further interest in the man. On October 8, 1936, the record shows, he was released to the Louisiana authorities, by whom he was tried for the murder of Warden Singleton of Angola Farm. There was a hung jury in that case, however, part of the panel being for a death sentence, while others stood out for life imprisonment. At present Charlie Frazier is still in the Louisiana Penitentiary. But he has not changed his ways. I have in my files a newspaper clipping which reads this way:

CHARLIE FRAZIER STILL A PROBLEM

Baton Rouge, La., Oct. 18 [1936] (AP)—With six new bullet holes in him and a leaden slug in one lung, Charlie Frazier, famed Texas desperado, will remain a "major problem" to the penitentiary officials at Angola, Warden D. D. Bazer said yesterday.

Frazier, who was shot in an attempted prison break last Friday, was sitting up this morning and will be out of the penitentiary hospital in a week or ten days, the warden said. Bazer said Frazier, who led a prison break at Angola in 1933, in which three persons were killed, is unchanged by his experience.

"I believe he'll make another attempt the first chance he gets," the warden declared.

Bazer said the one-time leader of Angola's "Red Hat" Gang was shot six times, instead of three, as first reported, suffering wounds in the back, in the chest near the heart, three in the abdomen and one in the hip.

Four of his wounds were received at close range when he tried to snatch the pistol of a guard riding with him in a truck, the warden said.

The outlaw, serving a life sentence for shooting with intent to murder, plus an additional 18-to-28 year term for burglary, has figured in prison escapes in both Texas and Arkansas.

I could vouch for the fact that Charlie Frazier had been an escape artist in Texas. I suspect that he has more lead in his body than any other living man, even more than Captain Frank Hamer. Hamer got his while enforcing the law; Frazier, while defying it. For hardened character and habitual crime, I never in my career as a law-enforcement officer saw Charlie Frazier's equal. Just to recapitulate, let me tabulate the official record, from the time he entered the Texas Prison System on January 13, 1917, with the prison number 40506, until the date of the death-cell break, when, as prisoner 76683, he was wounded.

1917

January	13–Received at Huntsville
August	11–Escaped
August	13–Recaptured

1918

January	6–Escaped
July	24–Recaptured at Hugo, Oklahoma; returned to Huntsville
October	10–Escaped; recaptured the same day

1920

February 23—Discharged at the end of his term

June   1—Sent up from Arcadia, Louisiana, for robbery and night burglary; sentenced to 8 to 10 years at Louisiana State Penitentiary as R. E. Johnson, number 12525

1922

July   1—Paroled

November 22—Sent up from Oberlin, Louisiana, for burglary, 4-year term; received by Louisiana State Penitentiary as A. W. Adams, number 14189

1925

December 4—Escaped

1926

June   9—Sent up from Marion County, Texas, for robbery with firearms, burglary and theft; 25-year sentence

July   7—Escaped

November 11—Recaptured at Columbia, Tennessee; returned to Huntsville

1927

October   13—Escaped; recaptured the same day

December 26—Escaped

1928

July   27—Sent up from Little River, Arkansas, for murder; life sentence; received at Arkansas State Penitentiary, number 25872

1931

December 23—Life sentence commuted to 21 years by Governor Parnell, of Arkansas

1932

December 23—Received 15-day Christmas furlough from Governor Parnell; never returned

Resettling Accounts

1933

April   12–Sent up from Benton, Louisiana, for robbery, shooting with intent to murder; life sentence plus 18 to 28 years; also charged with remainder of terms due at time of his escape from Louisiana State Penitentiary, December 4, 1925

September 10–Escaped, with eleven other prisoners, from Angola State Prison Farm

November   8–Received at Huntsville, number 76683

1934

January   12–Attempted escape, but prevented from getting over the prison wall

March   9–Escaped main prison; shot by guard while attempting to get to wall with ladder

July   22–Death-cell break; badly wounded

CHAPTER 18

Peace Officers

I FIND LIFE an interesting and eventful journey. But as I look back, certain experiences in my life appear to have been the result of previous planning, although they couldn't possibly have been. Take my getting acquainted with Frank Hamer, for example. I first met him during my first term as sheriff of Grayson County.

A sheriff often has to be in Austin on official business—getting requisitions for prisoners and so on. I normally made it a practice while in the capital to visit the office of the Adjutant General, where Captain W. R. Aldrich was quartermaster of the Ranger force. And then, too, I liked to visit with the old-time sheriff of Travis County, George Mathis. Sheriff Mathis was always ready to help his brethren over the state in any way he could, and he had many calls for help.

Having myself been elected sheriff without any background as a peace officer, I felt that I needed advice, and I sought it from those in whom I had confidence. After all, experience is the greatest teacher, whether it is crime you have to deal with or anything else. So I used to hunt up men whom I could trust, and I learned from them.

Thus it was that I met such seasoned officers as Captains Brooks, Hughes, and Rogers, besides many other famous men, in the office of Captain Aldrich. Many is the hour I sat in amazement and admiration, listening to their accounts of daring and almost unbelievable exploits. Yet never once did I hear any of them boast of himself or of his deeds. Their stories would usually be brought out by one man's asking another about some happening, and somebody on hand would join in. Maybe it would be Pete Crawford or Arch Miller, or somebody else—and then the story would begin to unfold. Those hours were worth much to me, and in them I learned much that guided me in my new duties as a peace officer.

Among the group I frequently noted a young six-footer who had little to say. He was a good listener, but I noted that when he did enter the conversation the old-timers all listened. The tactiturn young man was Frank Hamer. At the time, of course, I didn't dream that he and I would ever have business together, nor did I guess how fateful would be that business in years to come.

Hamer had a way of calling the turn. For instance, when the State Bankers' Association offered a $5,000 reward for bank-robbers, "alive or dead," Hamer told them that the offer would generate crime. Time soon proved he was right. And I myself was later to be caretaker of one of the criminals provoked to crime by that $5,000 reward.

A former officer hired three Mexicans, supposedly to work for him out in the country. Just at the break of day, he let them out of his car in front of a small bank, gave them a small sack of tools (a hammer, some chisels, and a few other such articles), and instructed them to wait there a few minutes for him. In a few minutes, sure enough, he returned, after having driven around the block, and opened fire on the innocent Mexicans with an automatic shotgun. He killed two of them, but, unfortunately for him, one victim lived to tell the tale, and when he did tell it on the witness stand, the jury believed him. The outcome was that, instead of receiving $15,000 for three dead "bank-robbers," the murderer got 99 years in the penitentiary. And that is where I met him.

But to go back to Frank Hamer. He was born of Virginia and Tennessee parentage in Wilson County, Texas, on March 17, 1884. The Hamer family moved to San Saba County in 1890, and there Frank grew to manhood. That county was then, as now, chiefly a livestock area, and Frank came naturally by his love of good horses and his fondness for the free, open life of the cow country.

By the time he was seventeen, Hamer was a good cow hand. While working on the neighboring ranches, he became a top hand. More than once he was called upon to assist in running down and capturing transient stock thieves. He turned out to be quite good at this sort of thing; sometimes he did it without being asked, acting completely on his own initiative.

Dependable Rangers were in demand at the time; and, when Sheriff Parker recommended young Hamer to Ranger Captain J. H. Rogers, Frank was enlisted on April 12, 1906, as Ranger Private Hamer, aged twenty-two. The career then started will long add luster to the record of the finest group of peace officers that ever existed in this nation.

Frank was not precisely of the old school of Rangers. But he followed right after them, took in the lessons he learned from them, and adapted their craft and experience to the rapid changes in criminal techniques which came with the automobile and the radio. Rangers in pioneer times dealt almost entirely with border outlaws and frontier Indians. Hamer had to deal with men of violent blood who sometimes ranged a thousand miles in twenty-four hours. In Hamer's generation, crime had gone to town, in fact, chiefly to the cities.

To be sure, the border was still there. Borders are always a field for thieves and smugglers and fly-by-night offenders of many sorts. Hamer had considerable contact with those who took advantage of the border in the Pecos country, and he had many a brush with death in the wilds. Indeed, so many were these encounters that I shall not try to go into detail about them. Hamer would not thank me if I did. You see, his outstanding characteristic is sincere avoidance of all appearance of seeking notoriety or praise. Let me give you an example of that quality.

As I have already told you, when Clyde Barrow and Bonnie Parker were killed, I hurried to the scene. Hamer and I were in our hotel room afterward, when the telephone rang at midnight. It was New York, calling Captain Frank Hamer. Hamer answered and what I heard was something like this: "Yes, this is Hamer————Yes ———— National Broadcasting Company?———— How's that?———— A thousand dollars for a few minutes' talk over the radio?———— Hell, no!————I won't do it.————What do you think I am? ———— Hell, no!"

He slammed the receiver on the hook, cussing a blue streak and mad as a hornet. I know men who would have leaped at the publicity, to say nothing of the thousand dollars. But not Hamer; he's not built that way.

In news articles and magazine stories about Hamer you will read that he was engaged in thirty-five to fifty gun battles and has been wounded thirty-three times. Nobody can get him to talk about such things. My guess is that he has engaged in about twenty-three serious shooting scrapes. Several times they almost got him, and he still carries surplus lead in his body.

On those rare occasions when he talks freely about his life, Frank Hamer is fascinating company. One of the most interesting visits of my whole life began at 9:00 P.M. in Hamer's hotel room and continued until 5:00 A.M. the next day. He took me into his confidence that night and told me, among other things, about an assassin's attack upon him that came near costing him his life at the age of sixteen. The family doctor stood by Frank's bed and told his father, "I hate to say it, but the boy is not going to make it."

"I knew he was wrong," Hamer told me that night. "I knew I was going to make it, but I couldn't say it, because I was so far gone I couldn't talk. I could hear, but I couldn't speak. But, you see, I had talked to 'The Old Moster' about it, and I knew I was going to get well." It was the first time I had ever heard Hamer speak in such terms, and I was surprised.

"Lee," he said to me earnestly, "I've done a lot of things, as you know; but, from that day to this, I've never gone to sleep a single night without first I have talked with 'The Old Moster.' "

I have done my best to get Frank to write the story of his life. Once or twice, I thought I had persuaded him, but so far I have had no luck at all. (*The Texas Rangers*, by Walter Prescott Webb, includes much of the career of Frank Hamer and is a deserved tribute both to him and to that great organization, the Texas Rangers.) I believe the full story of Frank Hamer, boy and man, would be one of the most fascinating accounts of crime and law enforcement ever recorded. I have known many men of his calling, but in my judgment no man in modern times has equaled the deeds of this man in protecting society and putting down crime. A large part of his secret is that

Hamer has the confidence and respect of the underworld. When Frank Hamer gives his word, he keeps it, even if it costs him failure on a case. Criminals understand a man like that.

Now I want to tell you about another remarkable peace officer. One of the few changes I made when I took over the Texas Prison System was to appoint Walter Waid to be warden, in place of E. F. Harrell. I had no quarrel with Warden Harrell, who was a good man. But I felt that he was not well qualified either to handle prisoners or to gain the co-operation of the many employees of the prison management. Waid met all my demands and satisfied all my expectations.

Walter Waid had been city commissioner of the small town of Wolfe City and later its city marshal for a number of years before he became sheriff of Hunt County in 1924, a post he held for four years. As Warden of the Texas Prison System, he set a record which is unsurpassed as far as I know. Prison guards soon learned he was a square-shooter, with no favorites. Convicts also, except for a troublesome few, respected him. They found that he treated all with equal fairness and that he wanted to be of help to men who, by reason of their situation, were unable to help themselves. Every prisoner who went to Waid with a justifiable complaint got an honest hearing.

Waid liked sports and heartily enjoyed his part in encouraging baseball, rodeo, and legitimate recreation within the prison area. The school program was his special delight, and he liked to show visitors through our school system, manned as it was almost entirely by the prisoners themselves.

The new Warden proved that he knew how to pick a trusty. Of course, no prisoner could be made a trusty without my approval as general manager. That was the rule. A convict would come up recommended for trusty by the warden or the farm manager or the cashier, as the case might be; then the decision was mine. While I did not approve all recommendations, I seldom turned one down. And after Waid had completed a year as warden, I never failed to approve his recommendations. I had good reason for my confidence in Waid and in the men he chose.

Waid had a system in presenting candidates for trusties. This was to call me down to his private office, or bring his man to mine. Then the first thing he would say to the prisoner-candidate would be something like this: "Now, I can't make you a trusty; there's only one man who can. To become a trusty is the highest honor a prisoner can obtain. When you become a trusty, you are in line for a parole or a pardon. Mr. Simmons has confidence in me; and if you betray me, he will lose confidence in me—and you have hurt the chances of other convicts to become trusties: you have betrayed them, too.

Then he would say to me, "Mr. Simmons, I don't believe this old boy will go back on me, and I am willing to risk him."

Then he would turn back to his man and say, "You'll stay with us and prove to us that we're making no mistake in trying to help you, won't you?"

I have seen convicts stand there and actually cry as they vowed: "I swear I'll never go back on you!" And most of them kept their oath.

The reason I have told you all this is to justify my statement that I believe Waid's record will never be surpassed. Out of 1,991 convicts that became trusties on his recommendation for the full five years after 1931, only 19 betrayed his confidence. Think of that!

Convicts who had been confined for years without any privileges were allowed on the outside, driving trucks all over Texas, delivering license plates for automotive vehicles and shoes and canned goods from our industrial unit, and riding horses on the farms as they looked after the livestock. Besides these, there were cooks and house-boys employed by the officials outside the Walls.

The record of these trusties was due in part to the general program of the prison board under the new regime, but it was due chiefly to Warden Waid's wonderful insight into prisoner character and to his gift for inspiring confidence. He made the men believe he was their friend, as indeed he was. Amid the thousand problems that confronted me in the prison system, Warden Waid's assistance was priceless. His co-operation in all things was instant and complete. I could not have had a better warden.

A third peace officer of outstanding service during my time was Bud Russell. I suppose Uncle Bud was personally known to more enforcement officers in the United States than any other man. He is worthy of a far longer account than I can give of him here.

Russell was born at Blum, Texas, on the Hill County farm and ranch of his father. As a young man his first employment was on the famed Matador Ranch in west Texas, where he worked for two years. Upon his return home he was elected constable, serving for five years. In 1908 he was appointed assistant to John Luther, transfer agent of the Texas Penitentiary. When Luther was succeeded by J. V. Cunningham, Russell was continued as assistant. In 1912 Russell became transfer agent himself, in which capacity he served the state for nearly forty years.

In that period Russell handled 115,000 prisoners. They were of every type, from the mildest to the wildest specimens known to crime. From time to time he gathered them from the 254 counties of Texas and brought them down to Huntsville. Moreover, from practically every state in the union, he brought back to us escaped convicts to the number of some 4,000 and more.

During these nearly forty years, Russell lost one prisoner by escape, a Mexican named Carlos Brazil. Bud and his assistant, J. J. Small, were bringing in thirty-six convicts from El Paso in their two transfer trucks, en route to Huntsville. They had arrived at Abilene rather late at night and were unloading their charges at the Taylor County jail when Brazil broke away. He had picked the lock on the chain to which he was fastened, so that he was free from the other prisoners.

Russell, a crack shot, could easily have killed Brazil. Instead, he shot him in the foot and for his forbearance suffered the embarrassment of losing the one prisoner of his whole career. How great was that embarrassment you may judge from the fact that, the morning after Brazil's escape, I received the following telegram:

Abilene, Texas

Lee Simmons
General Manager
Texas Prison System
Huntsville, Texas

Have lost my first prisoner. Am tendering my resignation.

Bud Russell
Transfer Agent

Although Russell was in dead earnest, his message was so amusing to me that for the first and only time in my tour of prison duty I got

Peace Officers

"smart." You see, I knew Russell well and believed in him, both as a man and as an official. I had turned over to him many prisoners while I was serving as sheriff of Grayson County. I had heard him make many interesting and sensible talks at the state conventions of peace officers, advocating total abstinence by all peace officers as an example to youth. So it struck me as very funny that I should get such a telegram from such a man; for if Bud had lost all his prisoners, instead of only one, I should have known that Bud Russell was in no way to blame. Accordingly, since I would not be in my office when Russell got in with his prisoners at the Walls, I told my secretary to take down the following on a telegram blank and hand it to Bud when he arrived. It read:

Bud Russell
Transfer Agent

Refuse to accept your resignation. Prefer to discharge you. Please go to hell.

Lee Simmons
General Manager

Of course, I never actually sent any such telegram as that. As it turned out, however, I got the worst of it, for when Bud came in, he took the message, stuck it in his pocket, and promptly left for west Texas again to pick up some more prisoners for Huntsville. At a stopover town in west Texas, the customary crowd gathered around Bud and his "one-way bus."

Naturally, the local newspaperman wanted to talk about the escape of Brazil, and Uncle Bud obliged him by solemnly pulling out my "telegram." The newspaper printed it, and other newspapers did likewise. Everyone obliged by sending me copies of the stories. I never tried to fake a telegram again.

Uncle Bud's helper at times—and a very capable one, too—was his wife. Whenever he had women prisoners to transport, he would generally take Mrs. Russell along with him on the trip. It was Bud's way of protecting his reputation. It showed also his common sense.

While Russell always had a little smile on his face, even when handling prisoners, only his closest associates knew how keenly he appreciated a joke. On one occasion, while he was taking a bunch of prisoners on the train, Mrs. Russell was in charge of the five women in the gang. It was necessary to lodge the prisoners in the Harris County jail at Houston between trains, and the jailer told the women in the group to stand to one side, which they did. Looking up, the jailer saw Mrs. Russell standing apart, and he said to Uncle Bud, "Who is this woman here?"

"I don't know," said Uncle Bud, "I never saw her until I picked her up on this trip."

The jailer then ordered her to get over with the rest. Mrs. Russell, of course, did nothing of the sort. It looked as if trouble was about to blossom out all over the place, so Uncle Bud finally admitted, "That's my wife." The jailer didn't shoot him, but I understand he felt like it.

For many years the only means of transporting prisoners was by train. I have known Russell to handle twenty-five to forty or even more prisoners in this manner—frequently with no assistance except that the sheriff or deputy would usually help Uncle Bud load them on the train.

Once his prisoners were aboard, Uncle Bud would handle them himself. He could take them off the train and even change trains with them and still not have the slightest mishap. How he could do all this, I never could understand. He seemed somehow to have "the feel of the situation." He told me he could tell when trouble was brewing. Often, he said, all he had to do was to call out: "Look out, down there. Don't get any wrong ideas into your heads!"

That seemed to quiet them down, he said. Of course, Russell early acquired a reputation by convict "grapevine," and part of his success was due to that. Prisoners knew in advance that he would treat them fairly and look after their needs, but they also knew that he would stand for no foolishness. Above all else, they knew he was determined to deliver them to Huntsville, once he headed that way. Because of this respect which he had earned, it was quite rare for Uncle Bud to have to "work over" a prisoner.

Harold V. Ratliff, of the Associated Press, filed this dispatch from Blum for the Sunday, May 28, 1944, papers:

Peace Officers

Blum, Texas. (AP)—Towering Bud Russell, rugged individualist whose favorite expression to tough guys was, "You're just forty years too late," won't be seen again with his "one-way wagon" in which he traveled a distance of more than fifteen times around the world.

Uncle Bud, known to every peace officer—and most everybody else—in Texas, has retired to the life of a stock farmer, after nearly forty years of service with the State's prison system, three decades of which he spent as chief transfer agent.

"Thirty-nine years and nineteen days," he said a little sadly, at his home here, in formally announcing that he had handed in his resignation because "I haven't much time left, at best, and I want to spend the rest of my life with my family; besides, there's a lot of work to be done around here now, and we can't get any help."

Russell and his one-way wagon traveled 3,900,000 miles. And from the county jails of Texas and other States, he delivered 115,000 persons to the prison system.

Perhaps it should be 114,999, because Uncle Bud lost one man. A little apologetically, he tells about it—about the little Mexican who hid a hacksaw in the sole of his shoe, cut the chain that bound him, and escaped when the one-way wagon stopped at Abilene. But Russell had the satisfaction of taking the Mexican to the penitentiary thirty-two days later, after he was captured by the border patrol while trying to get back to his native land.

Uncle Bud could have prevented even that escape, had he wanted to take a chance. He shot the Mexican in the foot and, when that failed to stop him, could have brought him down with another bullet (because Russell is a crack marksman) had the fugitive not run into a group of Negroes in a church. Russell didn't figure an escaped convict was worth the risk of hitting an innocent Negro.

Russell retired at the age of 69, which he certainly doesn't look. He quits one of the toughest jobs of them all, still with his humor intact, and with ill will toward none—not even the prisoners who gave him trouble.

Uncle Bud took a vacation in March, then on April 1 began a leave of absence with the understanding that he could return to his job any time he saw fit in six months. He didn't see fit, and Major D. W. Stakes, general manager of the prison system, regretfully accepted his resignation.

Letters came when the news spread. Typical of them was that from Lee Simmons, former general manager. Simmons said Russell had rendered a service that "has not and never will be surpassed by any State official."

Russell never killed a man, shot only two. One was the little Mexican who escaped, and the other was a prisoner he fired on at Temple to prevent his running away.

"Just creased his temple," Uncle Bud recalled. "He wasn't hurt, but he sure thought he was."

When he started to work with the prison system, he transported convicts on the trains and could take as high as 80 at a time. Then he switched to trucks, the capacity of which was from 26 to 28.

And did he watch those pennies for the State! He spent an average of nine cents a meal for prisoners by buying wholesale, and drove a truck 223,000 miles on two sets of tires.

"Of course meals are a little higher right now," he said. "Run from ten to fifteen cents."

Russell has handled practically all the noted prisoners of Texas—Clyde and Buck Barrow, Raymond Hamilton—just about everybody except Bonnie Parker. For some reason, Bonnie never made Bud's one-way wagon.

But they were all the same to Bud Russell. They had to behave themselves while they were on his truck, and, when they did, he had a word of praise. But he never really got mad at a prisoner until he mistreated a relative or annoyed the citizenship. He told the tough guys, "You're just forty years too late, if you think you are tougher than I am," and kept an eagle eye on his flock of jail birds every minute of the way.

That he was confident of his marksmanship was attested when he told an officer who examined his gun and found only one bullet: "Well, I came for only one prisoner, you know."

Before I close this chapter, I want to say a word about my prison guards. They were wonderful fellows. Their bravery and faithfulness protected the safety of the public and guaranteed the safekeeping of the prisoners in my general care. I owe much to them all. I have already told you of some of these stout-hearted, straight-shooting lads; but there is one family of which I ought to make mention here.

As far back as 1911, while I was sheriff, I took a prisoner to Huntsville, where I met two or three guards, all named Mayes. Later, as a member of the prison board, and still later, as general manager, I met yet other guards of the same family name.

There were seven Mayes brothers in the service, all of them quiet, unassuming, gentlemanly fellows. I came to know several of them quite well, and our acquaintance deepened into friendship, and friendship into downright admiration. Yet I never could understand how it came about that seven brothers should spend almost their whole lives guarding convicts.

Uncle Sam Mayes, for instance, began working as a guard on April 23, 1879, and remained in that job for fifty-three years. I did not get a detailed report on all seven brothers, but it is said of them that not one ever lost a "rank" prisoner, that is, a prisoner who was not a trusty.

At the time I resigned as manager of the Sherman Chamber of Commerce, on April 1, 1930, I was receiving a salary of $8,000 a year, with the privilege of looking after my own personal business. From that I went to the position with the prison system at $8,000 a year, with no time to look after my private business matters. Moreover, when the depression hit, all salaries were cut, and mine was cut considerably. My private affairs went from bad to worse, as I have already indicated. But I drew dividends from my work with and for the prisoners. Read this letter and you will see what I mean.

Huntsville, Texas
Jan 1, 1935

My best of oner to you cawrnel Simmons this is spiffie an warden wade an all the are fishell of the sisterm that has a say over me to let you Know how much I does preasih the xmex that youl prepared for me and not me a lone but all my en mates andwe Joied it so muc an I my silf so much and tell I dont Know how much oner I can gave youl but I will give all I does Know how the best of my Knorlege and to all of yours familys to   So I does hope I will have a chance to shore youl that I am not as bad as I have been sad to be and to I am sorry over my misstakes in this life and hope I can over com it with all of you here and elce whaire this has been a lessing to me the rest of my life I may live. I meain to be a better man here and elce whair Kind sir and I meain to shore to youl I can live it Kind sir so verry well sir yours umble sevent JOHN ROBERTSON
#43,257

Even if John Robertson's letter was not the best of testimonials to the prison education system, it was a spontaneous and unrehearsed expression of more than yuletide good feelings. I like to think it typified a spirit which had become prevalent among a large majority of the convicts under my administration.

CHAPTER 19

Prison Miscellany

I ALWAYS LIKED Bill Sterling, who once served with the Rangers. But I had one run-in with him. We had started a program of cattle-dipping on the Ramsey Farm, the 15,088-acre farm down in Brazoria County. Captain Jackson was farm manager, and he was supervising the dipping of cattle to rid them of ticks. As the representative of the law in that section, the Sanitary Commission Ranger backing up the dipping program knew that there had been a good deal of cattle-stealing going on in that area, the stolen animals being sold to "wet" butchers in Houston. So he laid a plot to see if he could catch some of my men, who he thought were stealing the state cattle. He got an ex-convict to approach Captain Jackson's livestock man with a proposition. The stockman, according to this scheme, was to pen up a few head of state cattle, and then outside parties would come in, get the cattle, and take them off to the slaughterhouse in Houston.

The stockman reported to Jackson, who advised him to "sit right in with them and go ahead." So the stockman passed the word to the ex-convict. In a few days the outsiders came to the stockman with twenty dollars in earnest money. We didn't know then that the brains of the plot were supplied by the Ranger, who was trying to run down the thieves, to be sure, but who, as it happened, didn't like Captain Jackson, either. Meanwhile, Jackson ordered six or seven head of cattle penned up at the large dipping-vat pens about a mile and a half from the highway. The site was chosen so that the thieves would have to come inside the farm property for the pickup.

There was a culvert at the place where the rustlers would have to leave the farm to get back on the highway. When they came out with the cattle in the truck, they found some logs had been placed across the road. As they stopped Captain Jackson rose up on one side and Brazoria County Sheriff John McKinney rose up on the other. With guns trained on the thieves, the officers shouted, "Put 'em up!" Then the sheriff took his prisoners off to jail—the livestock inspector along with the rest—and locked them up.

"Lee," said Bill Sterling (he was adjutant general of Texas then) in a hurried telephone call to me shortly thereafter, "what's the matter down there?"

"Nothing, Bill," said I. "Nothing at all. We've just got a bunch of cattle thieves in jail. That's all."

"Well," said Bill, "I'm going to send Frank Hamer down there to see what we can do about it."

"Frank," I told Hamer when he arrived, "Bill and the Governor got exactly what they deserved. It was coming to them. If they thought there was cattle-stealing going on on Ramsey Farm, they should have taken it up with me. I am responsible down here, and I'm the man to deal with. If they were afraid to take it up with me and thought Captain Jackson was in on any thievery, then they ought to have taken it up with the sheriff of Brazoria County."

The upshot of all this was that old Bill Sterling gave me a commission as a Ranger. I've still got it. Later on, I went in to see Governor Ross Sterling and told him just what I had told Bill, except that I added that if Captain Jackson was stealing any cattle, he surely was doing a fine job for the state, seeing that he had several hundred more head than when I took charge of the prison system. Everything about it was all right with Governor Sterling. He treated me fine. He and Bill and I were friends.

I was never closely associated with a finer man or a more courteous gentleman than W. A. Paddock, chairman of the prison board. He gave freely of his time and money for the welfare of our prisoners.

Like Chairman Baker, who preceded him, he accepted his responsibilities with all seriousness.

The trouble with both Paddock and Baker was that they knew about crime and criminals mainly from hearsay and theory rather than from practical experience. Paddock, in particular, was strong for our welfare program, schools, shows, and rodeos. He often took Mrs. Paddock with him to show her what we were doing in the system.

Now, you never know what to expect from a convict. One morning an ex-convict appeared at Mr. Paddock's office in the Second National Bank Building in Houston and told him how well he was getting on since his parole. He was married, he said. His wife was in the car in front of the bank, and he wanted Mr. Paddock to come down and meet her.

Kindly, benevolent Mr. Paddock consented, and, when they got to the automobile, the ex-con introduced his wife and insisted that Mr. Paddock get into the car, saying that he wanted to take him a few blocks to show him how he was fixed up at a tourist camp. Mr. Paddock obliged him by crawling into the front seat. They had barely got going when the "ex" stuck a gun in Paddock's ribs and told him to "stick 'em up." He threatened to pull the trigger if Paddock said a single word. At the prison board meeting later on, Paddock told his story:

"I felt a little suspicious when the convict insisted on my getting into the car, but I hated to refuse him. Immediately he pushed the gun in my side. I begged him several times to take that gun away, as I was afraid it might go off accidentally. The man was driving through heavy traffic all the time with only one hand.

"He drove out east of Houston about fifteen miles on the Beaumont Highway and turned off into the timber several hundred yards. There he ordered me out of the car. He told me that he had written out a check for a thousand dollars and that at first he had meant to take me into the bank and make me cash it, but he got afraid it mightn't work, so he had decided on this plan instead.

"Then he made me give him what money I had. Next he told me to give him my watch. I took my watch out and held it in my hand; I began to plead with him to let me keep that watch. My father gave it to me when I was twenty years old. So he let me keep the watch.

"He ordered me to march in front of him farther on down into the timber. I refused to do it. I told him that I had done nothing except what he had asked me to do, but I wasn't going any further. You see, I felt sure that if I should go on into that timber, the "ex" would kill me so that nobody could identify him later on.

"Well, he told me to stand right there for thirty minutes and not look up. And he drove off with his lady companion." (Paddock said it that way, "lady companion.") "After a while," continued Paddock, "I walked back to the highway and stood there a good while trying to thumb my way back to Houston."

And there he was, just about the principal civic and charitable worker in all Houston—and a millionaire into the bargain—standing by the roadside trying to thumb a ride. At last a friend came along, recognized him, and picked him up. When Paddock got into town, he reported to officers—and afternoon newspapers had headlines, and big ones, too.

A day or so after all this, a burglary was committed by Mr. Paddock's "friend" and another "ex." In their flight across the state in a stolen car, the two fell to quarreling. Just after they had crossed Red River north of Denison, the partner threw Paddock's highjacker out of the car while driving at high speed. The injured man was picked up by a passer-by and confessed his identity. He was taken to Denison, and Sheriff T. Binford came after him the next day. The physician in attendance said he thought the man could be moved without harm, so Binford carried him back to Houston, where, however, he died in a day or so.

When Chairman Paddock had finished his story of his experience, he wound up vigorously: "A convict like that—you ought to take him out in the Gulf, tie a rock around his neck, and pitch him overboard and let him drown!"

Dave Nelson, a capable prison board member, who always saw the funny side of life, promptly came back at Paddock: "You damned, hard-hearted old cuss, you! I move that the Chairman buy the dinner for us all. Who ever heard of a prison board member having that much money? He ought to have lost it!"

Mr. Paddock took us all down for a fine lunch; and, while he never did believe in mistreating prisoners, after this experience his attitude changed considerably in the matter of prison treatment and prison management.

In the discharge of his duty a prison officer is governed by law. He cannot allow personal feelings to enter too largely into what he does. But a man can't keep all sympathy out of his work. For example, I read one day in the newspaper that we were to receive as a prisoner a very prominent attorney whom I had known for many years. He had graduated in law with my brother's class during my freshman year at the University of Texas. I had visited in his home and had on occasion escorted his sister to literary-society meetings and other events. I shall not give his name.

This man was quite an orator and did well in his profession. He was elected district attorney and served his district admirably. Later he was appointed judge of the Court of Civil Appeals. But he became an alcoholic, and that ruined him. While under the influence of liquor, he committed a terrible crime. When he sobered up, he found that he had murdered a young stenographer.

After a long legal battle in the courts by friends in his behalf, he was given a three-year sentence. When he arrived in Huntsville, the Warden asked me what I thought we should do with him. Friends had brought him over and had delivered him to us, as was frequently the custom when the sheriff in charge would permit it.

I didn't see this prisoner for the first day or so, and my first meeting with him was out in the prison yard one morning. I did not stand upon my position but, instead, shook hands with him and called him by his first name. He called me "Lee," to which I took no exception. However, when I met him in the yard the next day, he apologized for calling me "Lee." He said it would not happen again, as he knew that he should recognize my official status. And thereafter he did.

The man was a physical wreck and some sixty years of age when we received him, but I knew in advance what I meant to do with him. I turned him over to Red Reynolds, and Reynolds made him an instructor within the Walls. But there was so much complaint against him there that his prisoner-pupils would not have anything to do with him.

Prison Miscellany

Red asked to have him transferred to the Harlem Farm, which had the best of all our schools, provided by this time with a commodious classroom. Accordingly, we transferred the man, but in a little while Red came to me and said that his teacher was in trouble again. Harlem convicts would have nothing to do with him. They were staying away from school, as was, of course, their privilege. Resentment, you will readily understand, was directed at this sheltered, favored man because he had been given only three years for murder, whereas the common run of convicts received from five to ten years for far less serious crimes.

What was to be done? I transferred the lawyer to the Ferguson Farm, where Manager Martin placed him in the kitchen as a flunky, for, indeed, he was incapable of any real physical labor. I shall never forget my visit a few days later, when I walked into Ferguson Farm kitchen. There, he sat, near the stove, peeling Irish potatoes—just an old "knockout," as we called men of his type.

Once a man of ability and courage, possessed of a moving mastery of words, he could have gone high and far, perhaps to the post of attorney general and then on to the office of governor or senator, for all I know. He could have rendered God knows what service to his state and nation. Yet there he was, peeling potatoes.

I was troubled all day about that man. He worried me. By the time I got back to Huntsville, I had made my decision. I ordered him back to the Walls, determined to make some use of him. For the time being, the Warden made a helper out of him at the prison commissary. Meanwhile, I prepared to employ him in a project which I had long had in mind.

Our prisoner's health had by this time improved considerably. Good food, early to bed and early to rise, no liquor, regular habits— prison routine had been good for his body, at least. I had him brought to my office, where I outlined what I had in mind. He responded immediately to my idea, and I put him to work at the one thing which he could do supremely well.

The Texas Prison System owned at this time some 73,000 acres of land and had held most of it for a long period of years. No one knew where the lines and corners were or what kind of title the state had to these lands. We set up a small office next to that of Tom Tennison, the cashier, and dug out the old abstracts of title from the huge safe where they had reposed. Then we put our convict-attorney to work on our land titles.

The service thus rendered, under Tennison's direction, could not have been surpassed, I am sure, by any legal firm in the state. Our prisoner was sent as a trusty to the various county seats, where, with the aid of various county officials, he brought those abstracts up to date. Meanwhile, I organized a surveying crew, and the State Board of Water Engineers appointed a capable engineer to help us. Thereupon we started out to locate the corners and the lines of the state's prison lands.

I had Mr. Johns, of the construction department, make some five hundred 3-foot concrete markers with "T.P.S." inscribed on all four sides of each marker. By the time we finished the job, every acre of the 73,000 was identified both on the ground and on the map, with a permanent marker at every survey corner and at appropriate intervals between corners. The state recovered about 800 acres of land in this operation, much of it an extension of the Ramsey Farm. Some of it was later leased for oil exploration, and the state received, and is still receiving, good revenue from this source.

So the old "knockout" did a good job, after all. I am not forgetting, however, that all he did could not return to stricken parents the lovely girl whose life he had taken.

I was a great admirer of Governor Pat Neff. Honest, fearless, he believed in obeying the law personally and in enforcing it officially. I used to tell him that I thought he knew more about the penitentiary and did less about it than any other governor I knew of. He blue-penciled the appropriation for the Pardon and Parole Board; and mighty few prisoners received clemency during his administration. If anything, he was worse about that than Governor Dan Moody. Both were wrong, in my judgment. They had been district attorneys, and their policy was, in the main, that when a man was sent up he should serve his full term.

But this does away with hope; and when hope is destroyed we are

Prison Miscellany

in a bad way. My theory of managing prisoners called for a liberal parole policy based on merit alone. That establishes a lively hope of reward and results in better conduct and better chances for rehabilitation. It was for these reasons that I urged a policy of credit for overtime work and a consistent parole program favoring those who earned it. The record under that policy justified it.

But I want to give Governor Neff credit for one act of clemency. He visited the prison farms frequently and especially enjoyed his visits with Captain and Mrs. Flanagan on the Central Farm. Their hospitality was well known, and they entertained more visitors than did any other farm managers within the system. On one of the Governor's visits an old Negro insisted that "Cap'n Buck" let him talk to His Excellency about a pardon, to which Flanagan agreed, for the old fellow had been with him a long time.

Old Mose approached the Governor with hat in hand and bowed again and again. Then he told his troubles: He had been in prison a long time, had given a lot of trouble for several years and had escaped a time or two; but he had changed his ways, and "the cap'n knows Ah's been a good Nigguh foh a long time, an', please, Moster Governor, won't you he'p dis ol' Nigguh convict?"

The Governor asked him how much time he had, and the old man replied that he had two life sentences to serve, and that he just didn't see how he could ever make it. And then the big-hearted Governor said: "Mose, I'll tell you what I'll do. When I get back to Austin, I'll take one of those life sentences off you."

The old Negro jumped into the air as best he could and exclaimed: "Bless de Lawd! Ah knowed if evah Ah seed de big Governor, he'd he'p me!"

Among latter-day criminals of note who passed through my hands were Tom Ross, Milt Goode, and Louis Dodd. Tom and Milt had been sent up for killing two cattle inspectors named Robinson and Allison at Seminole, Texas. On a Sunday night before the District Court was to open the following morning, the district judge, the district attorney, and Robinson and Allison had all been seated in the lobby of the small local hotel. Tom and Milt had come through the door with guns in hand and shot down the two inspectors, who were to be witnesses against them the next day.

The crime had aroused much indignation. Tom and Milt missed the electric chair but drew long prison sentences. Later, they tunneled their way to freedom under the prison wall at Huntsville. They fled to the Pacific Northwest. Tom Ross was finally killed in Montana on a ranch where he was hiding out. Milt was recaptured, but escaped again, this time over the wall, amid a hail of bullets, only to be captured again. Sheriff John Helms brought him down from where he was caught, near Antlers, Oklahoma.

Louis Dodd had been prosecuted and given a life sentence for murder through the efficient work of District Attorney Dayton Moses, of Burnet County. Louis was really a hard prisoner to control. He escaped several times and was in some bad shooting scrapes. Shortly after I took charge, Milt and Louis came to me and told me that they saw how things were going to be thereafter, that they had been mistreated but believed they were going to get a square deal from me, and that they were going to change their ways and do right from then on.

They kept their word, and both were model prisoners. In fact, Milt turned in $140 which he had obtained in some illegal manner. He said he knew that prisoners were allowed to have no more than $2 on their persons. Later on, Milt helped me organize the first prison rodeo. He himself was quite a rodeo performer at one time. Before his troubles arose, he had been the world's champion steer-roper.

At the request of Warden Waid, I let Milt drive for me for a month or so, and later he received a parole and then a pardon from Governor Ferguson. He did not make the best of this clemency, however, for in a year or so he was returned to Huntsville with a short sentence on some minor charge. But I believe he is getting along all right now in west Texas. His father and family were old-time cattlemen of the very best standing. A background like that helps a man get back on the right road.

Louis Dodd straightened out, also. It came about in this fashion. Dayton Moses, who had sent Dodd up for murder, became attorney for the Texas and Southwestern Cattle Raisers' Association, a posi-

Prison Miscellany

tion which he held for many years. He was instrumental in sending to the penitentiary many cattle and horse thieves during his long service with that fine organization. My friendship with Moses dated back to my University of Texas days, while he was studying law and I was studying how to get back home so I could go to work. (School did not appeal to me in those days.) One day Moses was visiting me at Huntsville. As we were going from place to place inside the Walls, he said to me: "Lee, whatever became of old Louis Dodd? He sure was a hard one. You remember I prosecuted him and sent him up for life."

"Louis is a fine prisoner," I replied, "and is getting along fine. I'll let you see him. He's a bootmaker in the shoe factory."

We went down to the shoe factory, walked in, and stopped at the bench where Dodd was working. As he looked up, I said to him: "Louis, you know this man."

He stood and looked at Dayton for a moment, then extended his hand: "Well, Mr. Moses, I sure am glad to see you." Quite a conversation then took place between them— one that I will always remember, although I had no part in it, myself. Dodd did most of the talking.

"You sure did prosecute me hard, Mr. Moses," he said. "But you were only doing your duty, and I never did criticize and condemn you, like most of the boys did. You never heard me say one hard word against you.

"I know I've been a hard man and I've caused a lot of trouble in my lifetime. But it was all my fault. And I've changed my ways, and Mr. Simmons will tell you that I'm working hard and will do anything he wants me to do. And I never intend to cause any more trouble.

"Now, Mr. Moses, I'm getting old and have been here a long time, and my mother is old. I give you my word, Mr. Moses, that I'll never cause any more trouble and that I am sorry for the things I've done. I know I can't get out of here without help from you, and I'm asking you please to help me and give me a chance to show that I can do right. And I'll go straight and take care of my old Mother."

It was hard for me to keep back the tears, but I never said a word. As for Moses, he didn't promise anything but merely said: "Well,

Louis, I'll think about this when I get back home; don't know what I will do about it. I'm surely glad you are getting along all right." And he shook hands and said good-by.

When we got outside the shop, Moses said to me: "Louis put me on the spot, didn't he? What do you think about it?"

"Dayton," I replied, "I believe old Louis will do what he said he would, and I'd like for you to give him a chance. We need him badly in the prison, because he's a good bootmaker; but I hope you write a letter to the parole board for him. That's what it will take to get him out."

Later, Moses did write a letter, and Louis Dodd was paroled. He started a little boot and shoe shop and took care of his mother, just as he promised to do. He and Milt Goode, along with a good many other hardened criminals, learned that I meant it when I told them I was going to give them all a square deal.

One never knows, however, what to expect with prison inmates. The only rule is that the unexpected is sure to happen. For instance, on one occasion the big clock on the prison tower got out of fix, and a guard took two convicts up to repair it. While they were up there, they overpowered the guard, took his gun, and forced him to change clothing with one of them. Then they came back down and went on out the front door. The convict who was dressed in the guard's clothing waved to the picket guard in the little picket across the street and shouted, "I got 'em, Boss," as he marched the two of them, his prison guard and his own comrade, right on down the street. They released the guard when they got to the edge of town and escaped, but were soon recaptured.

Then there was the escape of Matt Akers, foreman of the prison automobile-repair shop. Everybody within the Walls got a chuckle out of that. Matt was a good mechanic and a pleasant, agreeable fellow. So when Father Finnegan brought in his Ford coupé to have some work done on it, Matt was on the job at once. Father Finnegan wanted a partition of some sort in the turtleback. It was ready for him when he came the next day at ten o'clock to get it.

Father Finnegan got in his car and drove up to the west gate, where

Prison Miscellany

he stopped to let the guard look things over. Two guards work at the drive-in gate, and all vehicles, as well as drivers, are searched as they pass in and out. Close watch is kept for weapons and ammunition on all inbound cars. But outgoing cars receive only a casual inspection to make sure no prisoners are concealed.

Father Finnegan, of course, was not searched. The guards looked in, lifted the lid of the turtleback, glanced in and let the lid back down again. Then they waved the chaplain on. The padre drove out to the Wynne Farm, visited with Captain Wright for some time, then got into his car, drove back into town, past the prison proper, to stop in front of the home of N. L. Boudreaux, the master mechanic—just across the street from the prison wall. There he got out for another visit.

Within a few minutes, escapee Matt Akers crawled out of the back of the chaplain's car, only to turn and find himself practically in the arms of a prison guard, who happened to be passing by on his way home from his tour of duty. Matt had had a half-day's ride on a round-trip ticket. Old Matt never heard the last of that ride.

Of course, men penned up together always put in a lot of time thinking about escape. Practically every way, I suppose, has been tried. We used two large tanks into which kitchen garbage was emptied. Each morning one of these tanks was hauled away and the contents fed to the hogs on Wynne Farm. Our system was that each morning a trusty-driver would bring in the wagon containing the empty tank and leave it at the kitchen; later he would hitch his team to the wagon under the loaded tank and drive to the gate, where he would dismount and be searched by the guards.

It was standard procedure also for the guard to mount the sloptank, remove the lid, and probe the interior with an iron rod to make sure that no prisoner with an itching foot had decided to hide within. It seemed an unnecessary routine, for, of course, a journey of any length taken inside that tank would be—well, impossible.

The old Negro trusty's astonishment may be imagined, therefore, when, about halfway on his trip to the farm, a prisoner actually crawled out of the tank and fled into the timber. As the trusty told it, he was scared nearly to death when that man crawled out of there "all wet and frazzled up." However, the dog sergeant was soon on the trail, and the dogs had no trouble following the scent. Recapture followed within a few hours.

Still another escapee had a yet more harrowing experience. This man escaped from Harlem Farm, with the dog sergeant hard after him. He climbed a tree to get away from the dogs but was yelling loudly for help by the time the sergeant reached him. You see, he had selected a bee tree—and the bees were on the side of the law.

CHAPTER 20

Trusties

THE DRIVER for the general manager had by far the best trusty job in the prison system. He slept in a small cottage in the back yard of the large, old-fashioned residence assigned to me. I never told the driver when or where I was going but expected him to have the car serviced and ready to go any time I called him. I had an electric push button in my room, with a wire to the room of the driver.

I had the reputation of getting up early. If I was leaving at four or five o'clock in the morning to go to the farms, or to Austin, or to some state institution, I would push the button; and by the time I had shaved and dressed and got out to the car, my driver would be on hand with the car ready to go. I never had a driver fail to be ready by the time I came down.

Warden Waid always selected my drivers. There was considerable risk involved, of course, and Waid made it his business to know his men before he recommended them. The best and most dependable driver that he ever gave me was Luther Berwick, who drove for me for twenty-two months. I never had a complaint to lodge against him.

In the first trial of his case, Luther received the death penalty, but his case was reversed, and he obtained a change of venue for the second trial, which resulted in a fifty-year sentence. Although the thing he did was very bad, Luther was not a confirmed criminal. In shooting a young man he was unfortunate enough to kill with a single shot both the young man and Luther's girl friend, who completed the triangle. Luther, of course, had not the slightest intention of harming the girl.

I have already referred to Luther a number of times in my story, but I think you will be interested to know that he was paroled a short time after I resigned my position with the system and that he married and got a good job.

Another good driver I had was a man who had been district sales agent for one of the best automobiles on the market. His territory included several counties, and he was operating on a pretty big scale. But he got his finances mixed up, sold his loan paper to too many different bankers—and came down to be one of my boarders.

This man had a respectable family. He found it hard to realize that he was a prisoner and subject to prison discipline. In Houston he knew a lot of people, and on two different occasions when we were in Houston, he failed to be at the car at the appointed time. He never made any explanations or excuses—and I never commented. In one instance I intended to go off and leave him, but Mrs. Simmons talked me out of it. So we waited for him. But the next time, as we came from the lower farms, we drove into Houston, and I told him that I would run over to the office of Chairman Paddock for a few minutes. I was gone about an hour, and when I returned to the car, the parking-station attendant said to me: "Your driver is over at the hotel; he said he was going to write some letters. I'll go over and get him for you."

"No," I said, "just get my car out for me."

"Oh, I'll just run over and get him for you," he insisted.

"No," I repeated, "just get the car."

He did. And I drove on to Huntsville, reaching home about seven o'clock. After dinner the telephone rang: "Houston calling General Manager Simmons."

"This is he."

"Deposit 85 cents, please." (Business of the little bell ringing as the coins fell.) "Go ahead, please; party on the line."

"Mr. Simmons, this is John; didn't you forget me?"

"No, I didn't forget you."

"Well, uh—what do you want me to do?"

Trusties

"Just do whatever you please; finish writing your letters, if you like." And I hung up. John knew it was against prison rules to send out any letters, except through the warden's office, or to receive any letters except through the same office.

I was leaving for Austin the next morning at five, so I telephoned the Warden to have his driver sent over for me at that hour. Of course, the car was ready for me the next morning, with Mr. Waid's driver on hand. But John was there, too, busily polishing away on the car. I thanked Cotton (Waid's man) and dismissed him. Then I got into the car, and so did John.

The funny part about it was that I was expecting John to have something to say to me about not having been on the job, and I knew he was expecting me to have a word or two on the subject. We stopped at Brenham and ate breakfast, talking about things in general, and still nothing was mentioned about what was uppermost in the thoughts of both of us. In fact, John never did mention it, and neither did I. That man drove thousands of miles for me after that, and never again did he fail to be where I told him to be at the time I fixed.

After John left, the Warden gave me as my driver a former prominent funeral director from one of our largest cities. I always gave my new drivers full instructions about what I expected. I told them they must comply with all laws and traffic regulations.

But this funeral director must have had his mind on something else, for he rather consistently failed to halt at stop signs or traffic lights. I corrected him rather mildly about it several times. But one morning in Huntsville, when he drove right over a stop sign without paying any attention to it, I had enough. I told him to get his things together, as I was going to turn him back to the Warden.

I didn't tell him why. But he knew. He apologized at great length and said that, if I would let him drive for me, I would have no further trouble about his driving. "No," I said, "get your clothes and belongings up, and let's go."

And I turned him in. Mrs. Simmons had been after me for some time to get rid of that driver. But her reason was different from mine. One day she asked me what he was in for. Now the funeral director had received the body of a man who died without any known relatives and who left an estate of about $800. The probate judge having ordered the burial, the funeral director proceeded to officiate, later presenting a bill for $700 for funeral expenses. Either somebody talked, or else somebody acted on pure suspicion, for the judge had the body dug up, and it was found that it had been wrapped in a bed-sheet and buried in a plain pine box. Well, when I told all this to my wife, she said to me: "I just don't want to ride with him." And she didn't have to.

I never talked to any of my other drivers about their offenses, but I recall that I did ask this fellow, and he told me. Then I asked him how much time he was in for, and he replied: "Eight years; the jury gave me three and the newspapers gave me the other five!"

I had another John who drove for me. But he drove me only about two miles. He was a man of my own selection, at that, although we had the approval of the Warden. I never went over Waid's head about such things. I let him run his job, and recommending trusties was part of it.

This man had got into trouble, like Luther Berwick, with the result that he received a short sentence for murder. He had been a substantial and respected citizen in a small town. While I had never met him, I had read about his trial and conviction, as reported in the *Dallas Morning News*. After I had been in charge of the system for about thirty days, I sent for this man. When he arrived at my office, I told him that I would like to use his services in some worth-while employment, for I knew that the work he was doing around the prison yard was of little consequence.

"We need a man like you," I said to him, "over in the prison store, and I want to talk to you about it. If I were to ask the Warden to make a trusty of you and to put you in the store on a good overtime job, would you stay with me, or would you leave some time and cross the Rio Grande, and have folks saying, 'I wonder how much money that bunch got for putting him to work on the outside?' "

"Let me go down to my cell," he answered, "and get some letters of recommendation that I brought down here with me."

"I don't want to see any letters. Not a person has talked to me about you or about your case. I asked you a question."

"Mr. Simmons," said he, with tears in his eyes, "I give you my word I'll never betray you or go back on my promise to stay with you and the Warden, and I'll do everything in my power to assist you and to be loyal to you."

We placed him in the big commissary, and he made a wonderful helper. Actually, he was a more valuable man than the civilian who was managing the store at the time. I was sure he would be when I chose him for the job. I wanted to show my appreciation for the fine work he was doing. Accordingly, I said to him one day: "I'm going up your way in a day or so, and I'm wondering if you would like to drive me up, and see your wife and family?"

He said he would like it very much, especially as his father was getting very old and was in bad health; he had been afraid that he would never get to see the old man again while he was alive.

"Don't say a word about it to anybody," I told him, "and I'll let you know."

He was Warden Waid's man, not mine. (The only prisoners directly under me were two Negro houseboys, the yardman, and my driver.) So I spoke to Waid about taking this man as my driver, and he was pleased with the suggestion. When next I saw John, I told him to be ready the next morning. I had to go to Fort Worth on business, and his home wouldn't be much out of the way.

John was ready, of course, bright and early. He felt the car out a little, and then we started. I told him to drive slowly for a while, all the while expecting that I would be doing most of the driving. We got about two miles out on the highway, and then John began to look the world over as we rolled by. I understood that, of course. The scenery was different from what he had been looking at, in county jails and then at Huntsville with us.

"Stop, John," said I. "I'll do the driving and you do the looking."

He began to apologize, but I stopped him. I drove the remainder of the trip, some four hundred miles by the time we returned to Huntsville. When we got within about fifty miles of his home, I told him we would send his wife a telegram. (I had cautioned him beforehand not to write home about the trip.) I wrote the telegram and signed his name to it: "Passing through about four o'clock with General Manager and hope to see you."

At about four o'clock we did drive up in front of a really nice residence. I remained in the car while he went in. In a minute or so, he came back with his wife and introduced me. She said that she knew that John would want to see his father and mother, who had had an early supper prepared for us, and that it was only a mile up the road to his parents' house.

"I intend to leave John with you here tonight," I said. "But, John, I expect you to meet me at the Jefferson Hotel at seven o'clock in the morning."

About five minutes ahead of time next morning, John and his wife were at the hotel. She thanked me for permitting the visit. We drove over to Fort Worth and then to Sherman, arriving by early nightfall. We drove to the Grayson Hotel, where I went to register, leaving John sitting on the long hotel porch. "Huntsville's trying to get you," said the clerk.

I laid down the pen without registering and reported promptly to the telephone operator. I was afraid we might have to backtrack to Huntsville in a hurry. The operator soon had the cashier, Tom Tennison, on the line: "Mr. Simmons, Governor Moody has called here twice to know what John is doing out of the penitentiary."

"What did you tell him?"

"I told him that you were going home on business, and I guessed you took him along to drive for you, but that I didn't know."

"That's fine," I reassured him. "Don't let it worry you; everything will be all right."

When I came back out of the hotel, John asked me, "Anything bad happened?"

"No," said I, "not a thing. Mr. Tennison said Governor Moody has been calling over there to find out why you are out of the penitentiary."

"Mr. Simmons," said John, "you don't know how much I appreciate your letting me come to see my folks, but I'd rather not have seen them than to have embarrassed you this way."

"You haven't embarrassed me one bit," I replied. "I'm glad I brought you along. You know, John, it isn't anybody's business whom I make a trusty and use for a driver. Don't let this worry you at all."

"Mr. Simmons," he said, "I would die and go to hell before I would betray your confidence in me." He meant it, too.

What happened, I am sure, was that some of John's enemies had called the Governor to find out why this man was at home. Naturally the Governor was in order in trying to find out the facts, as there was no record in the office of the secretary of state to show that parole had been granted.

The next time I was in Austin, I went in and explained to the Governor. Said he: "It's none of my business whom you make trusties or whom you use for drivers. Some folks phoned and asked why that fellow was out, and all I could tell them was that I didn't know anything about it, that my office had not granted any clemency."

My "two-mile driver" continued to make good at the store, and after his release he returned home, where he made good again as a citizen. He is still making good. And he sends me a Christmas card every Christmas. Confidence and co-operation—they pay.

By way of further example, let me tell of an intelligent, fine-looking young prisoner in Tennison's office. This twenty-year-old was serving two years for forgery. Pleasing in appearance, attentive in his work, the lad was liked by all of us. One day he had a sudden attack of appendicitis. The prison physician said he was in critical condition and that an operation was necessary at once.

The patient sent for me, and I visited him in the prison hospital. He asked to talk to me in strict confidence. I assured him that he could do so. Then he told me that he was serving under an assumed name and gave me his real name. He gave me the name and address of his father, who was president of a large university in the Eastern part of the United States. "If I die," he said, "I want you to wire my father; if I get well, I want you to forget what I have told you."

He got well—and I have forgotten.

The lad served out his term and was discharged. His place in the farm's office was taken by an older, married convict. This man's friends were active in urging a pardon for him. When Governor Sterling looked over the application for clemency he noticed that one of the reasons for pardon was that the man's wife was in a family way. The Governor picked up the telephone and called me at Huntsville. "Lee," he said, "the next time you're in Austin drop by to see me."

When I went in to see him a few days later he showed me the pardon application and asked, "How is it that a man who has been in the penitentiary for five years is about to become a father?"

The Governor was half-joking and half in earnest. But when he gave me the convict's name I explained the situation. As bookkeeper for the Harlem Farm the man was a trusty. He had been assigned a small office opposite the manager's home, where he worked and slept and where he was allowed occasional visits from his wife.

Governor Sterling seemed satisfied with my explanation. "All right, Lee," he said, "I just wanted to know what this application was all about. It had me a little worried."

"I can understand that, Governor," I replied. "If we were to establish a policy of releasing every convict whose wife was in a delicate condition, the state would be guilty of contributing to immorality. And besides, under that policy we soon wouldn't have any prisoners in our penitentiary. But this case is a little different."

CHAPTER 21

Rodeo Reunion

ON NOVEMBER 1, 1935, I resigned as manager of the Texas Prison System. After more than five years devoted to maintaining "the peace and dignity of the state," it was high time I took up such matters as my overdue bank notes and business interests in my home community. I fully intended to devote all my time to such matters from then on. But it seemed inevitable that I should again be drawn into the business of law enforcement.

When Federal Judge Randolph Bryant, of the Eastern District of Texas, approached me the following year to take the position of district clerk, I protested: "I'm not a desk man. I've always been an outdoor man." But the Judge insisted that he had plenty of marshals and deputies to handle the paper work—he needed me because of my practical experience in law enforcement.

Some of my friends were also skeptical about my qualifications. "Why, Lee," they said, "as district clerk you'd have to wear a coat at work. That's something you've never had to do on any of your other jobs." But I solved that problem by keeping a coat hung behind the door in my office. I put it on when I had to make an official appearance in the courtroom then hung it up again behind the door when I went back to my desk. Without compromising the dignity of federal justice I thus preserved my comfort.

But throughout my tenure of office—and I served with six United

States district judges of the seven divisions of our district—I remained at heart an outdoor man, a livestock man. That was my natural bent, from the days when as a small boy I had sat on the rail fence watching trail herds go by our little farm. From that time to this I have been in the cattle game in some shape or fashion. It was never on a large scale, to be sure, aside from my period of prison management. But for some sixty-odd years I have handled and owned both cattle and horses.

I got to thinking about all this not so long ago and decided that I wanted to get back to the old-time, rough-and-tough business of handling cattle once more before it came my time to leave for the Great Roundup.

When I was in Stamford in 1954 attending the West Texas Cowboy Reunion, of which I am a life member, I ran into my long-time friend George Humphries, who was just the man to help me achieve this ambition. For thirty-seven years, since he was hired as a lad of seventeen by Burk Burnett himself, George has been the energetic and industrious manager of the 6666 ranches. I told him of my dream of participating in one final roundup, and he said, "Come right on to the 6666. We'll be glad to have you work with us. We start the wagon October 20, gathering our cattle to separate the calves from the cows."

Of course I accepted and began immediately to make plans for going. Former Ranger Tom Hickman, another lifelong friend, was my choice of companion. On October 19 Tom and I set out from his home in Gainesville and went to Ardmore, Oklahoma, where we saw a good rodeo that night and were guests at the home of Floyd and Florence Randolph, both famous rodeo performers, Mrs. Randolph having been World Champion Cowgirl at Madison Square Garden, in New York. The next day we drove back to Gainesville and loaded up for the trip to the 6666 Ranch headquarters at Guthrie, King County, Texas.

I went prepared, for if there is one thing a cowman wants when working cattle, it is his own rigging. So I took my saddle, which I had been riding for twenty years, along with chaps, spurs, "booger red" jacket of heavy canvas, and bedroll. At 4:00 P.M. Tom and I

Rodeo Reunion

drove up in our separate cars to the large, old-time, well-furnished headquarters. Mrs. Humphries, George's helpmeet all these years on the 6666, greeted us, and, after a brief visit, we went to find George and discover where the wagon was spotted.

When the cowboys began to come in they reported that one of their number had been injured. While running a horse that had broken away from the remuda of some 110 animals, this man's mount had stepped into a hole, fallen, and rolled over on the rider. The injury was so serious that he was taken at once to Paducah. He later died in a Lubbock hospital. This introduction to the roundup was not very encouraging for a man then nearly eighty-two years old.

The 6666 outfit consisted of an extra-large chuck wagon, with chuck box at the rear end and belly box underneath for cooking utensils (three large Dutch ovens, bean pots, skillets, coffee pots, and so on); an old-time cook in charge of four buckskin mules to haul the chuck wagon; a flunky cook to help out the chief cook, with a smaller wagon and two buckskin mules to haul wood, water, and supplies; twelve cowboys, including several old timers like Manager Humphries and myself; and the remuda of horses. Of course, I should add the wagon boss, Swede Swenson, Jr., formerly with the SMS ranches at Stamford.

I was strongly impressed with the sanitary arrangements of the camp. After bedrolls, equipment, and the like had been unloaded, a pit was dug, and heavy pipe was fastened in position with rods. In this the cooking was done. About ten steps away from this arrangement, the garbage pit was dug to receive all the leftovers and waste.

Although camp was moved three times, arrangements were the same in each case, and not once did I see any man throw waste or food of any kind on the ground. Without exception, each man walked to the garbage pit, cleaned out his tin plate into it, and returned to pitch his plate and cup, together with his knife and fork, into a huge washtub by the fire for the flunky cook to take care of.

Food there was in plenty and in variety, too. We had fresh beef for every meal except breakfast, which consisted of bacon, eggs, hot cakes, preserves, molasses, sour-dough biscuits, and corn bread. A young, fat steer was slaughtered the second day out. All food was well prepared, and cooking vessels, cups, and plates were all clean and sanitary. A huge pot of coffee was at all times hanging over the fire. Cowboys, you know, really drink coffee.

At 4:00 A.M. the cook's alarm clock went off. He then dressed and woke the two horse-wranglers. The latter saddled up the two horses tethered near camp and started out after the remuda, as the horses were all on the grass during the night.

It wasn't long before the cook was yelling, "Come and get it!" The boys came rolling out of their bedding, washed up, and grabbed tin cups for coffee. Before we had finished eating, we could hear the hoofbeats of a hundred horses coming down from the hills. And above the drumming of the hoofs we could hear the cowboys yelling. In a little while all of us gathered up ropes and bridles and surrounded the horses, closing in on them in a small circle, while two ropers lassoed the horses as they were called for by the riders. Meanwhile the wranglers, having chosen their own mounts, went in for breakfast. Each morning and each noon this process was repeated, as each cowhand had about eight horses in his string. This meant that each horse was ridden a half-day on about every third day.

With our horses saddled up, we all mounted, wearing chaps and gloves on account of the mesquite brush. Then we normally rode out a mile or two from camp, where Manager Humphries took over. I have seen him sit his horse for five minutes at a time, surveying the country and laying out his plans. Twelve of us lined up, without uttering a word until he gave his orders for the drive.

For example, he would say: "Swede, take so and so (two men) and make the drag through that country," indicating with his hands. Then in the same manner he would divide the tasks of the other older hands. Then he would say, "Taylor, you and Lee make the drag through here, and I'll take Prairie Dog (one of the hands), and we'll make this drag." Then finally: "Boys, we want a clean sweep. We're not coming back here again."

We would then separate, riding through the open and the brush country. As we ran on to the cows and their calves, we would drive them toward the corral or pens designated by George, slowly coming in to arrive at about the same time. There we would pen the cattle to await the arrival of three large trucks the next morning. The trucks were to take off the calves to a small 110,000-acre ranch, where they would be kept until they were three years old. Then they would be sold to feeders in the corn belt up North.

As it turned out, some fifty calves had been missed in the springtime, when marking and branding is generally done. It was fine to see Old George and Swede, or Taylor, or McLearin ride in, rope a calf, drag him out to the fire for the younger hands to down him and put that 6666 on him.

As we finished a 20,000-acre pasture and were riding along together, George remarked: "Lee, we put 567 cows in here last spring, and we have gathered 560. Pretty good sweeping—560 out of 567 in heavy mesquite and rough country."

Every once in a while, when first saddling up of a morning, a cowboy gets bucked off. Several times a cowboy would come in riding double behind a comrade because his horse had thrown him and got away. It was two days before one dismounted boy's horse was found—still wearing the saddle. So large was the range, so thick was the brush, and so much alike were hills and creeks that it was easy for a new hand to get lost. They told me of a fellow who was lost for two days before they found him. "If the darn fool had just built a fire, we would have seen the smoke and gone to him," they said.

Without saying a word, I felt in my "booger red" jacket to see if I had any matches. I do not smoke, and I found that I had only two or three. Presently I slipped around to the chuck-box table and picked up several. They might be needed.

The next morning, George pointed out a tall, bald hill and said: "Lee, we're going to hold up just to the right of that bald hill you see yonder. If you happen to get lost down below, you can get out somewhere so you can see that hill, and just drive toward that."

I ran on to two big white-faced cows and a big fat calf, drove them out, and ran into old Taylor, who had four or five head himself. So I didn't get lost. But the matches in my "booger red" were a great comfort to me, just the same.

All in all, I had a wonderful time. I tried to make a hand, and I know I made friends of the boys. All of them were considerate of me—offering to saddle my horse for me, pour my coffee for me, and the like. But I made myself one of them and waited on myself. George said I made a good hand. I hope I did, for he let me ride three of the best horses of his string. One of them was Jiggs, his prize cutting horse on which he has won first place in a number of contests. So if I didn't make a hand, I had no excuse.

I have an invitation from friend George to come back next fall for the roundup, and I may do just that. Certainly the hospitality of George and Mrs. Humphries is wonderful, and their friendship beyond compare.

Although it has been more than twenty years since I have had any official participation in the management of the Texas Prison System, I still make it a practice to attend at least one rodeo performance at Huntsville every October. With an exception or two I have been able to make it each year. For it just doesn't seem right to let a fall go by without returning to Huntsville for the rodeo. The occasion is something like a class reunion of alumni as we all go back to seek out old comrades and to exchange memories with those who shared with us an important period of activity.

Each year when the rodeo season is on I load up the five-hundred-dollar saddle presented to me when I left the system and head south. Each year the crowds are larger and the "take" for prison welfare from the gate receipts is bigger. The rodeo now plays consistently to crowds of over thirty thousand. Now, thirty thousand people suddenly crowded into a town of ten thousand sets up a big problem. Traffic is congested in all directions for miles around. People have to park their cars as far as a mile away from the arena.

Concessionaires have solved the problem of refreshments for those who do not bring their own lunches. I found that cottagers near the prison rent their front lawns to these stands for sometimes as much as two or three hundred dollars a day. It is not uncommon for concessionaires to sell completely out of stock within a few hours.

From the beginning of the prison rodeo until now, attendance has consistently overflowed seating capacity. Although the performance does not begin until two o'clock, every seat is taken by noon. I remember that the first rodeo drew fifteen hundred people. The last under my administration attracted between ten and twelve thousand,

and we turned people away every Sunday of the season. In 1956 crowds of thirty-two thousand were counted. Naturally, it pleases me to see how the rodeo has become an institution, growing from year to year.

But I do not go down each year simply to count the crowd and show my pride. I go to visit with old friends among both employees and prisoners, and to help out with handling the rodeo stock, just as I used to do in the old days. They give me a cow pony—nothing extra, just a good cow horse—and I go out and help the prison stockmen round up the animals who are to appear in the arena. We used to drive the cattle into town, but nowadays the highways are so crowded that it isn't safe to handle cattle that way, so we load up two trucks with the bulls, a third with the steers, and a fourth with the calves. It takes a bit of hard, stiff riding to round them up, too. The horses, however, we drive into town as in former years.

Albert Moore is still in charge of the rodeo. He introduces me to the crowd in the grandstand, as I ride in on my mount. But I take no VIP seat up there. Just as I have always done, I stay with the boys down in the arena.

But things are not entirely as they used to be. Many of the riding and roping stars of current exhibitions are hired professionals from the outside. There is a reason for that, to be sure. The prison population now tends to come more from the cities, so that there are fewer and fewer real cowboys among the convicts. In the old days we never let a man ride unless he knew his business, because rodeoing is dangerous. But in the tryouts we found plenty of men who knew that business and could ride with the best of them.

Today the professional ropers and riders have their own association, and it is practically a labor union. You have to conduct rodeos according to their rules, or else somebody in the association will object, and then no member will participate. That fact has radically changed the prison rodeo. Our original plan was to make the rodeo a show for the prisoners and by the prisoners, for their recreation and entertainment—with public attendance strictly a secondary concern. But now the public's part has become so big that the show has to be run for the public's benefit. And that means a professional performance.

One innovation at the 1954 show seemed to me all wrong. I asked Albert Moore: "What in the world has a parachute jump out of an airplane got to do with our Rodeo?"

"Well, Mr. Lee," he answered, "I was dead set against that, myself; but they insisted upon it. And so we've got a parachute jumper."

He explained that the jumper was a prisoner who had served with parachute troops in World War II. There was a spot marked in the arena where he was supposed to land. But he missed the entire prison plant. Albert reassured me about that. He said the jumper was a trusty and was really doing his best to land on prison property, but that the wind blew him out of bounds. In fact, the wind had blown him out of bounds every time he had jumped so far. His parachute, I suppose, was just naturally escape-minded. Probably it was just as well, for I kept worrying about what would happen in the way of a stampede if he happened to parachute down into the grandstands in the middle of those thirty thousand people.

The 1956 prison rodeo included as side attractions trained animal acts, a mounted quadrille, and "Marilyn Rich, the Original Helicopter Girl," doing "death-defying acrobatic stunts from rings and a rope attached beneath a helicopter." All of this was broadcast over NBC's "Wide, Wide World" program. It was quite a change from our modest beginnings.

The prison rodeo is still a good show, a wonderful show, and I don't want to find myself in the position of criticizing it. In many ways it is a more finished performance than it used to be. But I don't believe it is as rough. I don't see how it very well could be.

My annual return for the rodeo gives me a chance to note the steady advance of the prison system as a whole. The Legislature has come to recognize that expenditure of money on the prison plant is a justifiable outlay. Millions of dollars now go into things which the system has long needed.

It pleased me to find that the prison brick plant which I established is still in use and that every brick used in construction projects at the Walls is prison-made. But on the outer side of the Walls the rails of the stairs leading to the picket stations atop the walls are of brass. I never saw so much brass in all my life. It must take around a half-dozen men full time just to keep that brass shining.

Rodeo Reunion

I was glad to see that prison cattle production is getting straightened out. For much of the prison land is better suited for cattle-
raising than for crop production, although 1953 crops were very
good, the cotton crop the best the system ever harvested. Experiments
with cattle on the prison farms were for a time discouraging, owing
to the fact that fine Northern cattle were brought down into the hot
mosquito- and fly-infested pastures of south Texas. At first the cows
failed to breed well and the stock generally showed up to poor advantage. But now that the stock has been acclimated, results are much
better. I am sure the grade of cattle can be improved by introduction
of better bloodlines and that then the wisdom of turning to a cattle-
raising program will become even more apparent.

Meanwhile, the prison population is mounting steadily. The curve
of increase indicates that pretty soon we shall have more young men
and women at Huntsville than we have at Austin enrolled in the University of Texas. That makes me wonder: How is the prison system
going to find work for all the thousands of prisoners who are going
to be on hand in ever increasing numbers? There is no question but
that power farming is here to stay, and on the prison farms we have
great tractors and four-row machines but few jobs for prisoners with
hoe and ax. It is something to worry about.

At the last rodeo I was talking these things over with Joseph Wearden, who served on the prison board in my time and succeeded to the
chairmanship of the board upon the death of Mr. Paddock. When he
got home again he was kind enough to write me the following letter.

Victoria, Texas
October 23, 1956

Mr. Lee Simmons
Sherman, Texas

Dear Lee:

Lately, the Post Office Department has tightened up on its regulations,
so that when we write letters to anyone in cities the size of Sherman or
Marshall, they request us to use street address, but I am betting in this
case that Lee Simmons is well enough known in Sherman that no street
address will be necessary for this letter to reach him.

I could not resist the urge to write and tell you how very much I enjoyed seeing you and visiting with you and reminiscing some with refer-

ence to former days of the Texas Prison System, as a visit with you was an extra bonus which I had not anticipated when I arranged to go up last Saturday and Sunday.

My opinion of the operations as now being carried on, is that the program now in effect had its first inception in you. Circumstances forced beginning in a small way, but you did not fail to begin, and you must have laid firm foundations for the structure as it now is to build and expand upon. The state of Texas owes you a debt of gratitude for your abiding interest in the welfare of the Texas Prison System since 1914.

Yours sincerely,

[signed] Joseph Wearden

As I have said, I go back to the Rodeo not only to see the show but also to see old friends as alumni do at reunions. The warden at the Walls is now Emmett Moore, who was secretary to Warden Waid in my day, and I always enjoy a visit with him. It is only fair also to say a good word for General Manager O. B. Ellis. He is a good man doing a good job, and he has deserved and won the co-operation and confidence of the Legislature. He has an excellent name and an excellent record and has made good use of the handsome monetary backing he has received.

The most notable improvement to strike the eye is the new residence of the general manager. It is a truly handsome place of about fifteen rooms. Here all the members of the prison board can be entertained and can come and go as they like. It is quite palatial, compared with the old-fashioned residence Mrs. Simmons and I occupied.

Prison management has added another story to the hospital I built, and all within is spic and span. The classification department, at which I made a beginning, is now fully manned and organized. I understand it is doing splendid work.

It was, of course, pleasant to find that some of the old guards remembered me. While I was general manager I had the regular practice of visiting all the farms and of getting up early in the morning after spending the night with the farm manager. I always went to eat breakfast with the guards and, in general, made myself practically one of them. For, in truth, the success of my administration was largely in their hands.

I remember back in those days I was eating breakfast one morning and missed one of the guards. Naturally I asked about him and was told that he was at home with an injured leg. I went over to see him. When I walked into his bedroom tears came into his eyes as he said: "Ain't never nothing like this happened before, Mr. Simmons. I never thought a man like you would ever come to see an old guard like me."

"Why, I'm interested in you, of course," I said, calling him by name. "I'm not only interested in you but I'm interested in your family."

And so I was. When the farm guards and their families came into Huntsville, they all visited me at the manager's house, so that it was no more than natural that they should remember me and that I should remember them. Sometimes a name slips my mind, of course; but it comes back to me when they introduce themselves to me, as I'm glad to say they do. "You don't remember me," a big, fine fellow said to me as he came up to me in Huntsville one day, "but, by damn, I remember you!" With a little help I identified him as M. E. "Panama" Shiftlett, who now is a member of a contracting firm in Houston.

"Of course," said I. "And the next time you come to Sherman, don't go to the hotel—come to my house. I've got plenty of room." The alumni reunion was going on, you see.

I was driving along in traffic one day over in an east Texas town when I heard a shout. I stopped to see what was the matter, and a big old boy came over to talk to me. He was another of my former guards who had made good on a later job of a different kind. We had such a reunion there in the middle of the street that a policeman came over to see what the trouble was.

"Brother," said my fellow-alumnus, "this here is Lee Simmons."

"You're dern right," said my brother peace officer. "Everybody in Texas knows Lee Simmons."

That isn't so, of course, but a man wouldn't be human if he didn't glory in friendships that are old and tried and true. What greater earthly reward can a man hope to find? So you may understand why, at rodeo time, I go back to Huntsville to relive for a few hours some of the days gone by, and why the prison rodeo remains for one old man the high point of the year.

Afterword

Short of the possibility of global war, crime is the most serious problem of our nation. Crime is older than history, to be sure; and there will be crime, I suppose, as long as there are human beings to commit it. But our crisis is in the realm of juvenile delinquency, which increases so fast that it threatens the very survival of the United States. I am no alarmist; but I say the fears on this score entertained by the best minds are well-founded fears. They deserve our honest consideration.

Read the headlines: "Girl, 13, Admits Setting Fire to Churches" ——"Policemen Catch Three Youths in Chase for Stolen Car"—— "Juvenile Crime Tied to Bad Home Life"——"Juvenile Crime Age Dropping"——"141 Students Disciplined in Bridge-Burning Case" ——"Runaway Juveniles Jam Dallas"——"Eight Hundred Youthful Cons End Nine-Hour Riot"——"3 Youths Seized in Theft Ring" ——"Texas Youth Delinquency Shows Rise."

Is there no cause for alarm? Call the roll of criminals of the last generation and consider the fruits of juvenile delinquency.

Jesse Pomroy was a criminal at thirteen. When he was fourteen he murdered two children. He was saved from the electric chair by reason of his extreme youth, and died after spending fifty-five years in prison, forty of them in solitary confinement.

Henry Starr, an Oklahoma outlaw, headed a dynasty of crime and sponsored Matt and George Kimes and Al Spencer, the last a horse thief and robber who was killed while resisting arrest. Starr himself was shot to death after robbing a bank at Harrison, Arkansas.

William Harrison ("Little Jake") Fleagle was the leader of a gang of bandits who killed four men in the $219,000 bank robbery at Lamar, Colorado. He was killed by officers in a railway coach at Bronson, Missouri, in October, 1930. Ralph Fleagle, his brother, was hanged with two companions in Colorado in June of the same year. Their crime was the murder of three bank officials slain in the holdup. They had kidnaped Dr. William Wininger, a Kansas physician, to treat one of their wounded comrades, and then shot him so that there would be no identification.

The Dalton Gang—Bob and Emmett, aged nineteen, possessed of the ambition to rob two banks at the same time—got their comeuppance at Coffeyville, Kansas.

After many killings and robberies, Eddie Adams, a youthful desperado from Pratt, Kansas, was killed and two of his companions were wounded and captured in a running fight that cost two officers their lives at Wichita, in 1922.

In 1932 Harry and Jennings Young killed Sheriff Marcell Hendrix and five of his deputies who were trying to arrest them at their home in the Ozark Mountains for the slaying of a constable. The boys later fled to Houston, Texas, where they committed suicide rather than surrender to a posse who had surrounded them.

Harvey Bailey, Bob Brady, Jim Clark, Wilbur Underhill, Ed Davis, Frank Hawley, and Alvin Peyton took part in the big Memorial Day break at the Kansas State Prison. Brady, Clark, Underhill, and Hawley were killed or died of wounds a few days afterward. Harvey Bailey lived to be the brains of the Urschel kidnaping, along with "Machine Gun" Kelley, Kathryn Kelley, and Albert Bates. These four are serving life sentences now.

Take the Dillinger gang: John Dillinger himself, put on the spot by "the woman in red," was killed as he came out of a Chicago motion-picture theater; Harry Pierpont died in the Ohio electric chair; Jack Clitus was killed trying to escape from the Ohio Penitentiary; Charlie Makly was shot down by police outside Chicago; Homer Van Meter, Dillinger's "first lieutenant," was shot to death by Minnesota and federal officers; Herbert Youngblood (who helped

Afterword

Dillinger escape from an Indiana prison with a wooden pistol) and his pal Eugene Green were both killed.

"Baby Face" Nelson, "Pretty Boy" Floyd, Verne Miller, "Dutch" Schultz, Verne Sanky, Frank Nash, and so on down to Buck and Clyde Barrow, Bonnie Parker, Raymond Hamilton, and the rest whom you have already met in these pages—I could add another long list of criminals of the period. But those I have named suffice to show the tidal wave of crime that struck the country in the twenties and thirties. I have called the roll to warn you that another flood impends. Our current juvenile delinquency points to nothing less.

We are running now at the rate of two million grave crimes a year, with a homicide every five minutes, an automobile theft every two and one-half minutes, a criminal assault every six minutes. In this harvest of crime the police gather in more eighteen-year-olds than offenders from any other age group. Among crimes of prisoners under twenty, robbery comes first, automobile theft second, burglary third. From 1941 to 1950 arrests of women increased 109 per cent. We grow criminals faster than we can build prisons to hold them.

I have no criticism of psychologists, psychiatrists, penologists, and sociologists. In my prison work I availed myself of the aid of men of science. Their wisdom contributed materially to the reformation of many young criminals. I do not belittle it here. But in preventing crime science has had little success. As I venture into this field, I expect to be assailed and ridiculed by a pleasure-seeking generation. I have read the books; I have listened to the experts. But what I shall say is out of the book of experience. If I were more experienced as a writer, I might hope to be more orderly and perhaps more persuasive in what I have to say. In any case, I hope to be understood, whether I am convincing or not. At my age, egotism is to no purpose and pride of opinion utterly without profit. I aim only to be of some slight service to millions of boys and girls shortly to enter useful citizenship—or crime.

Heretofore I have described how I was reared, how I was disciplined, how I was early put to tasks and to responsibilities seemingly beyond my years, how I came to know life on both sides of prison bars, and how, for many years, I had firsthand dealings with some of the most desperate men of my time. I stand on the statement that few men have had the opportunity to see crime and criminals as I have seen and known them during these eighty-odd years of mine.

I don't mean that I have the answer to crime prevention. I haven't. But I hold that juvenile delinquency is the main source of crime. I believe it is possible to fix responsibility for that delinquency. I believe that we can look within man himself and find the cause of crime.

Every rational being has a conscious, or a subconscious, reason for his acts, some sort of intention, some kind of motive. His craving, his desire, may be for good or for evil. It may spring from real or imaginary sources. But for everything we do there is motive. Motive inside cannot be separated from action outside when we are dealing with crime.

Emotional forces, it is true, can overrule the mind, conscience, and will so as to destroy self-control, and crime results. But this type of offense plays but a small part in the great mass of crime. The real cause of crime is the criminal himself.

I have read page after page on heredity and environment, and you can take individual cases to prove that either is the cause of crime. Of course, any informed person knows that environment—bad influences, poverty—can have a telling effect upon crime and especially upon juvenile delinquency.

But I believe that body and soul constitute man. Man is not born evil. He is born an innocent baby and gradually develops into a thinking, acting, responsible individual who should be taught to know right from wrong, good from evil. He should be taught the fundamental principles of life and the meaning of the death to follow.

The child who is not taught kindness is cruel to animals. The child who has not learned sympathy is ruthless toward other children. The boy who has not been drilled in honesty, industry, and economy while he is a boy will become a youth with desires which inevitably lead him to steal. The young man or woman who has not accepted the responsibilities of life as they should have been learned in the family circle or from the reading of good books is ripe to become a forger or an embezzler or a hijacker in order to obtain money so that he or she can keep up with the pleasure-seeking crowd.

The first offender little realizes the punishment that he is to receive, punishment which by its very weight pushes him further and further into disgrace and degradation. The real punishment of the first offender does not come from his mere confinement in prison. If you would warn the youth of the land against crime, warn them that the real punishment of the felon comes after his discharge from prison. Oh, how I have seen that punishment, over and over again!

The convict completes his term, he is discharged, and he fares forth in a free world to seek employment. The first question asked him is: "Where have you been working lately, and what references can you give?"

If he tells the truth, the employer makes some excuse and the ex-convict is not hired. He applies elsewhere and does not tell his employer that he is a discharged felon. He gets the job, but before long the employer is told that he is an ex-convict. Nearly always he is then discharged. Having lost one job after another for this cause, he becomes discouraged. "Oh, what's the use?" he says. "I don't have a chance."

And again he commits a forgery, or a burglary, and returns to prison. And the public and press wonder why there are so many repeaters and why prison management has failed. Suppose you interview the recidivists and ask them why they return.

Most men in prison are not criminals—they are merely lawbreakers. Their first offense is usually due to lack of proper home training. But their second and third offenses are the result of the punishment that follows upon release, as surely as the night follows the day. I hope you stop and read that sentence over again.

I myself have asked hundreds of repeaters why they came back and have had practically the same answer from them all: "If I told the truth, I couldn't get employment; and if I said nothing or lied about being in prison, it was soon found out and I was discharged."

You are thinking now, of course, that it should be the duty of the state to provide employment for a reasonable time after discharge of prisoners or else to give them sufficient financial aid to tide them over for a short period.

I have read arguments pro and con on this subject and have heard it discussed by legislators and others. It would not be a sound policy, for honest men and women frequently seek employment to no avail. Surely a person should not be forced to become a felon in order to obtain work! As for financial aid, all prisons and reformatories are a burden on taxpayers, and most legislatures will not provide aid except for a few new and needed furnishings and a small amount of cash. There is merit in paying to prisoners a small per diem for their work, especially to those with long terms of service. But few prisons have this policy.

I have talked to many prisoners as they were being discharged and have often stood by the desk of Warden Waid to listen to the advice and admonition he was accustomed to give before handing out the discharge papers and a $50 check. Perhaps there are few men who could equal him in these talks. I doubt if any man could excel his handling of the situation.

Waid would boil over with enthusiasm as he cited the names and the accomplishments of prisoners who had made good after returning to the free world. Then he would call the names of some of the most notorious characters who had returned to crime and tell what the results were for each of them. He would hold his man by the hand and look him in the eye and say: "I've got confidence in you and I know you are not going to disappoint me. You are not going to disappoint Mr. Simmons, either. And I don't believe you are going to disappoint that father and mother of yours. They tried to raise you right. You've got plenty of time yet to show them and your friends that you can go straight. And I believe you're going to do it.

"You just made a mistake; we all make 'em. Now, you go home and get you a job and stay with it, and I believe you've got sense enough to see by now that there isn't but one way to get along, and that is to work and do right. And I believe you're going to do it. Good-by and good luck! If you find I can help you any, let me know."

I am sure that these talks by Warden Waid kept many a man from returning to prison. Words of encouragement at the right time can mean a lot, especially when they come from peace officers and friends at the time of a prisoner's discharge. I think it is their moral duty to exercise their influence in this way. It is an opportunity for a great service.

We are talking now of the cure of the criminal, such that his ways of living are changed from bad to good as he goes back into society.

Afterword

And this is where the churches, schools, YMCA programs, and other character-forming institutions can be of use.

Under the most favorable conditions, however, reform of the criminal is not the answer to crime. We must look to prevention. And the methods of prevention must do their work before the career of crime has begun—and see to it that it is never begun.

Once the first offense is committed, the responsibility falls on police courts, justices of the peace, probation officers, and all those officials concerned with the administration of our parole statutes. All of them have a duty of preventing further crime where that is possible. When the offender reaches prison, the penologist becomes the "man behind the gun." I know from experience that he is likely to have the "gun" turned on him by outsiders who know nothing of prison conditions and problems, nothing of prison disturbances and prison mutinies.

In my opinion, the warden or general manager of a penitentiary must have a knowledge of human nature as his first qualification. He must understand people. Next, he should know crime and criminals. After that, he must have courage—physical courage and moral courage. And I think moral courage is the more important of the two.

A man of such qualities and experience is prepared to rule and to command the respect of those whom he rules— or at least of the greater number of them. The psychologist, the psychiatrist, and the bureau of classification are of the greatest assistance. But the warden is the man in charge of the general program outlined for him by the prison authorities. There is no substitute for a good warden.

Now I want to say a word about prompt and effective law enforcement as a means of preventing crime. I regard many criminal lawyers as menaces to society. They are by law officers of the court in which they practice, and the oath they take does not require the dishonorable actions sometimes employed to obtain delay of trials. Delay is the lawyer's strongest weapon, and some criminal lawyers practice delay to defeat justice. For justice delayed is justice defeated.

If there is any money to be got out of the client or out of his relatives, a psychiatrist is employed and an attempt is made to prove that the defendant is insane or was at the time of the offense, although nobody had ever had cause to suspect insanity theretofore. Or else there is more swearing that this important witness or that one is unavailable. Or, again, the attorney suddenly becomes ill, or something else calls for postponement. Meanwhile witnesses are drifting away, forgetting their evidence, or dying. The case for the state, in other words, gradually melts away with the passage of time.

Forty per cent of juvenile delinquency is the result of the broken home. A few simple changes in the divorce laws might well have telling effect. If thirty days' notice were required before a marriage certificate is issued, fewer wild marriages would occur. And if after every divorce both parties had to wait a full year before remarriage, there would be less delinquency and fewer dependent children on the welfare rolls and less business for police courts, probation officers, and so on down to the penitentiary.

But if we are either to prevent crime or to cure it to any sweeping degree, it is going to take a jarring awakening of the conscience of this whole money-mad, pleasure-craving nation. The people as a whole will have to be brought to the realization of the perils of the situation and of the personal responsibility of every man and woman to do something to end those perils.

I cannot foresee what agency can bring such an awakening to America. It may take a Martin Luther or the combined endeavors of all Christian agencies. Whether this trend toward crime will go on to the point of revolution where all law and all morality will fall, I do not know. I have said I am not an alarmist, and I am not. But I do know that crime is on the march. So far as I can see, only the home can halt that march. And before that can happen, our homes must re-establish the altars of the ancient virtues known and practiced by the founders of this nation.

Index

Index

Index